Research in Criminology

Series Editors
Alfred Blumstein
David P. Farrington

Research in Criminology

Understanding and Controlling Crime: Toward A New Research Strategy
D.P. Farrington, L.E. Ohlin and J.Q. Wilson

The Social Ecology of Crime
J.M. Byrne and R.J. Sampson (Eds.)

The Reasoning Criminal: Rational Choice Perspectives on Offending
D.B. Cornish and R.V. Clarke (Eds.)

The Social Contexts of Criminal Sentencing
Martha A. Myers and Susette M. Talarico

Predicting Recidivism Using Survival Models
Peter Schmidt and Ann Dryden Witte

Coping, Behavior, and Adaptation in Prison Inmates
Edward Zamble and Frank Porporino

Prison Crowding: A Psychological Perspective
Paul B. Paulus

Off School, In Court: An Experimental and Psychiatric Investigation of Severe School Attendance Problems
I. Berg, I. Brown and R. Hullin

Policing and Punishing the Drinking Driver: A Study of General and Specific Deterrence
Ross Homel

Judicial Decision Making, Sentencing Policy, and Numerical Guidance
Austin Lovegrove

Marc Le Blanc
Marcel Fréchette

Male Criminal Activity from Childhood Through Youth

Multilevel and Developmental Perspectives

With 17 Illustrations

Springer-Verlag
New York Berlin Heidelberg
London Paris Tokyo

Marc Le Blanc
École de psycho-éducation, Université de Montréal, Montréal, Québec, H2C 1A6, Canada

Marcel Fréchette
École de criminologie, Université de Montréal, Montréal, Québec, H3C 3J7, Canada

Series Editors
Alfred Blumstein
School of Urban and Public Affairs, Carnegie-Mellon University, Pittsburgh, Pennsylvania 15213, USA

David P. Farrington
Institute of Criminology, University of Cambridge, Cambridge CB3 9DT, England

Library of Congress Cataloging-in-Publication Data
Le Blanc, Marc, 1943–
Male criminal activity from childhood through youth : multilevel and developmental perspectives / Marc Le Blanc, Marcel Fréchette.
p. cm. – (Research in criminology)
Bibliography: p.
ISBN-13: 978-1-4612-8160-3
1. Juvenile delinquency. 2. Criminal behavior. I. Fréchette, Marcel, 1932– . II. Title. III. Series.
HV9069.L33 1988
364.3′6′088041–dc19 88-26566

Printed on acid-free paper

Softcover reprint of the hardcover 1st edition 1989

Typeset by Publishers Service, Bozeman, Montana.

9 8 7 6 5 4 3 2 1

ISBN-13: 978-1-4612-8160-3 e-ISBN-13: 978-1-4612-3570-5
DOI: 10.1007/978-1-4612-3570-5

Preface

In the last 50 years or so – following the etiological and comparative works of the Gluecks, the ecological studies of Shaw and MacKay, the surveys on delinquent gangs and the first survey of self-reported delinquency by Porterfield – empirical criminology has succeeded in compiling a fairly exhaustive list of factors likely to lead to delinquency. Whether these factors are biological, psychological, sociological, or legal, their effect on delinquent behavior is now better known. On the whole, analytical and comparative studies have been fruitful, as evidenced by recent reviews of the literature, among them those of Rutter and Giller (1983) and Wilson and Herrnstein (1985), even though a number of ambiguities and numerous controversies still persist.

The history of investigation has given rise to a great number of theories explaining delinquency, as any self-respecting manual of criminology can confirm (for example, Empey, 1978; Feldman, 1978; Shoemaker, 1984; West, 1984). Each of these theories gives the impression of being *the* explanation of delinquency. Even today, in spite of the impressive number of so-called integrative theories (see The Albany Conference, 1987), each one asserts that it is the one that best explains the many complex causes of delinquency. Although most theories have an empirical base, rarely have they been submitted to thorough verification, such as systematic replication or cross-cultural and temporal comparisons.

On the basis of this rapid review, it is evident that there is a great deal of scientific material available. Its development, however, has been and still is beset by four conceptual and methodological stumbling blocks: disregard for the levels of interpretation, slow conceptual development of the notion of delinquency, inability to go beyond description, and difficulty in properly analyzing longitudinal data. It is not our intention to dwell on these problems here, since we will have occasion to come back to them throughout this book. It is well, however, to show how they have been solved within the framework of the research program that gave rise to this book.

Our Perspectives

The French criminologist Jean Pinatel (1963), in a masterly effort to define the bases of criminology, was the first to propose that criminologists should distinguish between three levels of interpretation of the criminal phenomenon, namely *criminality*, the *criminal*, and the *crime*, each level having its own perspectives, its own rationales, and its own methods. He defined criminality as the sum of infractions committed at a given time and place, influenced by demographic, economic, or political factors and occurring on a societal scale. The level of the criminal centers on the transgressor and involves personal characteristics and the factors that influence the formation and evolution of his or her personality. The level of the crime, the act itself, involves only a small part of the life or criminal career of the subject; it is an event that has a beginning, a development, and an end and there are factors or mechanisms that cause its appearance.

This basic rule, that there are three levels of interpretation, was rediscovered by American criminology recently, but the emphasis has been mainly on the two levels of the crime and criminality (Hirschi, 1979, 1987; Short, 1985, 1987), an emphasis Sutherland had suggested much earlier (Sutherland & Cressey, 1960).

Following this rule, we have chosen to devote this book to a single level of interpretation, what is traditionally called crime. To make sure that there is no confusion, we will use the term *criminal activity* to refer to the level of interpretation. This term offers a twofold advantage. First, it is universal and refers to a reality in constant movement rather than to the strictly legal category, crime. Second, it permits the use of three complementary perspectives that, like a nest of tables, fit into one another, namely, the perpetration, or the way the crime is executed; the offending (to follow the recent suggestion of Blumstein, Cohen, Roth, & Visher, 1986), the descriptive and evolutive characteristics of all the crimes committed over a given period of time; and the behavioral pattern or overall configuration of the parameters and mechanisms of offending linked in specified ways. By concentrating on one level of interpretation, as did Wolfgang, Figlio, and Sellin (1972) in their classic study, we sought to support as firmly as possible the explanatory perspective on delinquency, the search for correlates and causes of criminal activity. Consequently, large portions of this book will deal successively with these three ways of looking at criminal activity: how crimes are perpetrated at different ages; offending as seen from a descriptive, an evolutive, and a process point of view; and the characteristics of a limited number of behavioral patterns.

To follow the rule of levels of interpretation is not enough. It is clear that, at the present time, the idea of criminal activity is still subject to conceptual difficulties. A review of the criminological literature quickly and incontestably establishes that, on the one hand, descriptive concepts are numerous (prevalence, seriousness, crime mix, etc.) and some evolutive concepts have been identified (specialization, escalation, etc.), but, on the other hand, although data are abundant they are still insufficient. The report of the Panel on Research on Criminal Career (Blumstein et al., 1986) eloquently supports these observations. Furthermore, as we shall see, there is no significant consensus on the operational definition of most of the concepts used by theoreticians and researchers. Besides, although theories on the correlates and causes of delinquency abound, none has appeared that takes into account the development of offending and its internal dynamics. What is more, developmental models capable of integrating existing concepts are rare and simplistic. For example, the model proposed by Blumstein et al. (1986) is constructed with only four concepts: the frequency of the crimes, the age when criminal activity started, the duration, and the age when it stopped. In short, our objective will be to propose a better conceptual and operational elaboration of the dependent variable. This will be done with the aid of the empirical data at our disposal. While making an evaluation of the applicability of existing theories to one or another aspect of criminal activity, at the same time we will be seeking new explanations for one or another of the components of criminal activity. Chapters 3 and 4 will be devoted to this conceptual elaboration and its validation by empirical data. Not only will the concepts be strictly delimited, but a method or articulating the concepts will be proposed and tested so as to construct a model or an integrated theory of criminal activity.

Once we have clarified exactly what will be called delinquency, and once the components of criminal activity have been suitably established, we must avoid one of the stumbling blocks that has hampered many studies over the past 50 years. It is the fact that almost all studies describe the accomplishment of the crime, the offending, or the behavioral patterns using only one sample or a single method of ascertaining the degree of an individual's delinquency. Throughout this book, however, and particularly in Chapters 3 and 4, we will use a comparative approach: We shall compare hidden delinquency with official delinquency as well as a representative sample of the adolescent population with a sample of youngsters declared juvenile delinquents by the court.

Studies on criminal activity usually focus on official delinquency—arrests or convictions. We also study these aspects, but we add data on hidden delinquency obtained by means of three interviews set up at intervals between the beginning of adolescence and the beginning of adulthood. A comparative approach is necessary because, on many questions relating to the nature of the offending (frequency, escalation, specialization, etc.), the conclusions of different studies do not agree, especially those that include hidden delinquency and those that use only official delinquency. Those that compare the data obtained on the two types of measurements of delinquency are rare and deal only with some limited aspects, notably the validity of the reports of hidden delinquency (see the works of West & Farrington, 1977). Not wishing to state prematurely that one is superior to the other, we thought it would be interesting to systematically compare the two (which we have done in Chaps. 3 and 4) to determine the points of convergence and of divergence and to explain them.

The second comparison proposed throughout the same chapters is between a representative sample of the adolescent population and a sample of wards of the juvenile court. It has two complementary objectives: to verify the general scope of the conclusions derived and to further the comprehension of the mechanics of criminal activity. The sample of adolescents, because it is representative of a generation born around 1960, makes it possible to control whether the interpretations extend to the entire adolescent population. This type of inquiry, which uses a questionnaire and involves a large number of subjects, does not offer very detailed information about criminal activity. What is more, since delinquency is occasional and of no great seriousness, discovering the dynamics of the delinquency is difficult. The sample of wards of the court offers greater scope: The rates of prevalence and intensity are high for most types of infraction no matter what the age, and the interview can be used to obtain detailed information about the accomplishment of crimes over long periods. In short, it might be said that the adolescent sample offers a naked eye view, whereas the juvenile delinquents sample offers a magnified view, like that of a microscope. In this sense, as Cernkovich, Giordano, and Pugh (1985) noted, and with reason, samples of convicted juvenile delinquents are essential for the advancement of criminological knowledge. They make it possible to include chronic delinquents who are virtually absent from the studies on hidden delinquency that are based on representative samples of adolescents.

Finally, it is evident that, when in addition to using a comparative approach we use a longitudinal approach systematically to follow the whole evolution of criminal activity over time, we adopt a perspective that has been little exploited in criminology, as shown by the reviews reported by Farrington (1979) and by Mednick and Baert (1981). The recent work of Farrington et al. (1986c) also points to the lack of longitudinal studies, especially those that include several direct contacts with the subjects and use data from various sources. Consequently, we have compiled a list of all the crimes committed by boys recruited from among ordinary adolescents and delinquents, from the moment the crimes become apparent during puberty to the end of the 20s.

In criminology, a caustic debate is going on between the supporters of longitudinal surveys and the upholders of cross-sectional surveys. The advocates are Blumstein et al. (1986) and Farrington et al. (1986c), while the prosecutors are Hirschi and Gottfredson (1986, see also Gottfredson and Hirschi 1987a). The advocates of longitudinal research emphasize the numerous uses and advantages of designs with repeated measures on the same people. The prosecutors vigorously question the usefulness of such surveys. The argument of the prosecutors is that longitudinal research is not required for the study of crime. The demonstration of this argument is fivefold: There is an age invariance in crime (Hirschi & Gottfredson, 1983); the concept of criminal career is inconsistent with evidence (Gottfredson & Hirschi, 1986); and in their most recent article (1987a), Gottfredson and Hirschi document three new arguments – the features of the longitudinal design are not superior to the properties of the cross-sectional design, its superiority to measure the effects of intervention could be challenged, and a comparison of empirical results obtained from the two types of studies shows that longitudinal surveys have produced no really new knowledge concerning the causes and correlates of crime. While the first four demonstrations have been subject to much controversy, the last one, that the results of longitudinal surveys have been confirmatory rather than heuristic, is devastating. The prosecutors present numerous examples, and they are sound ones. They show that for standard causal variables such as sex, race, age, family variables, and peer group influences, the two sets of surveys produce facts that are confirmed one by the other. A reading of Farrington et al. (1986c) and of Blumstein et al. (1986) literature reviews does not demonstrate clearly that longitudinal surveys propose new outstanding results concerning the correlates of crimes.

Our position is that the debate over the usefulness of longitudinal surveys versus cross-sectional surveys will prove as sterile as has the qualitative/quantitative methods debate that was so prominent during the 1970s in the social sciences. We will argue throughout this book that cross-sectional surveys are sufficient to study the distribution and the correlates of crime, but that only longitudinal surveys can potentially help us to sequence events, crimes, and causal factors because each person acts as his own control. Even if we accept Gottfredson and Hirschi's conclusion that longitudinal research does not habitually address the question of sequence of events, we think that there are more urgent tasks for criminologists than debating research designs. It is particularly important to elaborate the notion of criminal activity and open ourselves to the concepts and methods of developmental psychology before we can come to any conclusions about the usefulness of specific research designs.

Acknowledgments. We wish to make note, in the present work, of results obtained in two research programs that began in the early 1970s and were carried out by teams of the Research Group on Juvenile Maladjustment of the University of Montreal. The two research programs had the same objective—to explain how delinquency develops—and the same method—longitudinal observation of subjects.

The first program, under the title "Diagnosis and prognosis of serious delinquency," followed the evolution of 470 wards of the Juvenile Court of Montreal throughout their adolescence, essentially by means of a sequence of interviews to measure their criminal activity, their social life, and their personality. The second program, "Structure and dynamics of delinquent behavior," measured the same aspects on a sample of 3,070 adolescents of both sexes living on the Island of Montreal.

This research would not have been possible without the help of the youngsters, who agreed to participate, and of the parents, professors, school authorities, and various practitioners from the social services and courts for minors. We thank them for their valuable assistance.

We also owe a great deal to the numerous collaborators who participated in this collective work and made it possible, whether our colleagues, Louise Langelier-Biron, Maurice Cusson, Daniel Élie, Jocelyne Forget, and Pierre-Marie Lagier, or the various research assistants who were responsible for the data collection and analysis. They are Jacqueline Bayreuther, Hélène Beaumont, Liane Bédard, Normand Bélanger, Lizette Bélisle, Diane Bourgouin, Aaron Caplan, Roger Charland, Claude-Nil Claveau, Gilles Côté, Renée Dedeker, Lorraine Drapeau, Marie-Claire Fabien, Françoise Frénette-Deschene, Marie Gagnon, Rosette Gagnon, André Groleau, André Lapierre, Jacques Lapierre, Marie-Josée Lavigueur, Suzanne Légare-Boisclair, Diane Maisonneuve, Bruno Marceau,

Martin Massé, Danielle Maurice-Hamel, Pierrette Trudeau-Le Blanc, Pierre McDuff, François Mourant, Elizabeth Mischlich, Hébert Parisé, Luc Parizeau, Michèle Perreault, Louison Pronovost, Lucie Rodrigue, Marie Sarrazin, Gisèle Séguin, and Pierre Tremblay. We are exceedingly grateful to them.

A research project of this magnitude could not have been carried out without the technical support of the secretariat of the Research Group on Juvenile Maladjustment, of the International Center for Comparative Criminology, and of the School of Psycho-Education, and in particular, without the patience of the secretaries who typed the manuscript–Nicole Pinsonneault, Marie-Christine Cohen, and Denyse Rompré.

This publication would not have been possible without the remarkable work of Dorothy Crelisten, translator of the International Center for Comparative Criminology, who, with her remarkable skill, undertook the difficult task of translating into English this scientific and technical manuscript.

An empirical and theoretical work such as this one could not have been undertaken without the direct or indirect intellectual stimulation of some eminent criminologists, such as Alfred Blumstein, Travis Hirschi, David Farrington, Rolf Loeber, Jean Pinatel, Albert Reiss, Denis Szabo, and Marvin Wolfgang. Some of them have inspired our work, while others have extensively commented on or discussed this manuscript. We would like to thank them for their support.

Finally, an enterprise as long and exacting as this one obviously could not be realized without the assistance of financial backers. Our thanks to the Quebec Social Research Council, the Social Sciences and Humanities Research Council of Canada, the Solicitor General of Canada, and the University of Montreal for their generous grants, for which we are deeply grateful.

Montreal, Quebec

Marc Le Blanc
Marcel Fréchette

Contents

1
From Delinquency to Criminal Activity

Is it possible to define delinquency, not only clearly and exactly but also in such a way that the term has an identical meaning for everyone? Is it possible, by this single word, to express the multitude of diverse acts that even the most superficial observation shows must be included?

Semantics tells us that the word comes from the Latin *delinguere*, "to make a mistake." The generic meaning of committing an offense has been specific since the 14th century; it refers to the activity of any person who evades the law, that is, in the etymological sense, who neglect the observance of what the criminal code calls a crime.

Current usage, whether in judicial practice or in the social sciences, is a source of confusion. In some circles the term is used to refer to crimes committed by both adults and juveniles. In other circles the term is reserved for the deviance of minors only, "minors" being identified in most legislation throughout the world as persons under 18 years of age.

The objective of this chapter is to review current definitions of delinquency and to elaborate operationally the notion of criminal activity. We will then present the data on which our analyses are based.

Definitions of Delinquency

Since a major task of this book will be to compare hidden and official delinquency, we thought it essential to review the evolution of the legal and scientific definitions of delinquency. Knowledge about changes in the legal definitions is helpful in understanding the significance of our results. We also felt it necessary to discuss the multiplicity of scientific constructs that refer to delinquency, in order to propose a new set of measures. As we will show, there is no adequate consensus on concepts, constructs, and measures.

A More and More Specific Legal Idea

Analysis of the concept of delinquency shows the importance of the law as the criterion for its definition. Obviously it is the legislator who determines what constitutes delinquency by deciding what acts are prohibited and their commission considered punishable and by stipulating the circumstances whereby the status of delinquent can be attributed to a given individual. It is also clear that such decisions and dictates are subject to the values, norms, and usages of the particular society. Every definition of delinquency, then, must necessarily be relative in time and space, as pointed out by a number of authors (see Cusson, 1983), even though striking constants emerge, constants that are obviously cross-cultural and historical.

A Recent Idea

Delinquency has only recently been of interest to the legislator. It wasn't until the end of the 19th century and the beginning of the 20th that the term acquired its specifically legal status, thanks to special legislation. Thus, even though delinquency has had a specific meaning since the 14th century, not until 5 centuries later did Western societies officially recognize the status of *minor* and enact special laws. In Canada, where we gathered our data, codification of the Criminal Code took place in 1892 and the Juvenile Delinquents Act was adopted in 1908.

It was also at the end of the last century, with what was called the "discovery" of childhood in society (Aries, 1962) and with the development of a new understanding of this idea (Empey, 1978), that the type of behavior adults should adopt toward children was codified. The official rights of children were declared, along with the concept of delinquency and the delinquent.

A number of U.S. states then decided to set up reformatories for young criminals and industrial schools for neglected children. This made necessary the creation of juvenile courts. Illinois had the distinction of being the first state to create such courts, in 1899. Platt (1969) recorded the history of what was an important innovation at the time. In practice, this court became a sort of "superguardian" with specific powers of restraint over both parent and minor.

In Canada, the same evolution took place (Corrado, Trépanier, & LeBlanc, 1983). As in the United States, the spirit motivating the changes was a humanitarian concern for abandoned, neglected, or delinquent children, a desire to "save" the children not only from the harmful effects of poverty, misery, cultural deprivation, and other bad influences, but also from the brutality of the adult criminal justice system. Furthermore, since ties with England were closer than they are now (Canada being part of the British Empire at the time), the influence of the doctrine of *parens patriae* was felt in Canada all the more strongly (Farrington, 1979).

Development of the Concept in Canada

The Canadian Juvenile Delinquents Act of 1908 was preceded in the latter half of the 19th century by a number of changes in criminal procedures (Gagnon, 1978). The first legislation calling for the application of different criminal procedures for youngsters under age 16 was passed in 1857; it called for speedy trials and punishments of young delinquents. However, until the Criminal Code was adopted in 1892, only small changes were made in the trial and sentencing of young people.

The 1892 Criminal Code included a first codification of the criteria and measures to be applied in the case of minors: (a) The age of criminal responsibility was set at 7 years, (b) children over age 7 and under age 14 could not be held criminally responsible unless they understood the nature and consequences of their acts, (c) special procedures were instituted for the trial of persons under age 16, and (d) the provisions of previous laws on sentences were maintained, such as use of the reform school in place of the penitentiary. In 1894, more rules for minors were passed, including the obligation to hold separate trials for juvenile delinquents and to not imprison them in adult institutions. These changes prepared the way for the establishment of separate courts for juvenile delinquents in 1908. Other new measures for minors included placing them in the care of an officer of the Children's Aid Society, finding them an accredited foster home, suspending sentence for an indefinite period, sentencing them to a minimal fine, and sending them to a reform or industrial school.

After the gradual institution of these many changes, the Juvenile Delinquents Act of 1908 did not appear very revolutionary. Rather it crystallized a renewed concept of delinquency and its treatment which made possible implementation of measures throughout Canada that had applied only in Ontario or Quebec. Let us look at the contents of this legislation, which remained in force to 1984.

The Act of 1908 marked a major turning point in the history of the Canadian judicial system. It instituted a court exclusively for juvenile delinquents; it delimited the range of delinquency; it specified the objectives to be achieved; it called for specialists to advise, enlighten, and support the court; and it determined procedures (referral to the adult court, notification of parents, etc.). This new justice system was based on a totally different philosophy of justice from that of the past and on a new view of delinquency, as pledged in the preamble. Delinquents were represented as products of their environment and as persons in need of help more than punishment. The state was a good parent who had to treat the delinquent youngster with justice, not like a criminal but like a child who, being on a downward path, needed counseling, encouragement, help, and support. To accomplish this, the state had to give a great deal of discretionary power to the persons in authority.

The definition of the delinquent advanced in this act merits special note, not so much because of its official content (it is, in fact, very simple and concrete), but because of its intention, since its object was to make the young offender a fully recognized subject of law. Delinquent here meant:

> . . . a child (under 18 years of age in Quebec or 16 or 17 in other provinces) who commits an infraction of any of the provisions of the Criminal Code, or of a federal or provincial statute, or a regulation or ordinance of a municipality or who is guilty of sexual immorality or any similar form of vice, or who commits any other infraction . . .

This definition, however, has the disadvantage of being rather elastic. It covers minor marginal behavior as well as serious criminal acts. The conduct described ranges from activities that adults consider improper for a minor (sexual promiscuity, use of alcohol) to the most serious crimes defined by the Criminal Code, from behavior prohibited by various laws and regulations (such as the municipal regulations on curfews) to those especially provided for juveniles (e.g., school attendance) or those passed in provincial legislations (against neglect, abandonment, situations of moral or physical danger, etc.) in which the child is a victim.

In this definition, delinquency emerges as an all-inclusive idea since, when all is said and done, a delinquent can be any young person who needs protection or who has contravened a law. This Canadian definition of delinquency, by the way, was not very different from the definitions adopted by most of the U.S. states and the Western countries during the same period or in the following 10 years or so (Corrado et al., 1983).

Contrary to this first legislation, the recent federal Young Offenders Act (1982), which came into effect in 1984, limits the concept of delinquency. A youngster who commits an infraction of the Criminal Code or of another federal law or regulation is called a "young offender," but this is not the case for one who is guilty of a departure from provincial or municipal laws. The very general concept of delinquency used by the previous Juvenile Delinquents Act, which included crimes committed by youngsters, situations in danger of leading to delinquency, serious disorderly conduct, and circumstances endangering the safety or development of the young person, is abolished. In addition, minors can no longer be prosecuted for acts considered legitimate on the part of adults or for acts for which the persons in charge of their education are responsible.

This tightening of the definition of delinquency was accompanied by a stricter distinction between childhood and adolescence. The Young Offenders Act applies only to minors from age 12 to 18, the age bracket corresponding to the beginning and end of adolescence. According to Zimring (1982), this position fits in perfectly with the evolution of juridic concepts as well as psychosocial theories. These concepts and theories led scientists first, and then practitioners and legislators, to differentiate clearly between childhood and adolescence, so that legally the second is seen as a phase of semiautonomy in which, despite the fact that the laws are identical with those for children, the obligations and responsibilities are much more demanding.

It is clear, then, that in Canada as well as throughout most contemporary societies, legislative developments have been determined by a considerable effort toward the conceptual specification and operational limitation of the idea of delinquency itself. Two types of infraction are finally differentiated. The first, infractions of the Criminal Code, seems to be more significant and constitutes official delinquency (referred to in this book, a little redundantly, as "criminal delinquency"); the second concerns infractions of the laws and regulations governing particular aspects of social life, such as driving a car, alcohol consumption, public order, and so on (these come under the title "statutory delinquency").

A Controversial Scientific Concept

For a scientific approach, it is not sufficient to define delinquency as the violation of a law by a minor. Too many questions are left unanswered. For example, violation of what laws constitutes delinquency? What must be the nature or seriousness of the infraction? Is the perpetration of the crime a behavior problem or a way of life? What distinguishes delinquency from other manifestations of opposition to the law? These many questions have been fiercely debated in scientific circles, whether in criminology, sociology, political science, or psychology.

Deviance Versus Delinquency

In sociology a distinction was made very early between deviance and delinquency. Most manuals on juvenile delinquency, whether early or recent (Cavan, 1962, 1969; Cusson, 1983; Empey, 1978; Gibbons, 1975; Reed & Baali, 1972; Robinson, 1936; G.W. West, 1984) have been unable to escape the debate over the legal versus the social definition of delinquency.

Partisans of the social definition say delinquency must be defined as (a) violation of current norms of conduct (Sellin, 1938), (b) conduct that is in conflict or at variance with the priorities of the community (Robinson, 1960), or (c) behavior that is totally contrary to normal social usage (Cavan, 1969). Delinquency and deviance thus become equivalent. The definition found in most manuals on general sociology (Rocher, 1968) likens delinquency to a violation of institutionalized norms that are shared and recognized as legitimate within the social system (A.K. Cohen, 1955).

To advocate such a perspective complicates the scientific approach enormously, since criminology has the ambitious mandate of studying and explaining all behavior that is socially inappropriate. This mission makes the basic problem of operationalization almost insoluble, since it requires choosing an object of study that can be sufficiently specific and minimally homogeneous and that can be explained by a limited set of factors. Furthermore, to equate delinquency with deviance accentuates the degree of imprecision—the fluidity, so to speak—of the phenomenon under study. As Walker (1977) explained, this is because there is more chance for the norms of conduct of a group to be relative and contingent than for the criminal laws or official regulations. A final difficulty is the lack of practicality of a nonlegal definition of delinquency, since a researcher's data will then be in danger of not accurately reflecting the current practices of the system of justice for minors.

The other choice is the strictly legal definition of delinquency, based on written laws and regulations sanctioned by the government. These regulations and the sanctions that accompany them have the advantage of a certain continuity (the Canadian 1908 law on juvenile delinquency lasted more than 75 years). At the same time, delinquency becomes a class of human behavior that has definite limitations and a variability that can be controlled consistently. Because the range of acts included in the definition is substantially restricted, scientific measurement is easier and affords comparisons over time and space; the pertinence and validity of the schemas of observation or explanation profit by it. The legal definition has enormous advantages for the scientific approach.

It is the legal definition of delinquency that seems to have had the systematic support of scientists, past and present, beginning with Durkheim (1956), who said we call a crime "any act sanctioned by punishment." There are also definitions, such as, ". . . all infractions committed, reported, brought to trial and sanctioned by punishment" (Tappan, 1949); ". . . behavior that violates the fundamental norms of a society and which, if reported to the agents of social control, would be judged delinquent by them" (Cloward & Ohlin, 1960); "Delinquency is defined by acts, the detection of which is believed can result in punishment of the person committing them by the agents of social control" (Hirschi, 1969); ". . . infractions committed by adolescents, punishable according to the terms of the Penal Code" (Cusson, 1983), and so on.

Recourse to the law did not solve all the problems of defining delinquency. The definitions just cited refer for the most part to behavior that is known to the judicial system. Some authors, however, speak of acts that "could" become known, thus introducing the question of the difference between hidden delinquency and known delinquency. This gives rise to the question, Is actual delinquency best represented by the former or the latter?

This debate has grown more bitter since the first studies on hidden delinquency (Murphy, 1946; Nye, Short, & Olson, 1958; Porterfield, 1946) showed that almost all adolescents commit crimes over a number of years. Those who believe that hidden delinquency is the better gauge of actual delinquency have always used the argument of the "purity of the phenomenon," since this delinquency escapes variations in the application of laws and the administration of justice (see Moyer, 1975, for a survey of the English literature on hidden delinquency, and Le Blanc, 1977b, for a survey of the French literature).

However, recent studies show that to compare known and hidden delinquency is to use two contrasting procedures that measure the same phenomenon—rather futilely, no doubt. Le Blanc (1983a) and Hindelang, Hirschi, and Weis (1981) showed that the conclusions obtained by both converge and that, despite important differences in degree, many are similar.

In short, whether deviance or delinquency, and whether official delinquency or hidden delinquency, the essential question is the extent of the phenomenon. In light of the many studies on the question and our own empirical observations, the law is certainly the best starting point. The legal definition has an express, and also a symbolic, meaning, implying a social consensus, a contract, and a conception of public order. It furnishes the most solid and consistent guidelines for determining what, among the multitude of inappropriate forms of behavior, is delinquency.

Symptom Versus Syndrome

While sociologists were discussing the distinction between delinquency and deviance, psychologists, placing the accent on the person rather than the behavior, were studying the delinquent person. Traditionally psychology has tended to consider antisocial behavior as the manifestation of a profound and general problem of adaptation.

From the psychological point of view, two main trends emerge. The first (and less recent) sees repeated acting out as a signal or, more precisely, a symptom. Crime is a symptom of certain unhealthy states of a psychiatric nature (Alexander & Staub, 1934; American Psychiatric Association, 1987; Healy & Bronner, 1936; Hesnard, 1963; Klein, 1955). The second is more directly criminological; it bases the criminal orientation on a specific configuration of psychological and social characteristics that influence this orientation and determine its intensity. It is a syndrome of a specific nature; it exists on its own and is not symptomatic of any other pathological condition.

Over the past 3 decades, this second trend has been strengthened and has become predominant. Several schools of thought, based on very different research models and with considerable clinical and scientific observations to their credit, have been working to show evidence of a syndrome of this kind and, by confirming its specificity, to construct a prototype of the antisocial individual. Let us first look at two contributions made by the group of so-called "psychoclinicians," the first by psychiatrists and psychologists of European tradition, such as Andersen (1963), Debuyst (1960), DeGreef (1955), Glover (1960), Hesnard (1963), Lagache (1965), and Mailloux (1971) and the second by North American researchers and practitioners, among them Cleckley (1964), Hare (1970), Karpman (1959), McCord and McCord (1956), and Yochelson and Samenow (1976). Then there is the group of "developmentalists," who are mainly interested in the stages of becoming a criminal. Among earlier authors are S. Glueck and E. Glueck (1970, 1974), Healy and Bronner (1936), and Robins (1966); currently there are Fréchette and Le Blanc (1987), Jesness and Haapanen (1982), Jessor and Jessor (1977), and D.J. West (1982). Finally, there are the authors of the sociological school (particularly the "culturalists"), such as A.K. Cohen (1955); Becker (1963), Cloward and Ohlin (1960), Jeffrey (1959), Wolfgang (1967), and others, who describe the criminal condition in terms of how the role and status of delinquent is acquired.

On the basis of all these contributions, the silhouette of the typical criminal emerges with increasing clarity. The formulations can be slightly different: Hesnard (1963), for example, spoke of egocentricity, personal immaturity, aggressive virulence, and psychic unreality; Mailloux (1971) saw the criminal as a person with an inflexible superego, marked narcissism, and an obviously negative identity; Pinatel (1970) described the four main traits of the criminal personality as ethical egocentricity, instability, aggressiveness, emotional indifference; Jeffrey (1959) described the criminal as suffering from "social depersonalization," which condemns the person to solitude and sterility. All of these authors recognized and demonstrated that individuals, when they become criminal, have endopsychic traits that are specific and stable and are responsible for the person's entry into the criminal role.

Definition of delinquency from this perspective has not been without criticism. It was first criticized for unduly limiting the delinquent group to those who have developed an authentic illicit lifestyle. Hence individuals who are not as deeply involved, who are occasionally delinquents, for instance; who haven't the official status of delinquent; or whose delinquency is hidden are not found in this model. The conduct of these subjects, wrote Hirschi (1969), is to all intents and purposes unexplained; therefore a conception of the criminal such as this cannot serve as the point of departure for the formulation of a general theory. A second criticism (no doubt the one most often heard but actually only a consequence of the first) argues that this extreme specificity, which exaggerates the difference between "true delinquents" and others by its excessive labeling, fosters a kind of redundancy and artificiality in the choice of the subject of study. Finally, a last criticism points out that reducing the phenomenon to a delinquency syndrome does not make representation of the reality any easier, since the heterogeneity of the act, persons, and situations is unquestionably very great; nor does it conform better with the data furnished by the system of justice for minors.

In answer to some of these criticisms, let us say that in this perspective, delinquency does not necessarily become a restricted or unidimensional phenomenon. It is seen here more as a complex and multiform reality whose diverse variants must be recognized. In fact, this criminological trend of thought is constantly enriched by the results of the taxonomic approach. Thanks to the contribution of numerous scientists, for example, Fréchette and Le Blanc (1987), Gibbons (1968), Megargee and Bohn (1979), Quay (1965), and Sullivan, Grant, and Grant (1957), among many others, there are an abundance of significant data. Their findings afford a thorough understanding of the delinquent reality, which is described in precise terms in all its different forms. At the same time, these authors recognize, despite the diversity of acts, an authentic basic structure. Since the work of Hirschi (1969), who was strongly against the statement that the only resemblance between different types of illicit conduct is in their illegality, recent empirical studies have shown that the personality of those seriously involved in delinquency is handicapped by specific deficiencies (Fréchette and Le Blanc, 1987).

In short, it seems clear that the concept of delinquency has become much more specific over the past 10 years. Delinquency, once likened to deviance, evolved to where the focus was on the illicit activity itself (that is, a violation of the criminal code) and then on the individual. This evolution shows an effort to link two "fields of analysis," as Sélosse (1983) put it, that is, to turn from the action to the perpetrator, from criminally oriented concrete behavior to the antisocial individual, or again from the "structure of behavior" to the "structure of conscience." In the comings and goings between these two levels, one guideline remains constant—the search for a clearer and more specific interpretation of delinquency, by dissociation of delinquency from deviance and by clear distinction between the real delinquent and the harmless transgressor.

Assessment of Criminal Activity

Criminology is concerned with both criminal law and social sciences. By amalgamating the two approaches, it seeks not only to achieve a more precise and dynamic theoretical framework, but also to better assess criminal activity. In that direction, the preceding section, with the aid of legal and theoretical historical arguments, have served to justify our choice of criminal delinquency as the subject of our study.

What made the criminological approach different from the start was the importance given to delinquent behavior as the primary basis for any conceptualization. As Cohen, a pioneer in modern criminology, stipulated in 1959, to construct a theory of delinquency one must always have the same point of reference, namely the illicit conduct. Farrington (1973) went further, stating that in criminology the key dependent variable is delinquent behavior. Furthermore, criminology has always stipulated what has practically become the golden rule: Only one of the three levels of interpretation (criminality, the crime, and the criminal) must be used to determine the dependent variable, that is, to attack the problem in an experimental way (Pinatel, 1963).

Levels of Interpretation and Levels of Analysis

First we must describe the level of interpretation that applies in our study. As we said earlier, we follow the fundamental distinctions that Pinatel (1963) suggested. The three specific levels, he stated, must be constantly differentiated in the study of the criminal phenomenon: the criminality, the crime, and the criminal, each requiring its own perspectives, rationale, and methods. Figure 1.1 shows these levels. Pinatel defined the first, criminality, as the sum of infractions committed at a given time and place, influenced by demographic, economic, political, and other factors and occurring on a societal scale. The second level of interpretation, that of the crime, should be studied only as a small part of the life or criminal career of the subject, as an event that has a beginning, a development, and an end; the factors or mechanisms that cause its appearance should be ascertained. The third level, the criminal, is centered on the transgressor and proceeds to a study of personal characteristics as well as of factors that influenced the formation and evolution of his or her personality and social roles. A number of criminologists have rediscovered this rule. Sélosse (1983) has applied it to

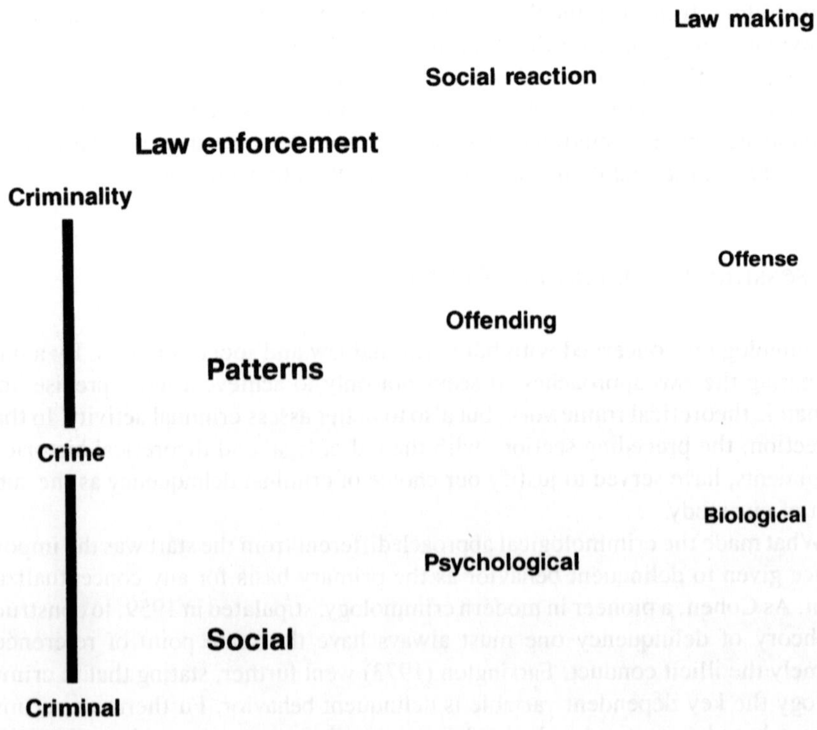

FIGURE 1.1. Levels of interpretation in criminology and levels of analysis in each.

juvenile delinquency by speaking of delinquency, the delinquent, and the crime; American criminology has emphasized mainly the two levels, crime and criminality (Hirschi, 1979, 1987; Short, 1985, 1987), and much earlier (Sutherland & Cressey, 1960).

This basic rule, however, is far from being obeyed by all criminologists. Many use the term delinquency when referring vaguely to one or another of the three levels (Matza, 1964; Mucchielli, 1965). Others formulate their theory without specifying the level they are addressing (Lemay, 1973; Mailloux, 1971) or convey a concept of delinquency that does not correspond to the level concerned in their analysis; A.K. Cohen (1955) and Cloward & Ohlin (1960) used a definition of delinquency that refers to conduct but in fact, they formulated a theory of the delinquent role. On the other hand, a number of recent authors have taken this requirement into account, from Hirschi (1969) to Cusson (1983), Arnold and Brungardt (1983), and Cullen (1985), who particularly stressed its application.

We chose to examine the second level in depth, that is, to acquire a thorough knowledge of the criminal activity itself (as authors such as A.K. Cohen, 1969; Farrington, 1973; and others have recommended). Our approach is based on the principle that criminal performance, in its factual sense, represents the primary point in criminology, the "irrefutable reality" (as Fréchette, 1970, put it), a reality that does not suffer speculation and can afford a truly scientific grasp of the phenomenon. To a large extent, this delinquency is established regardless of the ups and downs of social reaction, because it is an indictable offense committed by the subject and since identified as such by the courts.

Furthermore, it is not enough to choose a particular interpretation of the criminal reality; the very idea of delinquency must be adequately operationalized. In this regard, a large number of indicators represent the phenomenon: prevalence, incidence, persistence, development, gravity, duration, precocity, polymorphism, and so on. Authors often use different terms for these elements. For example, for *polymorphism* they use *variety* and *diversity*; for *intensity* they use *gravity* and *development*. Worse still, sometimes the same indicator is not measured in an identical way from one study to another.

To avoid these difficulties, recent works (Blumstein, Cohen, Roth, & Visher, 1986; Fréchette & Le Blanc, 1979, 1987; Le Blanc, 1986b; Loeber, 1982, 1985a, 1987) suggest better integrated and more consistent conceptual structures. Blumstein et al. (1986) proposed that to denote the level of interpretation in which we are interested here, criminal activity, the term *individual offending* should be used. In this way we get a generic concept that has the advantage of describing our subject of study while avoiding any ambiguity of meaning that the term delinquency often carries. It also makes it possible to go deeply into the reality by allowing us to identify three different but nonetheless connected concepts from which to approach the phenomenon: the offense, offending, and patterns (Fig. 1.1).

Beginning with the first, the offense, we find that European criminology, particularly in Germany (Göppinger, 1987; Seelig, 1956) and the Latin countries (Pinatel, 1963), has a large accumulation of studies that describe the cognitive, affective, moral, and material conditions governing the perpetration of the crime, both in general and in the case of particular types of criminals (perverts, the mentally ill, the professional, the emotionally inspired, etc.). The works of Erez (1980, 1987) on planning and of Cusson (1983, 1986), Felson and Cohen (1980), and Hough, Clarke, and Mayhew (1980) on utilitarian delinquency are in the same vein. This level of analysis concerns the description of a specific episode in a particular time period.

Offending, the second level of analysis of criminal activity, is a predominant study in North American criminology. Within this level are many concepts and measures of crime as an individual behavior, for example, prevalence, incidence, specialization, escalation, seriousness, duration, onset, variety, and so on. These are often redundant. For example, variety, diversity, and polymorphy refer to the heterogeneity of crime; intensity, aggravation, and seriousness refer to the gravity of crime; and so on. Further, the same concepts can be operationalized by very different measures. To clarify conceptually the situation, we propose to distinguish between descriptive and evolutive constructs of offending, and we will show that these parameters can be assembled to reconstruct the mechanisms of the development of offending.

The third level of analysis of criminal activity, patterns of offending, refers to a more abstract configuration of the characteristics of all the crimes committed. We will infer a typology from a large number of attributes of offending. Building on the distinction between classes and types (Hempel, 1952; Schrag, 1971), we will not propose a classification that refers to a number of logically possible combinations but a typology that attempts to specify the ways in which variables are empirically connected. This typology of patterns of offending will differ from existing criminal behavior systems such as those of Clinard and Quinney (1967) or of Gibbons (1965) because it will not incorporate any psychological or social role characteristics of the delinquents. It will be strictly a typology of behavior, such as that of Fréchette and Le Blanc (1980, 1987) or of Dunford and Elliott (1984). The construction of such a typology of criminal behaviors will be based exclusively on the descriptive and evolutive parameters and on the mechanisms of the development of offending.

Proposing three levels of analysis of criminal activity implies the use of three distinct perspectives. To study the completion of the offense, an analytical perspective should be used in which the criminal act is broken down into its most significant elements; to study the development of offending, a comparative perspective should be used in which the various illicit acts of the individual are looked at to discover the structures and dynamics underlying them; to examine the construction of behavioral patterns of offending, a synthetic perspective must be used that offers understanding of how long the penchant for crime lasts and the place it occupies in the life of the subjects.

The Offense

To account for the acting out, three kinds of facts must be considered: the type of offense that was committed, how it was carried out, and the external factors that triggered its commission. The last tells us where, why, and against whom the crime was perpetrated.

Type

An inventory as complete as possible of the delinquent acts generally perpetrated by youngsters who appear before the Juvenile Court (what we call criminally oriented delinquency) gave us a list of 14 categories for measurement purposes. Each category was given a precise definition (see Table 1.1). An effort was made to obtain the greatest homogeneity possible within the categories while maximizing the differences between them. All information gathered on the subjects of our research was then classified and codified with the aid of these 14 possible choices, enabling us to handle the data economically and effectively while organizing them with maximum consistency.

TABLE 1.1. Categories of types of offense.

Category	Description
Petty larceny	Acts of minor gravity such as the theft of sweets, cigarettes, toys, small amounts of money, school supplies; shoplifting (at corner store, for example)
Shoplifting	More serious offenses than preceding one because committed with a coefficient of greater risk (in department stores, for instance) or carried out in a well-planned and organized way
Common theft	Precise group of thefts excluding those involving breaking and entering or personal robbery; ranges from theft of various objects, including bicycles and sums of money, to receiving stolen merchandise
Burglary	All kinds of illegal entry; breaking and entering for purposes of theft whether successful or not; includes intention and attempt; theft inside a motor vehicle; possession of tools for purposes of burglary
Personal larceny	Crime depriving victim of possession by means of physical attack; principal offenses are theft with violence, aggravated theft, theft from delivery person, purse snatching, pickpocketing, etc. Implies the use of force in any form, but on condition that it is against one or several private individuals
Theft of motor vehicles	Theft of any motorized vehicle, from motorcycles and heavy trucks to trains, airplanes, and boats, etc.
Aggravated theft	Thefts of a more criminal nature: business or bank holdups; theft of arms, mail; etc.
Vandalism	Destruction or deterioration or private or public property, such as damage to property, fires, breakages, etc.
Personal attack	Physical attack against a person without any element of theft; main manifestations are assault, assault and battery, grievous bodily harm; by extension, can include threats, and possession of arms (with intent to threaten or attack someone)
Public mischief	Activities more deviant than delinquent: disturbing the peace, illicit presence, vagrancy, running away (if officially charged), possession of forbidden objects, sounding a false alarm, etc.
Drugs	Possession of drugs; trafficking
Sexual offenses	Indecency, indecent exposure, soliciting, rape and attempted rape, etc.
Fraud	Appropriation by means of trickery, such as the fabrication of false documents or forged money; use of forged checks or stolen credit cards; false representation, bank or business frauds; etc.
Homicide	Homicide and attempted homicide

This inventory clearly shows that the concept of delinquency is strictly empirical, since any act liable to incur a measure of judicial control is considered delinquent. Despite its limited character, the inventory offers the advantage of specifying the forms of illicit act under consideration from the most serious crimes to the most harmless. The amplitude of this nomenclature seems sufficient to cover all the criminal activity of interest here. It must be noted that in some of the categories there is marked heterogeneity because the characteristics of the behavior sometimes differ considerably.

TABLE 1.2. Descriptive and boundary parameters of offending.

Descriptive parameters	Boundary parameters
Participation Number of criminally active individuals in a population at a given time	Onset Age of the subject at the first crime
Frequency Number of crimes committed by an individual within a given period of time	Duration Interval between first and last crime
Variety Number of crime categories in which an individual is involved	Age of termination Age of the subject at last crime
Seriousness Degree of gravity of the crimes of an individual (for example, Sellin & Wolfgang, 1964, definition)	Transfer Transfer from juvenile delinquency to adult criminality
Direction Nature of the crimes committed	Crime switching Transfer from one type of crime or crime mix to another
Crime mix Mix of crimes, combinatory structures	

METHOD OF PERPETRATION

With regard to the modus operandi, every effort was made to find the principal components of each type of offense described by the subjects and in this way to discover what Pinatel (1963) called "the mechanisms of the crime." The investigation focused on the preparation of the crime, the use of technical means (arms, tools, vehicles, etc.), the physical conditions of execution, the presence of accomplices and their number and age, the role of the subject in the group, and use of violence, either physical or psychological, against the victim. These different facets of delinquent behavior constitute the facts on which our analysis of the delinquent act is based. In spite of their obvious interest, these kinds of data have been relatively rare in the criminological literature of the past few decades.

EXTERNAL FACTORS

Finally, particular attention was given to determinants of the delinquent behavior that played a role, if not in triggering it, at least in creating conditions favorable to it or even precipitating or accompanying its perpetration. Certain factors were controlled, such as the state of mind prior to the acting out, the preponderance of a hedonistic or utilitarian motive, tension experienced during the execution of the crime, the presence of intoxication before and/or during the act, the anticipated reaction of close relatives, and the consequences for the subject.

From this triple perspective, chapter 2 proposes an analysis of the completion of crime that will necessitate a thorough examination of the way in which each of the manifestations of delinquency was perpetrated.

TABLE 1.3. Process sustaining offending.

Activation
Acceleration: impact of age of onset on frequency
Stabilization: impact of age of onset on duration
Diversification: impact of age of onset on variety
Escalation
Stages in offending: relationship between types of crime, seriousness, age of onset, duration, age of termination, and time
Progression: from minor to more serious delinquency
Desistance
Deceleration: reduction of frequency before age of offset
Specialization: diminution of variety before age of offset
Culmination: remaining at a particular stage of criminal activity for the rest of the active criminal time

The offending

For this analysis, we propose three perspectives: descriptive, boundary, and process points of view. The first concerns the global indices of offending; through these a synthetical, statistical picture of a sample or a population can be drawn. The second refers to the markers of the frontiers of offending; these concern onset, duration, offset, and so on. The third is about the dynamic aspects of offending, the mechanisms of its development. Loeber (1982, 1985a), and Blumstein et al. (1986) used the first two types of approach but did not see the necessity of distinguishing between them in analyzing delinquent behavior. In our opinion, the triple analysis that we are proposing is essential because it helps to describe offending and facilitates understanding of not only the mechanisms that govern its development, but also the limits of its evolution. Table 1.2 presents the nomenclature of the descriptive and evolutive parameters and Table 1.3 lists the mechanisms of offending.

DESCRIPTIVE VIEW

As is traditional in criminology, we first distinguished between prevalence and incidence. Blumstein et al. (1986) suggested that *prevalence* denoted current or cumulative participation in delinquency, referring to the number of individuals who had committed a crime. *Incidence*, which Blumstein et al. (1986) called "frequency" and Loeber (1982) called "density," concerns the number of crimes committed by an individual within a given period of time.

These two descriptive measures, classic in criminology, can be complemented, according to Pinatel (1963), first by ascertaining the direction of the delinquent activities, that is, finding the number of individuals who have committed the different categories of offense [in this regard Fréchette and Le Blanc (1979, 1987) wrote also of the structure of offending or of the combinatory structure of offenses and Blumstein et al. (1986) wrote of the mix of infractions, or the "crime mix"]; second, by determining the intensity of the illicit activities, thus establishing the number of individuals for each different level of gravity involved (in conformity with the definition of seriousness adopted by Sellin & Wolfgang, 1964); and finally, by learning the diversity or variety of the illicit behavior, which makes possible finding the individual frequencies, given the number of categories of crimes accumulated.

Hence the study of offending depends on six types of indices – participation, frequency, variety, seriousness, direction, and crime mix. They will be called *descriptive parameters of offending* in this book. They are standard constructs in criminology and there are no great controversy on their definition and operationalization. Chapter 3 deals with them.

Boundary View

The evolutive parameters underlying this perspective are both old and new; they are listed in Table 1.2. Some go back to the works of the Gluecks (1930, 1937, 1943), such as the idea of precocity and desistance; others have more recently been refined, such as duration, which Blumstein and his collaborators (1982b, 1986) distinguished as partial, total, and residual; still others were either created or revised by longitudinal studies (Shannon, 1978; Wolfgang, Figlio, & Sellin, 1972; Wolfgang, Thornberry, & Figlio, 1987), such as transition from delinquency to criminality or the transfer from one type of criminal activity to another, which Blumstein et al. (1986) put under the heading of "crime switching."

Five constructs are proposed for the analysis of offending from a boundary point of view. They are onset, duration, age of termination, transfer, and crime switching (Table 1.2). These concepts are actually linked with a double dichotomy that is fundamental in developmental psychology, that of the continuity/discontinuity or stability/instability of the behavior (see Lerner, 1986). *Continuity* refers to the consistency over time of conduct of the same kind, whereas *stability* refers to the reproduction of identical behavior from one period to another. There are subtle nuances here, stable conduct being continuous (without the reverse being automatically true, however). Therefore, an individual can persist in delinquency by displaying juvenile and adult delinquency, but the nature of the offending can change in frequency, seriousness, variety, and so on. An individual can maintain the status of delinquent but the offending can regress or progress, become more or less serious, more or less frequent, and so on. Continuity is then very different from stability.

The boundary view is concerned with continuity. The continuity of the delinquent activity can be calculated in two ways: quantitative, where the data are the age at the time of the first offense (precocity), the total duration of offending (calculated by the time lapse, in years, between the first and last offense) and the age at the time of the last offense; and qualitative, the data being the transfer from one type of criminal activity to another. This transfer is measured in two ways:

Thanks to matrices of transition, it is possible to study crime switching, the changes in crime mix over time; it is also possible to study the continuity between juvenile delinquency, before the age of 18, and adult criminality, beginning from age 18.

Chapter 4 deals with the question of the continuity of offending using five constructs: onset, duration, offset, transfer, and crime switching. This point of view on offending has often been taken in criminology. This is not the case for the next perspective, the process view, where there is insufficient conceptualization and major controversies exist, as we will see.

Process View

With this perspective, a developmental analysis is used. It is concerned not only with the distribution of the crimes over the life span of an individual, but also with the processes that sustain continuity in offending. This perspective concerns the second distinction made by Lerner (1986), the problem of the stability/instability of delinquent behavior. The key question is, Does offending change over time? Attention is given to within-individual changes and to identification of processes underlying offending. This perspective is very different from the usual method of studying offending in criminology, the study of between-persons or group differences. A developmental approach implies concentrating on the dynamics of offending, for example, the processes of escalation, diversification, and so on. In the criminological literature, the developmental approach is generally simplistic because criminologists have not inspired themselves with the concepts and methods of developmental psychology. This is not to say that there have been no breakthroughs. Over the past 15 years, since the research done by Wolfgang et al. (1972), longitudinal studies have furnished interesting data on the relationship between several of the evolutive parameters we will be using, whereas syntheses, such as those of Loeber (1982, 1987) and of Blumstein et al. (1986) have led to clarification of the conceptualization of certain processes. All this work, however, is intuitive because it is not based on a well-thought-out procedure for reconstructing the natural dynamics of the development of offending. Our aim is to develop an approach that takes these concepts into account.

To do this we were guided by a general principle and a specific method. Lerner (1986), in his textbook on developmental psychology, recalled that the specialists of development had uncovered some general principles that should be helpful for the study of offending. One of them, the orthogenetic principle proposed by Werner (1957), is worth mentioning. It states that whenever development occurs, it proceeds from a state of relative globality and lack of differentiation to a state of relative differentiation, articulation, and hierarchic integration. This principle will serve as a background to the interpretation of our results on the development of offending. Duncan (1984) proposed a specific procedure to construct variables: A list of fundamental elements is compiled and then the variables are defined according to the combinations of these basic elements. By way of analogy, we propose to define the processes that encourage the development of offending as the result of the relationship between two or more descriptive and boundary parameters that are the basic elements of the offending (Table 1.2). The advantage of this procedure is that it offers clarity concerning the elements in question in the operational definition of constructs such as escalation, specialization, and so on.

With the guidance of this principle and procedure, the processes of activation, escalation, and desistance can be studied. Table 1.3 gives a definition of these general processes and of the subprocesses that constitute them. These three processes are perhaps not the only ones, but they seem to be the most important ones.

The activation process refers to the way the development of offending is stimulated as soon as it has begun and the way its persistence is assured. Once this process has begun, the result is delinquent activity marked by a high level of frequency, duration, and variety as well as precocity. This process is based on three separate, but closely interrelated, mechanisms–acceleration, stabilization, and diversification. Acceleration refers to the relationship between precocity and frequency; stabilization is inferred from the connection between precocity and duration; diversification is measured by the degree of variety in the criminal activity, taking precocity into account. This means that if offending starts early, it will probably be abundant, lasting, and varied. We will also show that the process of activation is the combined effect of acceleration, stabilization, and diversification.

Of these mechanisms, only acceleration is well known. Recent studies have shown that persons who are arrested early in life have a higher rate of frequency than those arrested later (J. Cohen, 1986; Farrington, 1983). On the other hand, those who start early commit more serious crimes later on (Shannon, 1978). It has similarly been established that early starters are more likely to become chronic delinquents (E.T. Glueck, 1968) and recidivists (Mannheim & Wilkins, 1955). In addition, Fréchette and Le Blanc (1979) were the first to describe the exact relationship between precocity and frequency on the basis of self-reported delinquency and Loeber (1982) on the basis of data on the official delinquency.

In describing the processes of escalation, we propose to clarify a question fiercely debated in criminological circles. Blumstein et al. (1986) proposed a clear definition: "Escalation is the tendency for offenders to move to more serious offense types as offending continues" (p. 84). In terms of the descriptive and boundary parameters we are using, we propose the following definition: Escalation refers to the appearance of a sequence of diverse forms of delinquent activities that go from minor infractions to the most serious crimes against the person as the delinquent increases in age. This sequence represents a more or less standard pattern of development among subjects who are heading for significant delinquency; the different parameters, types of crimes, seriousness, age of onset, duration, age of offset, are obviously contributing factors here. We will show that there are five sequential stages in offending, and we will verify if the delinquents are progressing to a more serious type of delinquency.

The last process we want to study is desistance, which depends on variety, escalation, and frequency of the offending. This means that the higher the frequency and the greater the variety and the seriousness, the greater is the chance of desistance due to saturation. It goes without saying that the mechanism of desistance should be studied only among persons whose delinquency is recurrent; one cannot speak of a process of desistance for the occasional delinquent. This process of desistance is composed of three subprocesses: specialization, deceleration, and culmination. Specialization implies desisting from a versatile offending into a more homogeneous one; it can be manifested when, with the passage of time, the person concentrates more and more on certain crimes or certain forms of crime. Deceleration refers to the reduction of frequency before offending is terminated. Culmination refers to the situation when a delinquent is blocked at a particular level of seriousness for a certain period of time before offending is stopped.

We will show in chapter 5 that offending develops according to these three basic processes in conformity with the orthogenetic principle. The changes in offending are systematic, organized, successive, and specific. They are not random. The theory of the development of offending that we will outline can be a guide for further studies.

The patterns

In the introduction, we set for ourselves the task of constructing behavioral patterns. These abstract configurations of the characteristics of all the crimes committed by an individual refer to the third, and more abstract, level of analysis of criminal activity. Having in front of us the recent criminological literature, in particular the National Academy of Sciences report (Blumstein et al., 1986), a question comes immediately to mind: Why did Blumstein et al. refer to criminal activity with the term *criminal career*? We have decided not to use this term to avoid confusion with its uses in sociology and criminology (especially with the criminological level of interpretation of the criminal).

When specialists of the sociology of occupation speak of a career, it is to refer immediately to the continuity of the activity, the successive stages during which specific expertise develops. Becker (1970), who expressed the thinking of sociologists on this question (citing Hall), defined the career as "... the patterned series of adjustments made by the individual to the network of institutions, formal organizations and informal relationships in which the work of the occupation is performed" (p. 165). Becker added (as Garfinkel, 1967, had illustrated before him) that these adjustments must be envisaged as ascending or descending movements between positions within the formal or informal hierarchies which may be based on prestige, influence, or income. This definition of a career is much more comprehensive than the meaning of "career" in criminology: It is concerned with the whole lifestyle, not only with highs and lows of criminal activity.

It is not restricted to behavioral patterns, and definitely not to criminal activity, the object of this book.

We must point out that the notion of career, in spite of its introduction in 1917 by von Mayr, is relatively absent from the early criminological literature. Empirical studies that describe one or several aspects of the criminal career did become more numerous in later publications. There are case descriptions (Shaw, 1931; Sutherland, 1937; etc.), numerous biographies and autobiographies, typologies of delinquent roles (Clinard & Quinney, 1967; Gibbons, 1965; Lemert, 1972; Schur, 1973) and more recently studies of chronic delinquents (Blumstein, Farrington, & Moitra, 1985b; Blumstein & Moitra, 1980; Chaiken & Chaiken, 1982; Dunford & Elliott, 1984; Farrington, 1981, 1984, 1985a, 1985b; Jesness & Haapanen, 1982; McCord, 1981; Petersilia, Greenwood, & Lavin, 1978; M.A. Peterson & Braiker, 1980; Polk, 1978; Polk et al., 1981; Rojeck & Erickson, 1981; West & Farrington, 1977; Wolfgang et al., 1972). Most of these works use a vague notion of career; the Blumstein et al. model (1986) is either very specific, when it is concerned with offense frequency (lambda), or unspecific, when it discusses offense seriousness. The criminal career is represented in a model within which four parameters interact–frequency, age of onset, age of termination, and duration. The seriousness dimension is not integrated into the model, but clear definitions of escalation and specialization are proposed following a literature review (Blumstein, 1986).

There is another reason to avoid the notion of criminal career–possible confusion with the level of interpretation of the criminal. As defined by sociologists, a career is an attribute of an *individual* or a way of describing his or her lifestyle. It is a set of successive adjustments in role, attitudes, relations, and so on, not only a set of behaviors. Because of this definition, the notion of a career should be used only when we are referring to individuals. When behaviors are the object of study, the notion of pattern seems more appropriate.

For these reasons, the term *patterns of offending* has been selected to represent the last level of analysis of criminal activity. In chapter 6, we will construct a typology based on a large number of attributes of offending. Being strictly a behavioral typology, this typology of patterns of offending will differ from existing criminal behavior systems, such as those of Clinard and Quinney (1967) and of Gibbons (1965), because it will not incorporate social role characteristics of the delinquents, and from typologies of delinquents, such as those of Hewitt and Jenkins (1946) and of Sullivan et al. (1957), because it will not include psychological traits.

This typology will not be composed of classes but of types. Following Hempel (1952), we will not propose a classification that refers to a number of logically possible combinations but a typology that attempts to specify the ways in which variables are empirically connected. The construction of such a typology of criminal behaviors will be based exclusively on the descriptive and evolutive parameters and on the mechanisms of offending. It will not be a statistical construction with such techniques as factor analysis or cluster analysis, but a logical construction based on our results. And it will respect the basic principles of typology construction: multidimensional, considering all aspects of offending; exhaustive, covering the whole spectrum of offending; and homogeneous, every type chosen to maximize its differences with the others and the resemblances between the cases it includes.

With this conceptual scheme outlined, we are now ready to pass to the empirical part of this book. We have defined three levels of analysis – offense, offending, and patterns; we have proposed a large number of constructs – descriptive and evolutive parameters and mechanisms; and we have chosen a method – combining the elements to accede to a higher level of analysis, from parameters to mechanisms or from offense to offending to patterns.

The Research Design

In this section we explain the essential characteristics of our research design. It is our intention to describe our sampling procedure and data collection in some detail, since this information is now available only in research reports written in French (Biron, Caplan, & Le Blanc, 1975, 1977; Fréchette, 1980; Lagier, 1983, 1988). This section is divided into two main subsections, the data and the instruments.

Data

Sources

The choice of a legal criminological definition of delinquency and our interest in the issues enumerated in the preceding section have guided the research initiative we began 15 years ago. From the start, we have taken indictable delinquency as our target, whether or not the case was brought to judgment in court, and in collecting information we have favored the version given by the subject. Further, we have directed our investigations to take into account the three levels of analysis in which we are interested.

To explain our choice of the legal criminological definition of delinquency, a number of details are needed. First, since data obtained by means of self-reported delinquency complement those furnished by official records of delinquency (see, in Hindelang et al., 1981, and in Le Blanc, 1983b, the arguments that support this), we needed to have recourse to these two types of data, particularly since we had decided to give strict priority to indictable crimes. The quality of these data of course depended on whether the delinquent conduct obtained with the data collection instruments was representative.

In addition, since we were interested in acts whose criminal nature was well established, we had to include a whole gamut of possible crimes (Fréchette, 1980; Le Blanc et al., 1973). With regard to measurement, this raised a problem of logical validity. We well know that in the social sciences this type of validity is the most difficult to guarantee. In the case of self-reported delinquency, this type of validity raises two questions: Is the conduct truly delinquent, that is, if it were to come to the attention of the official agencies of social control, would these agencies consider it delinquent conduct? And is the reported conduct representative of the criminal activity of the subject?

We note that the majority of surveys pay little attention to the representativeness of the conduct studied. Researchers either use someone else's instrument (the questionnaire of Nye and Short, 1957, is often used), they distort an instrument by removing or adding items, or they change the formulation of certain items. On the other hand, some studies (Elliott & Ageton, 1980; Hindelang et al., 1981; Le Blanc et al., 1973; Le Blanc & Pronovost, 1979) and our research discussed here have paid much attention to this question and have tried to achieve the best possible representativeness of types of conduct, from petty crimes to serious crimes, from crimes against property to crimes against persons (see Table 1.1).

Concerning the question whether the conduct is actually delinquent in terms of the law, studies (for example, Gold, 1970) and intepretations (see Hindelang et al., 1981) agree that the questions in most of the questionnaires generally concern acts punishable by law, but that the respondents also report experiences that could not be considered criminal according to customary juridical criteria. It must be said, then, that the self-report method gives an indication of the occurrence and prevalence of socially unacceptable behavior, but is not a certain indication of official delinquency. In short, we can consider that the logical validity of the questionnaire, although not perfect, is acceptable.

Given the fact that there has been no standardized police data on juveniles in Quebec since the 1970s, such records could not be used for our analysis. The official source of information was very inconsistent because of the number of police corps serving the areas where the selected subjects were living and because some of these areas had no files concerning juveniles. On the other hand, registration of the judicial data was much more stable, as were the data concerning placements in foster homes and dispositions of all kinds made by the juvenile court regarding children between the ages of 7 and 18. For these reasons, we rely on judicial data.

Data Collection Periods

Official reports and self-reported delinquency reports were gathered to cover the age range from onset of offending to the middle of the 20s. Our operational concepts, particularly our evolutive view, made longitudinal surveys necessary. We referred above to the debate going on between the supporters of longitudinal surveys and the upholders of cross-sectional surveys. The supporters of longitudinal surveys are Blumstein et al. (1986) and Farrington et al. (1986c); the upholders of cross-sectional surveys are Hirschi and Gottfredson (1983; Gottfredson & Hirschi, 1986, 1987a). The first emphasizes the numerous uses and advantages of designs with repeated measures on the same people. The second vigorously questions the usefulness of such surveys. Our position has been that this debate will prove as sterile as the qualitative-quantitative methods debate. Even if we accept the conclusions of Gottfredson and Hirschi that longitudinal research does not habitually address this question of the sequence of events, we think it is particularly important to elaborate the notion of crime, as we did in the preceding section, and experiment on different data-gathering intervals before drawing conclusions about the usefulness of specific research designs.

For many criminologists, the ideal design would be to apply the self-reported delinquency instrument every year [some ongoing research is using a 6-month time lapse between data gatherings (the session on Longitudinal Studies of the Development of Delinquency, Annual Meeting of the American Society of Criminology, 1987)] from late infancy to the middle 40s at least, if we are to have a life-span perspective. From our point of view, data gathering at such frequent periods is not necessary for economical, empirical, and technical reasons.

Gathering data at intervals of every 6 months or every year on large samples is very costly, even more so if we consider interviews of a few hours in length to gather comprehensive individual data, as we conducted. Empirically, it is also unnecessary. The data presented in the following chapters show that yearly changes are not very pronounced or regular before the age of 12. From 12 to the end of adolescence, the changes over a 2-year period are much more evident than those on a yearly basis; after adolescence, changes seem to occur at an even slower pace. Technically, there are no sound reasons to choose such a short recall period to counterbalance memory decay if we refer to Weis's (1986) discussion of empirical studies in cognitive psychology and survey methodology. It has also been shown by Hindelang et al. (1981) that longer periods of recall are even more efficient than a 1-year period in terms of reliability and validity of measures and in terms of association with correlates.

If there are no fundamental reasons not to have long intervals, even 3 and 4 years, between data gatherings of self-reported delinquency, it should be mentioned that the time lag must approximate the causal factors. Since we know very little about the sequencing of causal factors themselves, or in relation to delinquency, it is appropriate to be very prudent and to test varying intervals. Looking at the results of the London longitudinal study, particularly of West and Farrington (1973, 1977) and of Farrington (1986a), we would be inclined to conclude that broad factors (low social class or parent's criminality, for example) could survive through long intervals, whereas other factors must be studied at short intervals because their impact seems limited (labeling, leaving school, or getting married, for example).

In summary, the spacing of data gathering could be at more than 1 year, and preferably 2, but could also be at longer intervals, such as 3 or 4 years, since for salient events the respondents do not always make a rigid distinction between the last year and a longer period of time (see Weis, 1986). This strategy has been our choice.

Figure 1.2 illustrates our periods of data collection over time. First, it must be remembered that the official data on convictions were gathered over the entire

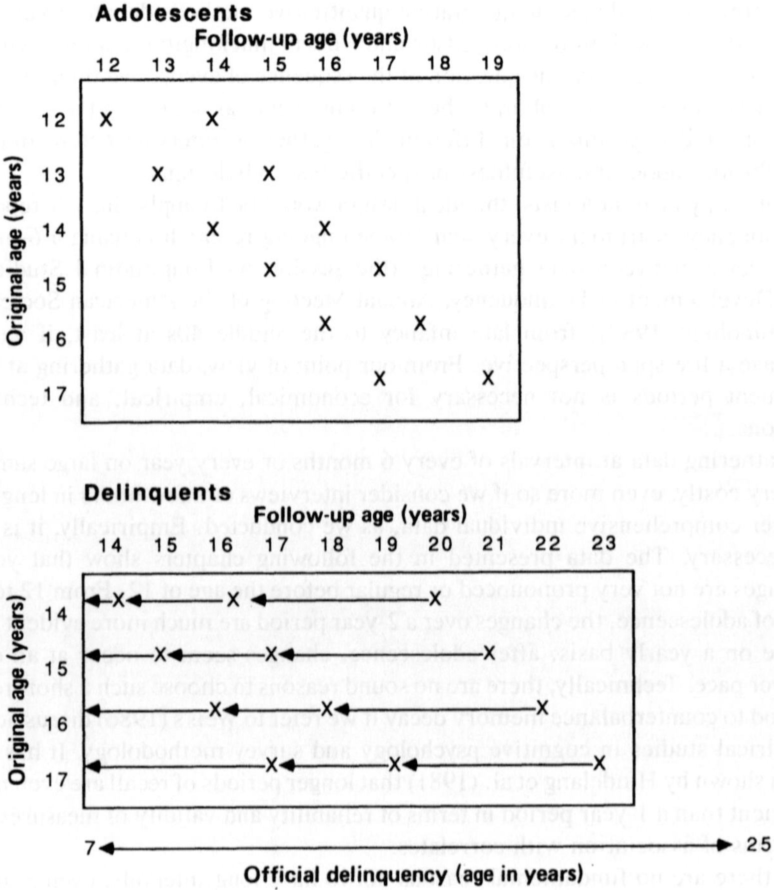

FIGURE 1.2. Data collections (X) for two samples – adolescents and delinquents.

period, from the age of 7, the minimum age of criminal responsibility in Canada, to an average of age 25. Second, for the self-reported delinquency, there were several successive waves of data collection, two for the adolescent sample and three for the delinquent sample. The spacing of each wave was 2 years during the period of adolescence for all subjects, and 4 years between the last interview during adolescence and the first interview during youth for the delinquent subjects.

It should be remembered that the 14-, 15-, and 16-year-olds constitute a group of subjects that are common to the two samples. Self-reported delinquency data covered the last year. A self-administered questionnaire was used for both samples, but the delinquent sample was also interviewed retrospectively concerning all their crimes since the beginning of their criminal activity and between each data collection.

The Samples

Two samples of males are constantly compared in the chapters of this book: a representative sample of 1,684 adolescents, called the "adolescents," and 470 convicted youths, called the "delinquents."

In general, studies of hidden or self-reported delinquency have recruited hundreds of adolescents to make up large samples. Nonetheless, it was hard to form fully representative samples because most such studies have drawn their clientele from the schools. The few studies that have tried for a truly random sample have run into the problem of how to include school dropouts, marginal populations, and institutionalized persons.

To offset these difficulties, we relied on the disparity and size of the two groups we recruited. Two random samples of French-speaking boys (including dropouts and other marginal populations) from the Island of Montreal, comprising 1,684 adolescents and 470 wards of the court, respectively, were constituted. These samples enabled us to make a complete and detailed inventory of criminal activity, both because we could compare the two groups and because of the representative nature of each group.

Since we are mainly concerned with processes in offending, for example, activation, escalation, and desistance, we favored a sample greatly at risk of chronic criminality. These processes do not stand out in a representative sample of the population because of the low base crime rate and particularly because of the low frequency for most crimes. Cernkovich, Giordano, and Pugh (1985) later recommended such a choice after showing that serious delinquents are too often absent from self-reported delinquency research based on representative samples of the population.

The Adolescents

The 1,654 adolescents were between the ages of 12 and 17 (Table 1.4) and represented all classes of society as well as all types of school and nonschool situations. The sample was stratified and randomized according to the five grades in secondary school and the different socioeconomic status of the school districts (see Biron et al., 1975). The adolescents completed a self-administered questionnaire in public and private schools, in various institutions, or at home during the spring of 1974.

During the spring of 1976, 2 years later, when the average age was 16.4, the same self-administered questionnaire was sent to a random sample of these boys by mail. Sixty percent (458) responded. The age distribution was not statistically different in this sample from the original sample (Table 1.4). Statistical tests for a large set of variables from different domains (family, peers, school, delinquency, etc.) have shown that these 458 boys very adequately represent the original sample (Biron et al., 1977).

The Delinquents

The delinquent sample comprised 470 boys from 13 to 17 years of age who had been taken under the authority of the court or given a sentence other than a fine

TABLE 1.4. Age distribution of samples of adolescent and delinquent boys, during completion of questionnaires 2 years apart and during interviews 2 and 5 years apart, respectively.

Questionnaire or interview	Total no.	Average age (yrs)	Age distribution (% of total)
		ADOLESCENTS	
Questionnaire 1	1,654	14.2	12 (9.4%), 13 (19.4%), 14 (28.9%), 15 (21.5%), 16 (20.8%)
Questionnaires 1 and 2	458	16.4	14 (9.3%), 15 (20.3%), 16 (32.1), 17 (21%), 18 (17.3%)
		DELINQUENTS	
Interview 1	470	15.2	13 (1.3%), 14 (27.9%), 15 (41.9%), 16 (23.6%), 17 (5.3%)
Interviews 1 and 2	396	17.4	
Interviews 1, 2, and 3	219	23.1	21 (6.4%), 22 (20.5%), 23 (29.2%), 24 (29.2%), 25 (14.6%)

or a compensatory measure. (For a detailed description of this sample, see Fréchette, 1980, and Lagier, 1983, 1988.) The boys were recruited between 1973 and 1976. All had appeared in court under the Young Delinquent Act (67.6%) or the Youth Protection Act (32.4%), and all had been declared wards of the court following that appearance. Some of the boys had just made their first appearance in court, some were reappearing, and some were the object of a placement by the social services. They were interviewed when they were on probation (43.6%), in detention (27.7%), or in an open institution (28.7%). As we will see later on, some were not sentenced for a crime or did not self-report any crime, but every one of them had been taken under the authority of the court when they were recruited.

The average age of the delinquent group was 15 years at the time of the first interview. The distribution of ages (Table 1.4) was quite similar to the age distribution of the population of the court of Montreal (Fréchette & Le Blanc, 1987).

Two years after recruitment, between 1975 and 1978, we reinterviewed 396 of the 470 subjects. The average age was then 17. Six boys had died during that interval. Of the remaining 68 subjects, 63 (13.6%) could not be located or a personal contact could not be made with their family or with them. Five boys chose not to collaborate with us. In sum, 84% of the original wards of the court (85% of those still living or 99% of those contacted) were reinterviewed. A comparison of these 396 with the original 470 showed no significant difference between them (Fréchette, 1980).

Five years later, in 1981–1982, we targeted interviewing 250 of the original 470 subjects, due to budget restraint in the context of an economic recession. The 470 had now been reduced to 456 through death – 8 more boys had died since the second interview); making a total of 14 (3%). To make sure that the sample of 250 subjects would be representative of the original sample, the following strategy was chosen (as described by Lagier, 1988). The original sample was divided into eight levels of persistence in delinquency according to records at different ages. We calculated the proportion that each level accounted for in the original sample of 470 subjects. Applying these proportions to our target number of 250 interviews, maximum quotas were set for each level of persistence in delinquency. Then subjects from among those interviewed twice were randomly interviewed up to the maximum quota for each level of persistence in delinquency.

The result was 219 interviews that represented very well the frequency distribution of the eight levels of persistence in delinquency in the original sample of 470 subjects. The average age was 23 in interview three. Table 1.4 shows the age distribution. This group, then, represents the original sample on the most important variable, delinquency (Lagier, 1988).

The Instruments

We cannot review here all the discussions on qualities that a good instrument of measurement of delinquency should have: the masterly evaluation of Hindelang et al. (1981) and Le Blanc's inventory (1983b) do just that. However, we must point out that we resorted to two kinds of approach—the self-administered questionnaire about delinquency in the last year used by both samples, and an interview about delinquency in the lifetime and since the last interview with the court sample.

The Self-Administered Questionnaire

The two samples were administered a self-reported questionnaire at a 2-year interval. This questionnaire consisted of about 220 questions, among which were 39 devised to represent a variety of types of delinquency, including serious acts (such as breaking and entering, fighting with a knife). The items were scored on an ordinal recency scale: never, once or twice, many times or often during the last year. The 39 delinquency questions (see Appendix A) were grouped into types of behavior on the basis of the results of a factor analysis showing six factors: status offenses, minor theft, major theft, vandalism, aggression, and selling and using drugs (Sarrasin, Caplan, & Le Blanc, 1977). These types were constructed using the items that loaded significantly (.40 and higher) on one of these factors only. These questions make it possible to judge the extent of the delinquency, its nature, its gravity, and its diversity. They refer solely to recent delinquency, that is, that occurring during the previous year.

The Semistructured Interview

With the second method, the ward of the court was asked to recall the offenses he had committed. To help him do this, a semistructured interview was introduced. Most of the analyses in this book are based on data from these interviews. Even if Hindelang et al. (1981) have shown that there is no major difference between the two instruments, the questionnaire and the interview, we chose to rely on the interview, for the following reasons.

We do not contend that an interview is superior to a questionnaire. That question has been discussed at length by many authors without any clear recommendation (Belson & Beeson, 1969; Gold, 1966; Hardt & Bodine, 1965; Nettler, 1974). It is, however, superior at this time in the development of knowledge about offending, because we do not know much about the dynamics of criminal activity. A standard questionnaire is too restrictive; an appropriate questionnaire would be too complex. Let us first present the advantages of a semistructured interview in relation to the need for heuristic studies of the development of offending. Then we will outline the complex instrument we used to elicit delinquency.

The advantages of a semistructured interview have been discussed by numerous authors (Belson & Beeson, 1969; Hardt & Bodine, 1965; Hood & Sparks, 1970; Nettler, 1974; Robins, 1966). Some interesting features of the interview are the following: Direct personal contact with subjects may help eliminate general or specific resistances to reporting crimes and may produce conditions that encourage communication. It may control for cognition, for example, reading or concentrating capacity, or for motivational errors, for example, interest or fatigue. The interviewer can also encourage high validity and reliability through being able, for example, to probe a frequency that seems surprising or for something that may have been forgotten, or to check on an understanding, say, when the respondent hesitates or shows signs of difficulty. The interviewer can also verify if the crimes reported are real crimes by asking questions about the modus operandi.

Two features of the semistructured interview are particularly important for the study we report in this book. These are the possibilities it offers for precision and for sequencing events. With the interview it is possible to explore in detail many aspects of the exact nature of the crime. Other information is also available, such as the occurrence of a series of crimes, the number and characteristics of accomplices, the presence of planning and instruments, the nature of intimidation and intoxication, and so on. In fact, it is possible to construct a time chart of the offending of an individual. This is related to the most interesting feature of the semistructured interview, the ordering of crime events. In a semistructured interview, the interviewer can situate rather precisely the location of transitional events in the life of the individual–when he left school, when his father left home, and so on–and can inquire about psychosocial factors–what was the supervision or the sanctions at certain ages, what were occupational aspirations, and so on. These types of information may be of great importance when a knowledge base is lacking, as in the case of the development of offending.

The use of a semistructured interview raises the question of the characteristics of the interviewer. Even if interviewer characteristics, such as age, sex, or race, do not seem to play an important role in distorting answers to survey questions about crimes (Hindelang et al., 1981), it is important to note that this has been found for adolescents but may not be the case for children or adults. In our experience and the experience of others, a mother-type interviewer has better rapport with young subjects and an older adult seems to elicit more valid and reliable information from young adults. Thus, not only should we control for the importance of these structural characteristics, but interpersonal skills should also be questioned. In particular, with a semistructured interview, it is our experience that more skilled persons produce more detailed data. We have tried to control for this impact by selecting highly skilled persons at the interpersonal level, by training these persons adequately, and by reviewing each of their interviews and giving them feedback on problems.

Such a defense of the semistructured interview as the most appropriate tool to study the development of offending is related to the state of existing criminological knowledge. Since it is definitely insufficient concerning conceptualization and data, a standard self-administered questionnaire would have limited us too much in this exploratory phase. To illustrate the potential of a semistructured interview, Appendix B outlines a protocol that we have used in Montreal.

The interviewer starts the part of the interview on delinquency with the first crime and has a set of 14 precisely defined categories of crimes (Table 1.1) to cover. To these categories can be added types of conduct disorders (use of drugs, fights, and so on). For each crime or set of crimes, the interviewer has a list of questions to cover: when the crime was first and last committed, the period during which there was a series of this type of crime, the frequencies obtained, how the crime was completed (planning, instrument, violence, accomplices, etc.). The interviewer knows the coding to all these questions, which helps to cover all topics. During the interview a report sheet is completed that orders all crimes and series of crimes with the appropriate information on each. With this type of data, it is possible to study the development of offending precisely.

Need for Data Specificity

It should be noted that in the delinquency measured by a self-administered questionnaire and the delinquency measured by a semistructured interview, the data were strictly *behavioral*, that is, they referred solely to the material aspects of the offenses, and the methods used. This level of measurement must be kept pure, uncontaminated by components of a different order, whether psychological, cultural, social or anything else, and essentially representative of what can be designated as the *delinquent fact*. It is only by maintaining such specificity that subsequent relationships with other measures, taken as dependent variables, can be accomplished. This orientation is the main thrust of this book.

2
Perpetration of the Offense

The first part of our analysis of male illicit activities concerns the perpetration of the offense. Sutherland and Cressey (1960) distinguished two types of explanation for crime: the processes operating at the moment of the occurrence of crime (the situational or dynamic explanation), and the processes operating in the earlier history of the criminal (the historical or genetic explanation). These authors rapidly went on to develop the second type of explanation, differential association, whereas they devoted merely a paragraph to argue that the immediate determinants of criminal behavior lie in the person-situation complex, which is the basis for the actual rational choice perspective (Cornish & Clarke, 1986). There is virtually nothing else in their book concerning the level of analysis of the modes of perpetration of the crime.

American empirical criminology has been mostly silent about that level of analysis, even if theoreticians have emphasized the utility of the situational explanation of criminal behavior (A.K. Cohen, 1966; Gibbons, 1968; Ohlin, 1969). The scant studies do not describe thoroughly the completion of crime, they mainly address questions of presence of planning and sophistication. They conclude that only a small fraction of offenses are conceived beforehand – the most serious profit-oriented ones. This is true of crime in general (Erez, 1980, 1987; Gath, Tennent, & Pidduck, 1971; Hindelang, 1972; Persilia et al., 1978) and for specific offenses (shoplifting: Bennett & Wright, 1984; Cameron, 1964; Carroll & Weaver, 1986; burglary: Maguire, 1982; Reppetto, 1974; robbery: Cocklin, 1972; Feeney, 1986; Gabor et al., 1987; homicide: Luckenbill, 1977; Wolfgang, 1958; rape: Amir, 1971). A recent explanation of the situational determinants of the perpetration of crimes was proposed as routine activities (L.E. Cohen & Felson, 1979, 1980; Felson, 1987).

European criminology has been much more active conceptually and empirically at this level of analysis. In Germany, much work has been done in that domain (see Göppinger, 1987), particularly careful case studies of the completion of specific crimes by criminalists. Seelig (1956) summarized that work and proposed seven basic questions to be addressed for each crime: Who? What? Where? With whom? Why? How? When? He also stated that for a crime to be committed there must be an individual with the proper predisposition and a specific situation that triggers the crime. Parallel to this development, in Belgium a psychiatrist, De Greef (1955, 1956) developed with clinical cases a theory of the process of the perpetration of a crime. And Pinatel (1963) classified the elements of the crime to be considered and proposed a comprehensive analysis of many crimes using this list of elements. More recently, English criminologists (Clarke, 1983; Clarke & Cornish, 1985; Cornish & Clarke, 1986) have revived that tradition with new empirical studies, proposing explanatory models and introducing the rational-choice theoretical perspective.

This level of analysis has attained a certain status in criminology with a textbook about criminal behavior (Hagan, 1987). We will devote our second chapter to this aspect of criminal activity. The data for our analysis are based on in-depth interviews with delinquents during mid-adolescence, at the end of adolescence, and as they entered their 20s. Using the measuring indices described in the preceding chapter, we evaluate the increased sophistication of crime.

The elements involved in the perpetration of the crime can be divided into three categories: the elements of the immediate situation, the subject's reaction to the offense, and the mechanics of the infraction. The elements of the immediate situation will be ascertained through the question, Against whom? (was the victim known?), and What? (what was the nature of the crime?). The reaction factors concern the perception of the act by the offender and his analysis of the pros and cons involved. These will be investigated through the offender's motives (utilitarian or hedonistic) and by means of the subject's reaction (tension during or after the infraction). Finally, concerning the mechanics of the crime, questions as to how and with whom will reveal some of these mechanisms, especially in terms of complicity (the presence, number, and ages of accomplices) as well as the modus operandi (the precipitating circumstances, that is, the presence of intoxication before or during the crime; the material preparation, that is, the use of tools; also the presence of psychological and/or physical violence and the role of the subject in the infraction).

One of the more valid ways of investigating the perpetration of crime is by means of a differential and longitudinal study. Rather than arriving at an illusory average conduct by means of descriptive operational concepts, the investigation must follow the many variations of completed crimes in order to grasp all of their diversity and complexity, both synchronically and diachronically. Consequently, we shall describe the elements of the characteristics of perpetration for each category of crime by covering a considerable length of time divided into three periods: beginning of childhood to middle of adolescence (470 male wards of the Montreal Court), middle to end of adolescence (396 of the original 470), end of adolescence to age of 23 (a representative sample of 219 of the 396).

The First Half of Adolescence

Burglary

As mentioned in chapter 1, this category of crime includes all types of illegal entry, breaking and entering, or the smashing of objects in order to commit a theft. More than three out of five delinquents (62%) admitted to having committed acts such as illegally entering a home to steal money and/or objects of value, breaking and entering warehouses and stores to steal merchandise, stealing from motor vehicles by breaking the lock, and so on. Before the age of fifteen they have committed an average of 11 burglaries.

The perpetration of this category of crime has some interesting characteristics (as shown in Table 2.1). The most striking is that almost all burglaries are group crimes, 88% of the boys having worked with accomplices. The groups are small, averaging two participants and rarely having more than five; in 9 cases out of 10, the boys are within a year or so in age. Thus, group support, most of the time by peers of the same age, proves to be an almost indispensable condition for the execution of the act.

It appears, too, that burglary is one of the categories of crime in which advance preparation is most frequent; 71% of the youngsters said they always prepared ahead of time. Such preparation involved planning and organization before the crime and/or recourse to a familiar and proven modus operandi. In addition, 56% of the boys said they carried instruments (burglar's tools, bars, blades, various objects). Thus, at an already early age, the subjects seem to have calculated the requirements of an efficient modus operandi and equipped themselves with the necessary tools.

Moreover, although the utilitarian motivation was predominant (67% of the group), a good half of the subjects (53%) were also looking for hedonistic gratification. The situation is the same for all the categories of theft that have a pronounced acquisitive character, such as common theft, personal larceny, and aggravated theft; percentage levels for utilitarian and hedonistic motives do not vary much from one to the other. On the other hand, what seems to be specific to burglary is the presence of tension during and after the act; a fair amount of subjects (47% during and 32% after) said they experienced feelings of stress almost every time. Perhaps this is because, on the one hand, the perpetrator of a burglary runs a fairly high risk, and on the other, this is one of the first serious crimes undertaken by very young adolescents. A good many subjects, however (49% in the first case and 57% in the second) felt no tension during a burglary, remaining relatively cool and collected; this accounts for the small percentage (always in comparison with other categories of crime), 27%, who felt the need to bolster themselves with alcohol or drugs.

In general, burglary is strictly an appropriation of goods and is done furtively during the absence of the owner, as evidenced by the fact that more than 90% of the subjects never had to resort to violence, threats, or intimidation to get what they wanted. This preference for anonymity is borne out by the observation that in three quarters of the cases, the victim was unknown (the word *victim* here includes places known or familiar to the subject). However, the presence or arrival of the owner or some other person does not always cause the youngsters to run away; 23 subjects had become violent under such circumstances, fighting with their bare fists, and 12 had fought with weapons on one or two occasions.

TABLE 2.1. Characteristics of perpetration of crime during the first half of adolescence (n = 470).

		Method of Execution							Conditions of Execution					
			Preparation			Complicity			Use of Violence		Tension		Motivation	
Type of Crime[a]	Total	Victim Known	Psychological (intoxication)	Material Planning	Instruments	Presence	Number (one)	Age (same)	Physical (force/ weapon)	Psychological (intimidation)	During	After	Hedonistic	Utilitarian
Burglary	62%[b]	24%	27%	71%	56%	88%	46%	93%	9%	3%	47%	32%	53%	67%
	266[c]	64	77	188	150	235	122	216	23	9	124	86	141	177
Shoplifting	54%	8%	10%	52%	13%	67%	46%	92%	3%	1%	47%	28%	63%	48%
	232	18	24	120	30	155	106	137	7	3	139	66	145	112
Common	40%	31%	17%	52%	19%	62%	56%	90%	4%	1%	31%	26%	47%	66%
theft	172	54	29	89	33	107	97	155	6	2	54	45	81	113
Motor	35%	13%	36%	52%	40%	83%	62%	93%	5%	1%	39%	27%	82%	29%
vehicle theft	152	19	54	79	60	126	93	141	7	2	59	41	125	44
Vandalism	23%	39%	22%	34%	65%	77%	49%	86%	13%	5%	22%	18%	75%	33%
	98	38	22	33	64	75	48	85	13	5	22	18	73	32
Personal	22%	10%	45%	56%	30%	83%	47%	90%	63%	50%	38%	28%	40%	77%
larceny	96	10	43	54	29	80	45	86	60	48	36	27	38	74
Petty theft	21%	58%	2%	29%	2%	37%	56%	97%	1%	0%	34%	32%	60%	57%
	89	52	2	26	2	33	14	32	1	0	30	28	53	51
Aggravated	13%	28%	30%	76%	72%	53%	76%	76%	19%	56%	35%	26%	41%	67%
theft	54	15	16	41	39	41	18	31	10	30	19	14	22	36
Personal	8%	44%	44%	47%	67%	47%	57%	86%	83%	42%	28%	22%	50%	53%
attack	36	16	16	17	24	36	8	18	30	15	10	8	18	19
Drug	8%	8%	75%	58%	0%	50%	58%	93%	0%	0%	6%	0%	39%	67%
trafficking	36	3	27	21		18	7	13		0	2	0	14	24
Public	8%	24%	39%	33%	15%	55%	73%	94%	18%	6%	18%	15%	61%	21%
mischief	33	8	13	11	5	18	8	16	6	2	6	5	20	7
Sex crime	2%													
	9	7	0	4	0	3	3	–	0	0	2	1	7	3

[a] Listed according to the number of delinquents committing the crime, greatest number to least number.
[b] Percentages calculated on 470 subjects.
[c] Row total; all the numbers and percentages in a row refer to these totals.

Shoplifting

This category of crime took second place in terms of the number of delinquents involved, 54% of the sample admitting to shoplifting with an average of 18 offenses each. Shoplifting was slightly less widespread than burglary but nonetheless adopted by one of every two adolescents. It was much more frequent then the other categories of crime.

Many of the crime characteristics studied do not apply to shoplifting for obvious reasons: No tools are needed, the subject mainly requiring manual dexterity; violence, whether physical or psychological, is unnecessary; and the victim is anonymous most of the time. Concerning intoxication before or during the crime, it seldom occurs in this category of theft (only 10% of the subjects), although it is hard to explain why. It could be that the subjects, once under the influence of drugs or drunk, tend to think of more serious crime, or again, as experience has shown, adolescents do their drinking mainly at the end of the day or at night, when most stores are closed. Shoplifting is preferably a group effort, more specifically a small group, generally composed of youngsters of the same age; it is first done for kicks or adventure, then for material gain. Only half the group had prepared for the crime in advance, the other half having acted on impulse or because the opportunity presented itself. This explains the tension reported by a good number of subjects.

Common Theft

This category ranked third, involving 40% of the delinquents with an average of nine offenses each. It covered a gamut of diverse acts, generally of medium gravity from the legal point of view, with the common characteristic being strictly theft, with no element of breaking and entering or of personal attack. It chiefly involved theft of money, clothes, electrical appliances, or bicycles and occurred in schools, in public places, and on private property.

The most striking characteristic of common theft is the fact that there is preparation in over 50% of cases (Table 2.1), an all the more significant percentage in that this form of delinquency depends largely on the subject finding favorable circumstances more or less by chance. Thus, preparation by at least half the subjects means they are constantly on the watch for the chance to "do a job."

The presence of accomplices seems to be fairly common (in 62% of the cases, one or several accomplices participated in carrying out most of the crimes). Most accomplices are about the same age as the subject, with the exception of about a quarter of the group, whose accomplices are significantly older. On the whole, however, the number of accomplices is fairly limited, for in about half the cases the subject had only one partner and in another 30% there were only two. This corroborates the probably widespread "inclination toward delinquency" behind these crimes, that is [especially considering that almost all the subjects (99 of 107) admitted to an active role in the preparation and execution of the act], that these youngsters get together with a maximum of one or two friends to look for, if not create, opportunities to steal. Conversely it might be said that the small number of accomplices greatly reduces the effect of group pressure and its power of suggestion, and consequently may show the possibly more gratuitous or more impulsive nature of the crime.

In such a context it was easy to foresee that the motivation would be utilitarian, which was actually the case; gain was the motive much more often (in 66% of cases) than hedonism (47%). Similarly, there was a certain amount of risk and adventure involved, since 69% of the subjects did not know the victim nor were they familiar with the place in which the theft was perpetrated. Few, however, experienced any tension before or after the crime (31% and 26%, respectively), nor was there much recourse to intoxicants (17% of cases).

The very small percentages under the headings "Instruments," "Physical Violence," and "Psychological Violence" were also foreseeable and have little meaning, because by definition this category of crime excludes contact with others and concerns acts that do not require the use of tools.

Motor Vehicle Theft

This category of crime is without doubt the most homogeneous of all 12. It includes not only theft of an automobile, which is by far the most frequent crime, but also theft of a motorbike, a motorcycle, a truck, and so on. However, in the final count no distinction will be made between "borrowing" a vehicle to take a joyride and stealing it for resale or dismantling. This category involved 35% of the sample.

Looking at Table 2.1, two characteristics are outstanding. These are the presence of accomplices (83%) and hedonistic motivation (82%). The number of accomplices varies considerably; 67 boys mentioned only one, 23 two, 10 three, and the other 15 four and over. The accomplices of a quarter of the subjects, incidentally, were much older. Regarding the percentage obtained under the heading "Hedonistic motivation," there is no doubt that it concerns the high rate of "borrowing a car for a joyride." The offense, which gives the youngster excitement and status (taking a ride even for a few moments in a big car one wants and can't afford), does not appear very serious to him, since the vehicle is borrowed temporarily and will not be used after the joyride.

It is possible that from the subjects' point of view, motor vehicle thefts are not as criminal as they are objectively perceived to be. The facts that the crime, even though prepared in 52% of cases, is committed by a group most of the time (that is, at the incitement or at least with the support of the group, and often even under the influence of older partners); done largely for kicks, and in the absence of the victim, and with no violence of any sort; and is accompanied by the consumption of alcohol and/or drugs (35%) and by tension during its commission (39%) show that motor vehicle theft is perhaps not committed in a context of a firm intention or with a criminal capacity. The recourse to tools in a relatively limited number of cases (39%), even when this is a type of theft in which tools could prove useful, shows the lack of method and organization with which it is usually executed.

Except for a small group of subjects (approximately 15 to 20%), who act out regularly, are out for material gain, prepare in advance, have tools, can operate on their own, know the victim, and so on, the theft of a motor vehicle, despite its presumed gravity, turns out to be more of a group venture having no antisocial significance for the guilty parties; for a good number of subjects it is limited to one, two, or three occurrences in the search for excitement or for the symbolic gratification it affords.

Vandalism

This category of crime includes misdemeanors, damage to property, fires, breaking things, and so on, that is, acts whose common denominator is the destruction or deterioration, most often pointless, of public or private property. It is principally a criminal activity that, much more than any other, is a futile discharge of aggression or frustration by means of destruction.

Even though the number of subjects given to vandalism was a good deal smaller than the number in the two preceding categories of crime, there were still 100 boys, or 23% of the sample, who committed an average of nine offenses each. On examining the characteristics of this category of crime in Table 2.1, we find a preponderance of cases where the acting out was a matter of physical release—"letting off steam." The dominant characteristic, then, and the one most evident in the 13 characteristics studied, is hedonistic motivation, which triggers the act for 75% of the subjects. The gap between this percentage and that acting for utilitarian reasons (33%) is very pronounced. In the majority of cases the act is gratuitous, impulsive, or at least opportunistic, given the fact that only 34% of the group mentioned having prepared ahead of time.

About the same proportion of subjects who admitted to a utilitarian motive (33%) also mentioned preparation (34%) and said they knew the victim (39%). Taking these three characteristics together would indicate that the aim was vengeance (which is included in the definition of utilitarian motivation). These subjects constitute a rather special group in which the search for vengeance, while necessarily classified until utilitarian motivation, presupposes a knowledge of the victim and premeditation as well as preparation.

Furthermore, as in the case of the categories of theft described previously, the presence of accomplices turns out to be an extremely important characteristic. Accomplices numbered between three and four on the average, all about the same age as the subject or within a year or two. On the other hand, barely 20% of the subjects mentioned feeling tense during the commission of the act, vandalism no doubt being seen as a rather amusing pastime.

Considering the nature of these acts, it was logical to find that there was little personal violence involved, even though the use of tools was predictably widespread, acts of vandalism being committed much more easily with heavy objects or pieces of metal than with the bare hands.

Personal Larceny and Aggravated Theft

A parallel can be drawn between these two categories of crime, since they share several determinant traits. Personal larceny comprises theft with violence—robbing a messenger, purse snatching, pickpocketing—whereas the second involves business business and bank holdups, the theft of weapons, and so on. Both have a more pronounced criminal connotation than the types of crime just discussed, the dominant element being the appropriation of another's goods by direct coercion. In stealing from a person, the methods are physical, involving violent manipulation of the victim; in the case of aggravated theft, the pressure is more psychological and proceeds by intimidation, the very real threat of bodily injury or even the life of the victim.

A total of 129 subjects, or 30% of the group of delinquents, were engaged in these forms of theft (108 committed one or the other, and 21 committed both). This is a large proportion considering the age of the subjects and seriousness of these crimes. For personal larceny, which was committed by the largest group, or 96 subjects, the average was fairly high, 7 offenses per person, whereas in the case of aggravated theft, involving 54 subjects, the average is quite lower, with 4 offenses per person.

Looking at the dominant characteristics of these two types of theft (Table 2.1), it is obvious that, compared with the other categories of crime, these are definitely the most serious; not only do the indicators of criminal gravity abound, they are also found to be the most frequently associated with one another. This is why the degree of utilitarian motivation is higher than in the other categories of crime (77% for personal larceny and 67% for aggravated theft), whereas the degree of hedonistic motivation is lower. Similarly, the presence of physical or psychological violence is considerable in these two types of theft. The offense is also prepared in advance in a great number of cases (56% for personal larceny and 76% for aggravated theft); instruments, which in these two cases tend to be fairly dangerous, are often used especially for aggravated theft. These two forms of theft, more than any other manifestation of delinquency except burglary, are the result of a group effort (83% in the case of personal larceny and 76% in aggravated theft).

Regarding the matter of accomplices, in both kinds of theft the number of partners is limited to two or three and most commonly to only one; it is interesting to note that a large number of subjects worked with one or several accomplices older than themselves. The large majority (especially in the case of aggravated theft) said they (the subjects) played an active role in carrying out the offense.

Concerning the other characteristics, tension either during or after the act is not prevalent, even less so than in other forms of crime although these two are far more serious. On the other hand, in the case of personal larceny there is a marked incidence of intoxication, which means that this type of theft is more likely to be an impulsive act or, more exactly, triggered by favorable circumstances once the subject has bolstered his courage with alcohol or drugs.

Considering that the crime involves a personal attack, this increases the potential dangerousness of the act. Finally, even though the percentages are not high, we note that aggravated theft is committed against a known victim three times as often as personal larceny, leading to the belief that the former tends to have elements of a high level of personal aggression, whereas the latter seems more impersonal.

Personal Attack

This category of crime completes the series of activities that can be considered most authentically delinquent. It is a special kind of delinquency involving almost pure aggressive reactions having nothing to do with theft. Its concrete forms are assault and battery and bodily harm. Given the particular nature of this crime, their insignificant material gain, and the potential risk to the perpetrator, it was evident to us that this crime would be much less prevalent in our group than the other truly delinquent acts. The figures we obtained confirmed this. In fact, only 36 subjects (8%) had engaged in this type of crime, with an average of 4 offenses per subjects.

An examination of the characteristics of this category of crime (see Table 2.1) offers a rather ambiguous picture. Approximately half of the subjects prepared the crime, had accomplices, and were intoxicated before and/or during the crime. This makes it impossible to detect dominant tendencies for the entire group.

On taking a closer look at how the various characteristics are combined, two fairly different subgroups emerge. The first, with about 30% of the subjects, has the following characteristics: commission of one or several personal attacks in a controlled rational manner; preparation for the crime and intentional use of violence, even with a precise end in mind; no intoxication; essentially utilitarian motive; work with a small group (which shows a need for premeditation and combines well with the fact of planning and making the act a profitable one); and no previous connection with the victim. In this context, personal attack would be a strictly criminal activity, which means that it would be structured, implemented, and contingent on objective advantages. In the second, which includes 25% of the group, the subjects' aggressive reactions are more impulsive, explosive, and no doubt more excessive than in the first case, since they are not planned or premeditated; are carried out while the subject is intoxicated; are personal, directed against a known victim (probably a vindictive reaction to a conflictual situation); and are motivated by an immediate need to let off steam. This second form of attack against the person is perpetrated blindly and brutally in a fit of anger and with much more danger to the victim.

The characteristic "Physical violence" is almost redundant, since it is difficult to attack a person without using physical violence. Only 6 of the 36 subjects did not use it—five used psychological pressure and strong threats and a sixth made two attempts at suicide. Twenty-four subjects, or 67% of the group, used instruments that in the majority of cases were dangerous (knives and firearms). A finding that is rather surprising considering what is necessarily involved in attacking a person is the small proportion of subjects who experienced tension during and after the act – 28% and 22%, respectively. This lack of reaction (as common only in the case of vandalism) can perhaps be explained by a certain callousness and indifference to violence, whether directed at persons or things, which would be typical of these youngsters.

Other Crime Categories

The four remaining categories in order of frequency are petty larceny (21% of delinquents), drugs (8%), public mischief (8%), and sex-related crimes (2%); except for the last one, a fairly large number of adolescents engage in them. Furthermore, they have special characteristics that differ not only from one another, but also from those of the preceding categories.

By definition, petty larceny comprises only minor infractions, such as the theft of candy, cigarettes, toys, small amounts of money, articles at school, money left in milk bottles, and so on. This crime had often been committed when the subject was younger in age, and it therefore had not had serious legal consequences. Concerning the category drugs, two offenses are considered indictable under Canadian criminal law—possession and trafficking. These are relatively recent forms of crime and may be difficult to put on the same footing as the more classic forms of crimes. Public mischief covers a heterogeneous group of activities that could properly be called misconduct, such as disturbing the peace, being in a state of drunkenness, causing a disturbance, holding up traffic, serious contravention of the traffic code, possessing illegal objects, and so on. Finally, sexual offenses, which by definition can include serious acts, are so few in this sample that it is hard to come to any conclusions about them. The few cases that were reported were involved mostly in homosexual prostitution.

In the category of petty larceny, we find quite a substantial proportion of cases: 89 subjects indulged in this type of pastime, generally starting at prepuberty, or the beginning of adolescence. It is perhaps strange to find that, in a group of delinquents such as this, the number admitting to petty theft is not much larger. It may be that the youngsters, when asked about previous delinquency, did not consider such acts true crime and simply omitted them from their narration. This is one of the limitations of the interview technique. It seems that, from the point of view of a good many subjects, these minor thefts are insignificant; the more serious a subject's current criminal activity, the more apt he is to scorn such earlier activities as "childish."

Regarding the principal characteristics of this type of crime, none is particularly outstanding, except perhaps the presence of hedonism (60% of cases) and knowing the victim (58%). Both indicate the immaturity and pettiness of these acts, since the subject, in seeking fun and excitement, commits them at the expense of family and friends (parents, neighbors, etc.). At the same time, he gets some material gain (the reason for acting out in 57% of the cases).

That there is very little social danger in this type of offense is shown by the almost total absence of violence, prior intoxication, or use of instruments.

Similarly, only a small proportion of these crimes were prepared (29%) and the proportion in which accomplices were present is only slightly higher (37%). We can conclude that probably, in at least three out of five cases, acts of this kind were committed without premeditation and the subject was alone and acted to satisfy a need of the moment or because the temptation was too strong. We found, as well, that in spite of the little objective gravity involved in petty theft, a third of the subjects were nervous or anxious during and after the act.

The possession and trafficking of drugs concerned only 36 subjects, or 8% of the sample. The average number of offenses was 12 per subject. This total does not include those who simply used drugs, and certainly does not account for the extent of drug consumption for the entire sample. Quite possibly it is not at all a reliable representation of the true proportion of "pushers" or adolescents "in possession" among our subjects. It shows the kind of control that the courts exercise on these two manifestations of the phenomenon, for the chances are that those who mentioned it are almost exclusively those who had been questioned by the police for one offense or the other. Furthermore, if we refer in Table 2.1 to the 27 subjects appearing under the heading "Intoxication," only 9 (out of 36) remain who could have been in possession or trafficking without themselves being consumers.

Examining the other headings in Table 2.1, a significant 67% had the characteristic "Utilitarian motive," indicating a practical, if not mercenary, goal. This, at least partially, justifies the distinction we established between possession or trafficking and the use of drugs. Besides being utilitarian, drug crimes are organized, as shown by the high rate of subjects who prepared in advance (58%) and the 50% who worked with accomplices. The victim is unknown most of the time and there is almost complete absence of tension, probably because these crimes have become part of daily routine. With regard to the other characteristics, the presence of instruments and the presence of violence, they cannot properly be applied to this category of crime.

Concerning public mischief, 33 of the group admitted to this offense but more than two thirds mentioned only two occasions or less on which it occurred. By definition, this category of crime is much more common among youngsters than are other manifestations of delinquency, and it is much more an infraction than a crime. The disturbance has to be very serious before the police intervene, and here the selective nature of the charges laid is very evident, for it is mainly the known troublemakers who are apprehended. If we rely on the frequency of these acts as stated by the subjects, the first possibility (an infraction) seems most accurate, with the element of danger here evidently determining the measure of social control.

Table 2.1 shows that this type of crime is largely due to a search for excitement (hedonistical among 61%) rather than for practical reasons (21%); it is committed fairly regularly in the presence of accomplices, the group facilitating the act, either because it supports the instigator or urges him on (accomplices here tend to be more numerous); from time to time it is committed under the influence of alcohol or drugs and, in the majority of cases, requires no preparation and even less often the use of instruments. Violence, in both its forms, is rare; the victim is unknown to three out of four subjects; and again, there is seldom any tension felt during the preparation of the offense.

As we just mentioned, the last category, sex-related crimes, cannot be used for purposes of analysis. There were only nine subjects in this category, five of whom admitted to only one offense. This category will therefore be eliminated in our subsequent analyses.

The Second Half of Adolescence

For the second part of adolescence, the characteristics of crime will be examined by comparing their evolution with the first part, in other words comparing the data in Table 2.2 with those in Table 2.1.

Burglary

Many components of the modus operandi of burglary prove to be identical during the first and second half of adolescence. They are the presence of accomplices (here again, small groups composed of two or three partners of about the same age, who according to the subject played an active role), the almost total absence of violence (whether in the form of physical restraint or psychological intimidation), and the presence of tension among a large portion of the group during the execution of the act. It must be remembered that a good number had committed only occasional burglaries and were inexperienced. On the other hand, differences emerge on a number of characteristics. There are fewer burglaries for hedonistic reasons (53% of the subjects before mid-adolescence, 31% later on), less preparation (71% against 57%), less use of instruments (56% against 46%), and fewer known victims (24% against 15%), whereas there is a big increase in utilitarian motivation (66% against 83%), and the presence of intoxication (27% against 41%).

The overall picture that emerges from these data is the following: At the end of adolescence, burglary continues to be carried out almost exclusively with the collaboration of one or two accomplices of the same age, to involve no violence, and to cause no tension for about 60% of the group. However, by contrast with the preceding period, it tends to have a more utilitarian goal, so that it is committed less frequently for pleasure, excitement, or kicks; it becomes more impersonal (an anonymous victim); it is less often prepared; there is less recourse to instruments; and the frequency of intoxication is markedly increased.

In short, burglary in the second half of adolescence becomes more and more acquisitively oriented; is characterized, paradoxically, by less preparatory organization; and is of a more impersonal nature. Perhaps such offenses become routine (which would explain their less frequent organization), or perhaps they are a sign of increased personal maladjustment (which would explain the more frequent intoxication). Interestingly enough, these late-adolescent burglars seem

TABLE 2.2. Characteristics of perpetration of crime during the second half of adolescence ($n = 396$).

			Method of Execution						Conditions of Execution					
			Preparation			Complicity			Use of Violence		Tension		Motivation	
Type of Crime[a]	Total	Victim Known	Psychological (intoxication)	Material Planning	Instruments	Presence	Number (one)	Age (same)	Physical (force/ weapon)	Psychological (intimidation)	During	After	Hedonistic	Utilitarian
Burglary	36%[b]	15%	41%	57%	46%	87%	43%	83%	9%	1%	40%	39%	31%	83%
	140[c]	21	57	80	65	122	49	102	13	1	56	55	43	116
Shoplifting	6%	0%	31%	46%	9%	41%	71%	78%	9%	0%	36%	41%	59%	77%
	22	0	7	10	2	9	5	7	2	0	8	9	13	17
Common	8%	29%	23%	29%	23%	65%	68%	70%	0%	0%	32%	33%	45%	74%
theft	31	9	7	9	7	20	13	14	0	0	10	12	14	23
Motor	27%	11%	47%	39%	35%	70%	67%	87%	3%	3%	32%	32%	59%	54%
vehicle	108	12	51	42	38	43	66	40	3	3	35	34	64	58
theft														
Vandalism	2%													
	8	1	4	2	1	5	1	5	0	0	1	2	5	3
Personal	9%	3%	49%	46%	41%	87%	72%	84%	65%	38%	24%	27%	43%	76%
larceny	37	1	18	17	15	32	21	27	24	14	9	10	16	28
Petty	2%													
larceny	7	4	0	1	1	1	1	1	0	0	1	3	3	4
Aggravated	14%	16%	55%	73%	79%	88%	52%	80%	32%	48%	43%	39%	25%	84%
theft	56	9	31	41	44	49	29	40	18	27	24	22	14	47
Personal	4%	41%	47%	47%	47%	47%	40%	71%	65%	12%	24%	24%	18%	88%
attack	17	7	8	8	8	8	2	5	11	2	4	4	3	15
Drug	7%	8%	38%	77%	8%	62%	67%	56%	12%	4%	27%	23%	50%	65%
trafficking	26	2	10	20	2	16	6	9	3	1	7	6	13	17
Public	4%	21%	36%	7%	21%	57%	57%	75%	21%	0%	0%	7%	43%	43%
mischief	14	3	5	1	3	8	4	6	3	0	0	1	6	6
Sex crime	1%													
	4	2	1	2	0	3	2	2	1	0	2	2	0	1

[a] Listed according to the order in Table 2.1.
[b] Percentages calculated on 396 subjects.
[c] Row total; all the numbers and percentages in one row are referring to these row totals.

to be no more daring, no more proficient, and no more sophisticated than they were earlier.

Motor Vehicle Theft

As in the first part of adolescence, the most widespread characteristic in this category of crime is the presence of accomplices (70% of subjects at the end of adolescence against 83% before). In each case over a quarter of the subjects who work with accomplices have three or more, most of the same age.

In late adolescence there is a marked reduction in hedonistic motivation and an increase in utilitarian motivation—motor vehicle theft seems to be less a means of deriving pleasure and excitement than a means of obtaining material gain. However, for a good half of the subjects, the two remain associated.

Two other variations occur often enough to warrant attention. The first is an appreciable reduction from the early period to the late period in the number of subjects who prepare the offense. Given the fact that in the second half of adolescence the majority of those who commit motor vehicle theft are still beginners, the increased lack of preparation does not seem to be due to habit; it seems to be due more to greater impulsiveness and perhaps a greater ability to act on the spur of the moment at this age. The second variation is the slight increase in intoxication during the crime, which could be an important reason for the general lack of preparation just mentioned.

Aggravated Theft

In comparison with the first half of adolescence, aggravated theft is one of the few categories of crime that increases markedly in criminal gravity. The most significant increases occur in the presence of accomplices, with a spectacular rise of 35%, and the presence of intoxication, with another large increase of 25%. Then comes utilitarian motivation, with an increase of 17%, and physical violence, a 14% increase. Thus, during the second part of adolescence, those who commit aggravated theft are even more motivated by material gain, organize their crime regularly with the participation of a limited number of accomplices, are often in a state of intoxication prior to the offense, and, for many of them, are not afraid to resort to physical violence. Moreover, the convergence of a number of these characteristics, namely, the increase in physical violence (and simultaneous decrease in psychological intimidation), the consistent presence of preparation, the recourse to instruments, the greater impersonality of the crime, and the lessening of hedonistic motivation, indicates that aggravated theft takes on a more pronounced criminal aspect and is probably becoming more risky (which could explain the increase in tension and the frequency of intoxication). At the same time, it is also more technical.

Personal Larceny

For personal larceny, comparison of the percentages between the two periods of adolescence shows few changes, as though this type of theft acquired its distinctive features at the very beginning of adolescence. It is still about the same majority of subjects who attack an unknown victim, form small groups to execute the crime, are activated by utilitarian motives, and have no feelings of tension. Again, more than two thirds prove capable of using physical violence (compared with the other categories of crime, this is a high percentage); nearly one half act regularly in a state of intoxication, and about 40% seek hedonistic gratification. Moreover, whereas preparation and recourse to psychological violence diminish slightly, the use of instruments becomes a little more frequent.

These characteristics, taken together, depict what is probably the most dangerous form of delinquency (more so than aggravated theft, because of the high incidence of physical violence against an almost always unknown victim) and the most sudden (because of the lack of preparation and more frequent intoxication as well as the quite frequent search for excitement). An interesting fact is that, no matter what the age of the subjects involved, the gravity of the crime does not vary. We find that even a large number of 14- and 15-year-old subjects are already marked by the most significant characteristics of perpetration.

Common Theft

Study of the characteristics of theft shows that, at the end of adolescence, it has changed little – it is most often committed without instruments, without violence and without intoxication. Only the planning category shows a sharp decrease, from 52% early in adolescence to 29% at the end of adolescence. This reinforces the impression that it is a relatively commonplace form of crime, probably executed because of an opportunity that presents itself, often within the subject's own neighborhood (the victim is known in almost 30% of the cases).

Drugs

As pointed out previously, this category covers possession and trafficking rather than use of drugs. Table 2.2 shows how the characteristics of this crime have now changed for the worse. There is less intoxication and more of almost everything else – planning, use of instruments, complicity, use of violence, and tension. This supports the hypothesis that there are two different kinds of crime here, that of the first part of adolescence, which is more a risky act committed by several youngsters, and that of the second part of adolescence, which is a more organized, skilled, and networked crime.

Shoplifting

For the small group of subjects who persist in shoplifting during the second half of adolescence, there are some important changes. First, there is a significant rise in utilitarian motivation (which supersedes the hedonistic motivation), there is a marked increase in intoxication during the offense, and there is a relative increase in tension after the act.

The general impression is that this crime, too, changes from one period of adolescence to the next. For the few persons still involved, it seems to become a rather more individual enterprise, whose acquisitive purpose increases considerably. According to subjects, there is an element of greater risk, since it more frequently requires prior intoxication and creates some tension. When we recall that for the younger adolescent shoplifting was somewhat in the nature of a game, its manifestations after the age of 16 give it a different aspect. It is now more an occasional act committed to satisfy a material need and bolstered by intoxication. It is no doubt a situational crime most of the time.

The Beginning of the 20s

Similar to Tables 2.1 and 2.2, Table 2.3 contains data on the sample of wards of the court already studied over the years, but this time at the beginning of their 20s. Our observations of the methods of perpetration during the second half of adolescence have led us to conclude that the style of offending changes as the subject increases in age. Offending seems to become more integrated into the lifestyle – it becomes more individual, more utilitarian, and more premeditated. Does this trend continue in the 20s, or are there new developments? The answer lies once more in examining each category of crime.

Burglary

This type of illicit activity continues to dominate the other forms of crime. At the same time, it continues to change to a more personal, more sophisticated act and to become easier to perpetrate and more utilitarian. It is more personal because it is often done without accomplices (24% at the beginning of the 20s against 13% at the end of adolescence) or with only one (68% versus 43%), and the accomplices differ in age (24% versus 17%). It is more sophisticated because the victim is almost always anonymous (89% versus 85%), but above all because the offense is prepared much more carefully (79% versus 57%) and instruments are used more frequently (49% versus 46%). The level of intoxication remains stable, but the burglary appears to be easier, since tension during and after the crime decreases. Finally, gain is the motivation in more cases (92% versus 83%) while the hedonistic motive does not increase.

The technical and utilitarian nature of burglary already noted from early adolescence is now more generalized. What happens after the age of 18 is a definite increase in its routine occurrence as well as in the conditions for the greatest chance of success; this is seen in the fact that careful planning of the crime appears more frequent.

TABLE 2.3. Characteristics of perpetration of crime during the beginning of the 20s ($n = 196$).

		Method of Execution							Conditions of Execution					
			Preparation			Complicity			Use of Violence		Tension		Motivation	
Type of Crime[a]	Total	Victim Known	Psychological (intoxication)	Material Planning	Instruments	Presence	Number (one)	Age (same)	Physical (force/ weapon)	Psychological (intimidation)	During	After	Hedonistic	Utilitarian
Burglary	52%[b]	11%	45%	79%	49%	76%	68%	76%	10%	10%	32%	30%	33%	92%
	102[c]	11	45	81	46	78	50	22	10	10	42	30	33	93
Shoplifting	11%	0%	22%	80%	5%	48%	50%	100%	0%	0%	40%	26%	45%	72%
	21	0	4	16	1	10	5	4		0	8	5	9	15
Common theft	21%	23%	15%	86%	10%	50%	82%	43%	5%	5%	33%	21%	27%	85%
	41	9	6	36	4	22	14	3	2	2	13	8	11	35
Motor vehicle theft	24%	9%	49%	76%	22%	55%	66%	89%	9.5?	6%	37%	19%	80%	54%
	48	4	21	35	10	25	15	8	4	3	16	8	37	25
Vandalism	3%													
	5	2	2	4	3	5	0	1	1	1	0	1	5	1
Personal larceny	10%	33%	42%	79%	50%	75%	57%	80%	53%	79%	60%	71%	44%	67%
	20	6	8	15	8	15	8	4	10	15	9	12	8	12
Petty larceny	1%	2	0	0	0	0	0	0	0	0	3	2	3	1
	3													

Aggravated	37%	6%	35%	88%	87%	89%	51%	59%	50%	90%	51%	40%	23%	100%
theft	72	4	24	61	59	62	29	20	34	61	35	27	15	67
Personal	15%	42%	56%	46%	39%	56%	69%	75%	82%	79%	38%	40%	76%	56%
attack	29	10	14	13	11	15	9	3	23	22	9	10	19	14
Drug	30%	44%	20%	97%	4%	55%	82%	25%	20%	20%	29%	15%	21%	90
trafficking	58	4	10	55	2	28	9	3	10	10	12	6	10	43
Public	10%	11%	60%	72%	33%	37%	63%	100%	33%	28%	29%	29%	81%	38%
mischief	20	2	9	13	6	7	5	2	6	5	4	4	13	6
Sex crimes	3%													
	6	4	3	5	2	5	0	0	2	3	1	1	3	1
Homicide	5%													
	10	6	6	4	7	4	4	0	8	8	6	3	4	4
Fraud	16%	11%	3%	94%	32%	53%	66%	50%	10%	10%	35%	22%	20%	97%
	32	3	1	30	10	16	7	2	3	3	9	6	6	29

[a] Listed according to the order in Table 2.1.
[b] Percentages calculated on 196 subjects.
[c] Row total; all the numbers and percentages in one row are referring to these row totals.

Aggravated Theft

The figures in Table 2.3 clearly show that aggravated theft, too, increases in criminal gravity when the subjects reach youth. Whereas the incidence of intoxication prior to or during the crime diminishes substantially (35% versus 55%), physical violence (50% versus 32%) and psychological violence (90% versus 48%) are used by a greater number of subjects. At the same time, for a slightly larger proportion of cases, the victim is unknown (94% versus 84%), instruments are more widely used (87% versus 79%), and planning is done more often (88% versus 73%). Further, perhaps because of the increased gravity of the crime, tension is intensified during its perpetration.

Again we can conclude that, by the beginning of the 20s, aggravated theft takes on a more pronounced criminal significance. It is more frequently planned and technically prepared; it is more dangerous for the victim with its elements of physical and psychological violence; it is more impersonal; and it is probably more daring, since the tension is accentuated. In short, aggravated theft, when it occurs between the ages of 18 to 25, makes it less and less possible for its perpetrators to escape becoming involved in what might be called criminal aggravation.

Possession of and Trafficking in Drugs

This illicit activity is practiced by a much larger number of subjects when they reach youth than during adolescence (30% versus 10.5% and 8.4% at the middle and end of adolescence, respectively). The method of operating also changes between the second half of adolescence and the beginning of the 20s.

A comparison of the data in Tables 2.2 and 2.3 reveals the nature of these changes. The level of intoxication among the perpetrators of this crime goes from 38% during the second half of adolescence to 20% at the beginning of the 20s; this means that the number of traffickers who don't take drugs themselves increases. The crime is more often prepared (97% versus 77%) and more structured, the buyer being known (44% versus 8%). It is supported by a network of large numbers of accomplices (82% versus 67%) of different ages (75% versus 44%). In addition, the use of physical violence (20% versus 12%) and above all intimidation (20% versus 4%) is more frequent. In short, this is a type of activity that tends more and more to look like an organized illicit business.

Motor Vehicle Theft

During adolescence, automobile theft was a group activity. It was also the result of a search for excitement and was usually acted upon impulsively and under the influence of alcohol and/or drugs. After the age of 18, motor vehicle theft loses many of the characteristics that gave it the appearance of a game. Preparation is more consistent (76% against 39%) and there is an increase in the use of specific instruments (35% against 21%); the activity seems more integrated in the subject's lifestyle, the tension after the act diminishing substantially (31% against 18%).

Automobile theft at the beginning of the twenties continues to be an exciting activity. However, as time passes, an increasing proportion of these offenders tend to make it a profitable venture.

Common Theft

Common theft evolves in the same direction as aggravated theft; for a greater and greater number of offenders it becomes a routine activity that can assume considerable proportions. Among young adults, common theft depends less on opportunity, is more often prepared (86% versus 29%), and is accompanied by intoxication a little less frequently than during adolescence (15% versus 23%). It is also more often determined by utilitarian motives (85% versus 74%). The modus operandi changes as well, the young adults operating more often with very few accomplices (82% versus 68%) of different ages (57% versus 30%). Planning is common (86% versus 29%) and instruments are used less often (9% versus 23%). Common theft eventually becomes a mainly acquisitive criminal activity, prompted by the lure of gain and encouraged by a simplification of operation that no doubt increases its effectiveness.

Fraud

Fraud is one of the few illicit activities that occurs only in later youth. However, the extent of participation (16%) and average number of offenses (seven) make this crime category one of the least important. It is much more impersonal than the other categories of crime, since only 11% of the victims are known. On the other hand, it is not committed under the influence of drugs or alcohol, the rate of intoxication (3%) being the lowest of all the categories, and the proportion of those who carefully prepare this crime, is one of the highest (94%).

Far more than crimes in any of the other categories, fraud is based on cunning. It is perpetrated through the use of trickery and requires a certain technical sophistication, but very rarely the use of force or intimidation. In a little more than half the cases, it is a group enterprise [a very small group since, in the majority of cases (64%), there is only one accomplice, often of the same age (50%)]. It is interesting, too, that this cunning type of offense, compared with other categories, involves very little tension during or after the commission of the crime. A last characteristic places fraud in a group apart, and that is the almost universal presence of utilitarian motivation (98% of cases) and almost total absence of hedonistic motivation (20%). Fraud is the only crime category, other than aggravated theft, where the gap between the two types of motivation is so great. In short, because of the diverse characteristics of its perpetration, fraud clearly belongs in the group of activities considered the most serious or the most truly criminal.

Personal Attack

Personal attack was relatively limited in the sample of delinquents we studied. It shows progressive increase from adolescence to youth. It is particularly interesting because it evolves in the opposite direction from most of the crimes against property, becoming less organized and more impulsive.

Among young adults it is more often accompanied by the use of alcohol or drugs (56% versus 47%) and is carried out in collaboration (56% versus 47%) with one other person (69% versus 40%). Physical violence increases, but the victim is still unknown to the subject as often as before (about 60%). There is also an increase of the use of intimidation (12 to 79%) and more tension during (37% versus 23%) and after (40% versus 23%) the crime. Finally, the crime is committed more on impulse—hedonistic motivation is dominant in 76% of the young adults against 18% of the adolescents while utilitarian reasons are decreasing (88% to 56%). The impulsive nature of the crime is also demonstrated by the fact that, on reaching youth, instruments are used less often (39% versus 47%).

In the final analysis, personal attack is an impulsive and potentially dangerous act, generally committed in a state of intoxication. It is accompanied by violence and/or intimidation and the subject derives pleasure from its perpetration. Considering that most attacks are done in collaboration with others, that the doers feel no tension during or after the offense, and that the victim can be known or unknown, it is plausible to believe that this type of crime is in keeping with the lifestyle of these young offenders (for example, frequenting bars where all the determining elements are present—the group, intoxication, intimidation, impulsiveness, and so on) and is due to a kind of propensity to aggressive acting out.

Homicidal Attack

Because of their special nature, homicidal attacks were not included with personal attack but were analyzed separately. As was to be expected, they are much less prevalent and less frequent than the latter and are characterized by a lack of planning, a state of intoxication, recourse to intimidation as well as physical violence and surprisingly little tension after commission of the crime. A number of traits are in direct contrast with other attacks against individuals. In the case of homicidal behavior, the relationship with the victim is often more personalized, the crime is perpetrated without accomplices, and an instrument is used in all cases. A larger number of subjects suffer tension during the execution of the crime, but as far as motivation is concerned, neither hedonistic nor utilitarian motive is predominant.

Homicidal events, like personal attacks, seem to be impulsive and unorganized; however, they differ in the fact that, for the first ones, there is more personal involvement on the part of the subject, their perpetration is more individual, and there is more use of a dangerous weapon.

Overview

Characteristics of the Perpetration of Categories of Crime

Because of the very detailed descriptions of the modus operandi obtained during our data collection, it was possible to get a clear picture of the perpetration of crime by both adolescents and young adults. Taking the most significant characteristics of perpetration, we find that generally speaking, the Montreal delinquents act out in the following way.

1. They attack an anonymous victim, a little more often at the beginning of the 20s than during the second half of adolescence or earlier. This considerably increases the attacker's impunity, both regarding his milieu, since he has less chance of being identified, and no doubt for himself, because this anonymity helps him to maintain a certain indifference to the victim while executing the crime. This observation confirms the position of authors such as Matza (1964), who pointed out the usual anonymity of the victim even though the latter is generally chosen from the offender's own neighborhood. This tendency is also confirmed by Reiss' (1988) review on the territorial concentration of crime.
2. They operate with a small number of accomplices, who most of the time participate in the crime. Curiously enough, accomplices tend to be scarce, only casual acquaintances and they change from one crime to another. Furthermore, the ages of the accomplices vary: During adolescence they are usually about the same age as the offender, but at the beginning of youth, the ages are more diversified. The group nature of criminal activities— what Matza (1964) called "the situation of company"—has been clearly stated in theories on juvenile delinquency from Thrasher (1927) to today (see Reiss, 1988 for review on that question). Our data, like those of Sarnecki (1985), show that the accomplishment of the crime is the work of microgroups, flexible and transient; it is not the result of organized gangs in most cases.
3. They are motivated by a curious mixture of utilitarianism and hedonism. This means that these young people try to give direction to their activities, by appropriating some lucrative object or releasing tension, on the one hand, or by deriving pleasure and excitement or even a sense of pride from them on the other. (It must be pointed out that since the delinquent is often emotionally involved in his act, the search for gratification, concrete or symbolic, plays an important role.) This mixture varies considerably from one category of crime to another, the most "utilitarian" being personal theft (larceny), aggravated theft, the possesion of and trafficking in drugs, and burglary. West and Farrington (1977) arrived at similar conclusions, saying that motives are usually purposive and that enjoyment comes second. We have also shown that the mixture varies from one period to the other for all the categories of crime, with hedonism diminishing and utilitarianism increasing (it seems this is one of the most important effects of a person's age). This conclusion makes it

possible to tone down the position of those who, like Cusson (1983) or Clarke and Cornish (1985), believe that the criminal act is primarily rational. The position of Bennett and Wright (1984) or of Walsh (1986) seems much more sensible – a limited or a temporal rationality. Delinquents do not calculate in the Bentham style, weighing and planning all angles. Rather they consider particular elements of the situation and disregard others, giving more attention to immediate critical factors.

4. They generally feel no tension during or after the act, as though the perpetration of the crime were of little consequence. The youngsters remain or try to remain indifferent to the stress of the moment, even in a crime as serious as personal attack. This relative absence of tension could be the result of the use of neutralization techniques, as hypothesized by Matza (1964), or it could be the result of the psychological process suggested by De Greef (1955), which implies a tolerance and/or consent to the idea of committing a crime.
5. They prepare for the perpetration of their crimes. This shows that, even among young subjects (sometimes at the beginning of adolescence), there is a true penchant for delinquency, a capacity to act out consciously and intentionally. The crime is organized in order to increase its efficiency. In the data presented by Erez (1980, 1987), even though they indicate that the planning is not detailed, a total absence of preparation was observed in only about two fifths of infractions. The planning of the crime increased between adolescence and youth in the Erez (1987) data and in our sample.

A comparison of the various characteristics of perpetration from one category of crime to another shows pronounced variations between the three periods of life under study. Two are particularly striking, the more frequent utilitarian motivation as time goes on and the corresponding reduction in hedonistic motivation. Two other changes are the fairly substantial increase over time in the choice of an anonymous victim and the presence of intoxication. Thus, with the increasing preponderance of utilitarian goals over hedonism, with the more frequent choice of indiscriminate victims and with the increase in the potential gravity of the offense (due to the greater frequency of intoxication), we have an activity of a much mroe criminal nature at later ages.

Moreover, of the only three categories of crime that have a large number of adherents – burglary, motor vehicle theft, and aggravated theft – the latter is the most prone to increase in gravity. Its utilitarian aspect increases as time goes on, as well as its preparation, the use of physical violence, and the choice of an anonymous victim. Burglary and motor vehicle theft also become more acquisitive, more utilitarian, more impersonal, more solitary, better prepared and organized, less associated with intoxication, and therefore more "criminal." In all of these cases the crime loses it rudimentary quality. These offenders, by the time they reach their 20s, are involved in criminal activities marked by gravity and sophistication.

This description of the way crimes are perpetrated leads to two definite conclusions. First, from adolescence to the beginning of youth there is a distinct increase in criminal propensity. Crimes against property becomes more and more technical and utilitarian and the modus operandi becomes more and more routine and individual; crimes against persons also become more dangerous, but for different reasons, in particular because of the perpetrators' potential for greater impulsiveness and lack of preparation. Second, many categories of crime clearly become a way of life. For acquisitive infractions (burglary, common theft, fraud, and so on), all requirements for the execution of the crime and assessment of the financial gain are consolidated; for crimes against persons, there is repeated recourse to violence as a means of self-expression and interaction with others. The fact is that the general profile of illicit activities changes considerably between adolescence and youth to show what may be called more thoroughly skilled methods with which to commit crimes or what Petersilia et al. (1978) have called criminal sophistication.

Increased Criminal Sophistication and Seriousness

Until now our analysis of the changes with age in criminal sophistication was specific and interpretive. We have described the modes of perpetration of each type of crime, but our conclusions about changes came from an overall reading of the data. To make a more rigorous check of the changes, we factor analyzed the 11 variables concerning the modus operandi (presence of instruments, material planning, presence of accomplices, number of accomplices, age of accomplices, use of physical violence, use of psychological intimidation, presence of intoxication, acquaintance with the victim, having hedonistic or utilitarian motive). These analyses were done using the principal component method and a varimax rotation. The results—factor loadings and proportions of variance—are presented in Table 2.4.

It can be noted that the factor structure and the content of the factors change over time. During the first half of adolescence there are two independent factors, a dominant (utilitarian) and a secondary (hedonistic) way of committing crimes. The utilitarian way of acting out implies—if we look only at the loadings that are significantly superior on one factor compared with the loadings on the other factor—the use of instruments, psychological intimidation, knowledge of the victim, and utilitarian motives. The hedonistic way of perpetrating a crime implies the presence of numerous accomplices and a search for excitement. There are, then, two very distinct modus operandi before the middle of adolescence.

During the second half of adolescence there are three factors instead of two, reflecting simultaneously stability and changes. There is still a hedonistic factor, but it accounts for less variance, 8% instead of 12.5%, and its group nature is less well affirmed. And we find two utilitarian modus operandi, a dominant one with most of the variance and a secondary one. The dominant utilitarian way of committing crimes is an aggravated way—it implies the use of instruments, material planning, the presence of a greater number of older accomplices, the use of physical violence and of psychological intimidation, and the presence of intoxication. The second type of utilitarian way seems more impulsive, since it

TABLE 2.4. Changes in the mode of perpetrating crimes with age, factor loadings.

Variable	First part of adolescence		Second half of adolescence			Beginning of the 20s		
	Factor 1	Factor 2	Factor 1	Factor 2	Factor 3	Factor 1	Factor 2	Factor 3
Use of instruments	0.60	0.36	0.71	0.34	0.14	0.56	0.45	0.22
Material planning	0.55	0.52	0.73	0.40	0.29	0.30	0.84	0.33
Presence of accomplices	0.42	0.77	0.86	0.81	0.32	0.29	0.42	0.74
Number of accomplices	0.20	0.63	0.53	0.40	0.26	−0.04	0.12	0.60
Age of accomplices	0.37	0.31	0.52	0.53	0.13	0.04	0.11	0.59
Physical violence	0.46	0.38	0.55	0.21	0	0.82	0.13	0.12
Psychological intimidation	0.52	0.28	0.56	0.06	0.21	0.98	0.14	0.19
Intoxication	0.46	0.41	0.62	0.29	0.07	0.20	0.17	0.26
Victim known	0.32	0.07	0.17	0.26	−0.03	0.32	0.17	−0.07
Hedonistic motive	0.11	0.61	0.21	0.06	0.60	0.08	0.48	0.11
Utilitarian motive	0.82	0.15	0.75	0.54	−0.06	0.40	0.65	0.41
% total variance	42.5	10.1	42.1	9.9	9.6	41.6	14.3	9.8
% variance for factors with eigenvalue 1 or more	87.5	12.5	81.8	10.3	8	71.5	19.7	8.7

implies only the presence of older accomplices and the victimization of places or persons they know.

From the first part to the second part of adolescence the hedonistic modus operandi is fading away and the utilitarian modus operandi is diversifying. Does this tendency continue during the 20s? The answer is yes, since the hedonistic factor as a main motive is being replaced by a nondominant factor combining hedonistic and utilitarian motives (19.7% of the variance) tied to crimes that are more frequently perpetrated with accomplices and are planned. The dominant factor refers to much more serious types of crime, committed with instruments, the victim being often known and with the presence in most cases of physical and psychological violence. The relative absence of planning and the continual presence of violence are signs of an impulsive and violent modus operandi.

As for the last factor, it refers to a specific modality of perpetrating crimes. It is done with a large group of accomplices, some of which are older; intoxication is present; and the motive is utilitarian. This type of modus operandi does not imply a search for excitement, as with the younger adolescent; it is committed for power, recognition, or material gain or as part of a lifestyle and it is not violent as in the dominant factor.

This comparison by means of factor analysis was very instructive. It permitted patterning of the ways crimes are perpetrated and it validated our conclusion that as delinquents grow older their modus operandi become more sophisticated and more aggravated. The perpetration of crime is dominated by a utilitarian modus operandi at every age; this dominant type divides itself over time into a more violent and impulsive way of committing crimes and into less violent group activity. A hedonistic modus operandi characterizes the younger adolescent. This tends to disappear or transform itself into a more profitable search for excitement. Young adults plan crimes to be done generally with one accomplice that result in material gains and include some form of thrill, but they are also involved in violent crimes of an impulsive nature. These two tendencies—more violence and more rationality—indicate an aggravation of the crimes committed by adults.

Explanations

Looking at psychopsychiatric theories on the process of acting out (De Greef, 1947, 1955; and Pinatel, 1963, for example), we find they are clearly inapplicable to most of the data we have presented. In these theories the completion of the crime is presented as a process with three phases: the reserved approval, when the idea of the crime is indirectly present in the mind of the future criminal; the formulated consent, when the individual is clearly thinking about the crime; and, the crisis period, when the individual is actively preparing the crime. Crimes against persons, which are relatively infrequent but become more and more impulsive as subjects get older, conform somewhat to this classic model, but this model cannot serve as a general explanation of the forms of acting out we have described. Complementary theories, however, can be applied to the perpetration of both hedonistic and utilitarian crimes (Clarke & Cornish, 1985; Cusson, 1986).

The first of these explanations of utilitarian crime is that of Cohen and Felson (1979, 1980); referring to the living habits of subjects, they believe the probability that a crime will be committed in a given place depends on the spatiotemporal convergence of a potential delinquent, worthwhile targets, and the absence of anyone capable of protecting the targets. The second, that of Hough, Clarke, and Mayhew (1980), states that the person involved proceeds with a cost/benefit analysis of the crime in terms of the material conditions favorable to the infraction and the low-risk gains to be made. According to our observations, the first of these theories does not adequately explain fully the hedonistic offenses that we found so prevalent at the beginning of adolescence nor the predatory activities observed at all ages. The second theory seems more compatible with the descriptions of the more and more technical and utilitarian offenses that characterize the delinquency of young adults.

Cusson (1986), Clarke and Cornish (1985) and Cornish and Clarke (1986) combined these theories in a single conceptual model, that of the rational criminal. According to this model, the subject makes a rational choice to commit a crime, given his past and immediate situation. Considering the characteristics of perpetration we described as typical at the beginning of adolescence, it is quite evident that no more than a minority of offenders fit this type; we found that there was limited preparation, that instruments were rarely used, and that the motivation was most often hedonistic. During the second half of adolescence and the beginning of the 20s, there are many more rational criminals, since crimes are committed with greater technical skill and with a much more utilitarian motive, but there is also a significant group of delinquents that progressively chose a more violent and impulsive way of committing their crimes.

In short, if we want to account for all criminal activity, the explanation of its accomplishment requires two theories: one for the rational criminal and one for the impulsive criminal. But theories that describe the accomplishment of the crime are not enough. A theory of criminal patterns must be added, since we have seen that with age, there is an increase in routine crimes and a definite tendency for illegal activities to become a way of life or at least a true "occupation."

3
Descriptive and Comparative Views of Offending

In chapter 2 we presented an analysis of criminal activities at their most elementary level, that is, at the level of perpetration. Chapter 3 undertakes an analysis at a higher level, based on the aggregation of the total number of infractions committed by a person over a given period of time. In chapter 1, five descriptive parameters were proposed to measure different facets of an offender's criminal activities–participation, frequency, variety, gravity, and violence. All five will be used here to further our study of male offending. To this end, three comparisons are particularly important: (a) between hidden delinquency and official delinquency; (b) between the criminal activities of a representative sample of the population and those of a sample of wards of the court; and (c) between the first half of adolescence (between ages 12 and 15½) and the second half (between ages 15½ and 18) as well as the beginning of adulthood (from 18 to the mid-20s). These three comparisons will shed light on the consistency of the criminal activity, its intensity, its diversity, its gravity, and so forth. Do observations regarding the two major perspectives on delinquency, the two samples, and the different periods of life lead to the same conclusions? Are the trends the same for the adolescent sample and the wards of the court? Does hidden delinquency vary in the same way as official delinquency? Are the same movements to be observed during adolescence and youth? Are the participation, frequency, variety, gravity, and violence interchangeable aspects of the same phenomenon? These are important questions. Tables 3.1 and 3.2, giving data for the different descriptive parameters, will allow us to answer them.

Before going ahead with these three comparisons, it is useful to recall certain characteristics of the two samples. The first sample, called the adolescents, was made up of 1,684 male subjects 12 to 17 years of age representing the Montreal population in this age group. For 1,611 of them, we could control the official delinquency record (convictions by a court for a criminal infraction) up to the mid-20s; in addition, 458 of them answered a self-administered questionnaire on two occasions concerning their hidden delinquency. The second sample, the delinquents, included 470 wards of the court between 13 and 17 years of age who had been sentenced to probation or to placement in a training center, either under

TABLE 3.1. Official male offending: five descriptive parameters.

	Adolescents (n = 1,611)			Delinquents (n = 470)		
Parameter	Adolescence	Youth	Total	Adolescence	Youth	Total
Participation (%)	4.1	10.7	14.2	81.5	72.1	92.3
Frequency*						
Cumulative						
Mean	3.32	4.8	4.91	8.09	13.94	15.35
SD	5.05	7.05	8.04	10.57	16.78	18.31
Median	1.42	2.54	2.46	4.29	8.77	8.68
Annual						
Mean	1.75	2.05	1.67	2.98	3.09	2.56
SD	1.5	2.15	1.5	3.18	2.63	1.95
Median	1.02	1.49	1.01	2.01	2.34	2
Variety						
Presence (%)	40.88	44.2	46.9	73.84	75.8	86.2
Degree†						
Mean	1.09	1.94	2	3.06	3.73	4.48
SD	1.42	1.48	1.57	2.03	2.34	2.69
Median	1.35	1.4	1.44	2.56	3.32	4.81
Gravity‡						
Total						
Mean	18.7	29.68	29.12	51.78	75.48	104.95
SD	30.23	53.56	56.33	73.31	82.61	129.39
Median	6.44	13.22	12.72	26.36	52.06	62.4
By crime						
Mean	4.78	4.83	5.71	5.91	6.3	7.16
SD	0.33	0.32	0.38	0.21	0.14	0.31
Median	5.07	3.7	5.07	5.14	6.16	6.43
Violence (%)	0.6	2	2.4	28.1	34.9	47.7
Frequency¶						
Mean	2	3.5	3.42	3.02	4.09	4.77
SD	1.12	4.72	4.44	4.16	4.29	6.51
Median	1.75	1.87	2	1.5	2.47	2.53

SD, standard deviation.
*Cumulative frequency: number of infractions committed; annual frequency: number of infractions by years of involvement.
†Number of different crimes.
‡See text for explanation of how gravity was estimated.
¶Cumulative number of crimes.

the Juvenile Delinquents Act or the Youth Protection Act. We have a record of all official and hidden delinquency to their mid-20s, for 219 of them who were interviewed three times and to the end of adolescence for 396 who were interviewed twice.

Our three comparisons are based on two types of data—total convictions and total reported delinquency. Two instruments were used to discover hidden delinquency—a self-administered questionnaire given at different times to the two samples (appendix A) and a retrospective interview with the delinquent sample on three different occasions (appendix B).

TABLE 3.2. Hidden male offending: five descriptive parameters.

	Adolescents (n=458)			Delinquents				
Parameter	Age 15	Age 17	Total	Age 15 (n=470)	Age 17 (n=396)	Age 15 & 17	Age 23 (n=219)	Total
Participation (%)	91.2	89.5	96.9	100	100	100	81.3	100
Frequency*								
Cumulative								
Mean				64.32	124.9	131.9	1,075,46	545.05
SD				122.73	302.1	269.95	2,202.05	1,539.62
Median				21.29	7.33	33.17	30	47.6
Annual								
Mean				15.99	143.47	31.17	283.54	134.17
SD				22.65	275.9	72.08	471.72	233.83
Median				7.51	20.12	8.27	16.61	16.82
Variety presence (%)	64.5	59.1	68.1	81.4	54.9	86.1	77.2	89.4
Degree†								
Mean	2.08	2.05	2.2	2.96	1.91	3.27	2.79	4.13
SD	1.05	1.13	1.09	1.51	1.04	1.64	1.72	2.25
Median	1.93	1.8	2.05	2.78	1.66	3.07	2.4	3.7
Gravity‡								
Total								
Mean				1,106.39	1,727.45	2,241.85	15,065.8	14,558.95
SD				3,764.55	4,790.72	5,483.56	34,637.8	33,571.07
Median				79.05	57	159.45	255.94	491.79
By crime								
Mean				15.12	18.72	19.19	9.71	20.43
SD				3.62	6.95	6.35	0.41	5.95
Median				5.03	6.7	5.77	7.52	6.43
Violence (%)				31.9	19.8	39.9	46.1	50.6
Frequency								
Mean				39.82	22.68	36.28	25.55	40.61
SD				145.68	70.79	119.21	104.28	132.99
Median				3.5	3.44	4.35	3.43	5.37

SD, standard deviation.
*Cumulative frequency: number of infractions committed; annual frequency: number of infractions by years of involvement.
†Number of different crimes.
‡See text for explanation of how gravity was estimated.
¶Cumulative number of crimes.

Participation

Blumstein et al. (1986) recommended use of the term *participation* instead of *prevalence* to describe the proportion of the population that is criminally active over a given period of time. Their recommendation was based on Gordon's (1976) argument to the effect that the adaptation of the epidemiological concept of prevalence, in criminology, has been a source of confusion rather than clarification.

The degree of participation, then, will be measured throughout this section in two ways – cumulative participation, or the number of persons who have committed at least one criminal infraction during a given period, and annual participation, or the proportion of the sample that has been involved in criminal activity during a specific year. Only infractions of the Canadian Criminal Code are included here; infractions of the highway code and also federal, provincial, and municipal statutory infractions are excluded.

Cumulative Participation

Cumulative participation has been divided into three parts: participation before age 18, participation during the 20s, and total participation for the period covered by the study. These data are reported in Tables 3.1 and 3.2.

It turns out that 97% of the adolescents and obviously all of the delinquents report at least one criminal infraction during their adolescence (Table 3.2). However, only 4% of the former have been convicted by a court before the age of 18, in comparison with 82% of the latter. After age 18, 11% of the adolescents and 72% of the delinquents have been convicted by a court for an infraction under the Canadian Criminal Code, whereas 81% of the latter said they had committed at least one infraction of this type before the average age of 22. In terms of the total official cumulative participation, 92% of the delinquents and 14% of the adolescents have been convicted for a criminal infraction before they reach their mid-20s.

These data reveal four major findings. First, the degree of participation, as reported in the questionnaire, is quite similar (a difference of at most 10%) for both samples, the adolescents and the wards of the court; this was also the conclusion arrived at by Erickson and Empey (1963) and by Follman (1972). Second, participation decreases from adolescence to youth among the delinquents (among the adolescents it increases slightly). Third, among the wards of the court there is a disparity of around 20% when participation is evaluated with self-reported as opposed to official records. Fourth, data on the degree of official participation show that very few adolescents have to appear in court in comparison with adults, who appear in court 2.5 times more than adolescents. This difference may be due to the policy of diversion and its application to adolescents by the police and the judiciary (see Le Blanc, 1971, 1977b; Le Blanc & Beaumont, 1985).

These findings have been compared with results of other studies on the proportion of cumulative participation in criminal activities. Looking at those surveys conducted in other Western countries, and in spite of differences in the composition of the samples and the content of the questionnaires, we find that a degree of over 90% participation among the Montreal adolescents is not surprising. Elmhorn (1965) reported 93% among youngsters aged 6 to 14 in Sweden; Williams and Gold (1972) cited 88% for a national sample of American adolescents from age 13 to 16 [the more recent surveys of Bachman, O'Malley, & Johnston (1978), Hindelang et al. (1981), and Elliot Huizinga (1983) confirm this degree of participation]; Farrington (1973) reported 96% for his sample of English working-class youngsters; in France, Morange (1979) reported 89%; finally, Remschmidt (1978) in Germany, Podgorecki (1976) in Poland, and Hausman, Beaufils, Boniver, and Kerger (1982) in Belgium cited proportions of participation as high as that observed among Montreal adolescents during the years 1960 (Le Blanc, 1969) and 1970 (Le Blanc & Côté, 1986).

As for cumulative participation measured on the basis of official delinquency, the level in Quebec is lower by about half than the figures reported on referrals to court before or after the age of 18 in the United States (Blumstein et al., 1986). It is difficult, however, to interpret this difference. It could reflect a real difference in the situations or it could be due to variations in the definitions used. Furthermore, the proportion of 14% official participation in criminal activities up to the mid-20s is equivalent to the proportions obtained by Wadsworth (1975) in England (15%) and Jason (1982) in Sweden (14%), using a similar definition of participation.

Annual Participation

Our conclusion on cumulative participation has already been established in the criminological literature, namely, that criminal activities are widespread among the adolescent population and that few are brought to the attention of the courts. Moreover, we have been able to study a question about which data are scarce in the report of Blumstein et al. (1986), and that is, how participation varies according to age (see Table 3.3).

When we look at the average annual participation, the difference between adolescents and delinquents is not great, since the percentage is 89% for the first group and almost 100% for the second. The difference is much more striking when we take into account the average number of convictions (official delinquency); this number is nine times higher among delinquents (16.6) than among adolescents (1.7). It reflects the fact that only 1 of 45 adolescents who reported having committed at least one infraction during the preceding year appeared before the court, whereas the proportion was 1 of 6 for the delinquents. This confirms the fact that the difference between the adolescents and the delinquents increases as the observations go from self-reported delinquency to official delinquency. This difference cannot be explained by methodological factors: The same questionnaire on self-reported delinquency was used in the two samples and the official data were obtained in the same jurisdiction and at the same period. The explanation of the increasing difference can only be the result of substantial differences in the frequency and gravity of the crimes committed by each of the two samples.

A closer scrutiny of the annual participation, hidden and official, shows both differences and similarities (Table 3.3). In both samples, for instance, the maximum rate of persons convicted by the courts occurs at the age of 20 (4% among adolescents and 45% among delinquents). In the case of hidden delinquency, in the adolescent sample it is at the age of 15 that we find the highest percentage of subjects who admit having committed crimes, whereas in delinquents the

TABLE 3.3. Annual participation in criminal activities by age (%).

Age (years)	Adolescents (n=1611) Hidden	Adolescents (n=1611) Official	Delinquents (n=470) Hidden	Delinquents (n=470) Official
7		0		0.9
8		0.1		1.7
9		0.1		3.6
10		0.1		5.5
11	80	0.1		7
12	89.9	0.3		9.4
13	89.1	0.2	100	15.3
14	92	0.5	100	27.4
15	96.7	1.4	99.7	31.9
16	90.8	1.6	100	29.6
17	89.5	1.4	99.5	20.6
18	86	2.1	100	27.2
19	90	4	100	43
20		4.2		44.7
21		3.4		36
22		2.4		28.9
23		2.4		17.9
24		2.2		9.8
25		2.9		3.41
26		7		1.75
27		0		0.29
28				0.55
29				3.03
Average	89.4	1.7	99.9	16.6

*The participation for hidden delinquency is what the subjects recount at each age rather than the participation of all the subjects in the sample when at the age concerned; for official delinquency it is the participation of all the subjects at each of the ages.

percentage is already at its maximum at the age of 13 and stays there. However, when we consider only official delinquency before age 18 for this group, the highest level, 32%, occurs at age 15. With regard to official participation, the percentages increase for the two samples to about the age of 20. They do so more slowly and more consistently in the case of the adolescents and more eventfully in the case of the delinquents. In this group two peaks are followed by an appreciable drop, one after mid-adolescence, the other at the beginning of youth. We can therefore speak of cycles of participation in criminal activities.

As to differences between the two samples, the first concerns the evolving cycle of participation. With adolescents, the increase occurs only at the very end of adolescence with a reduction later on, whereas with delinquents, the increase begins much earlier, at age 14, and does not decline until 23 or 24. Moreover, there is a difference in timing of peaks in the cycles of official delinquency and hidden delinquency; as could be expected, the peak for the latter precedes that for the former. In the adolescent sample the difference is only 1 year, the highest level for hidden delinquency occurring at 15 years and for official delinquency at

16 years, but for the delinquent sample it is 2 years, participation is already at its maximum at 13 years, whereas according to official delinquency it reaches a peak only at 15 years.

The time lag between the participation in delinquency reported by the youngsters and that based on actual convictions deserves comment. It is no doubt largely due to the legislated policy of diversion and to the practices of the justice system for minors. By looking for alternatives to conviction and by showing a certain amount of tolerance toward the offender, the justice system contributes to the lag. The longer lapse of time in the case of delinquents is probably related to the fact that in Quebec almost three quarters of cases reported to the police and other social and judicial agencies are diverted (Charbonneau, 1982; Le Blanc & Beaumont, 1985).

The trends of participation in juvenile delinquency and adult crime have been well known to criminologists for several decades (see Blumstein et al., 1986; Farrington, 1984; Fréchette & Le Blanc, 1987; Glueck, 1940; Hirschi & Gottfredson, 1983). They show that the number of juvenile offenders begins to diminish a year after the end of compulsory schooling, whereas among adults, the number of active criminals diminishes appreciably after the age of 25. The data reported in Table 3.3 are in agreement with these findings. In Quebec, compulsory schooling ends at age 15, and after age 16 participation in hidden delinquency drops slightly in the case of the adolescents just as participation in official delinquency drops in the case of the delinquents. Using a panel study of adolescents (Le Blanc & Pronovost, 1979, 1980), our studies showed that, when youngsters leave school, they lessen their criminal activities.

Our analysis of the cumulative and annual participation in criminal activities led us to a number of conclusions. First, a major scale difference occurs in the degree of participation between the representative sample of all adolescents and the one composed of delinquents; this difference is observed whatever measurement is used. It is interesting to note that a similar difference had also been found with comparisons of other aspects of the social life and psychological functioning of adolescents (see Fréchette & Le Blanc, 1987). Second, participation persists from adolescence to youth, even if it diminishes both cumulatively and annually. Third, the difference between hidden participation and official participation is marked; this seems to be a direct result of a high level of tolerance and of the broad application of the doctrine of diversion. Finally, it is interesting to note that there seems to be much less participation in criminal activities in Quebec than in the United States, but about the same amount as that observed by various researchers in western Europe.

Frequency

The frequency of criminal activities, and more specifically the number of infractions committed by an individual over a given period of time, is a method of measurement that has just begun to be used adequately and only in a limited

TABLE 3.4. Annual crime frequency by age: Mean and median.

Age (years)	Number of crimes			
	Adolescents		Delinquents	
	Mean	Median	Mean	Median
8	1.00	1.00	3.67	2.20
9	3.00	3.00	2.65	2.23
10	7.00	7.00	2.77	2.27
11	1.00	1.00	3.09	2.11
12	1.60	1.67	3.79	2.17
13	1.67	1.50	3.15	2.19
14	3.13	2.17	4.05	2.45
15	2.96	1.92	4.09	2.53
16	2.15	1.43	5.19	2.90
17	3.09	2.17	3.87	2.30
18	3.18	2.41	5.26	3.17
19	2.94	2.13	4.37	2.41
20	3.11	2.25	3.25	2.02
21	3.86	1.79	3.10	1.95
22	2.04	1.92	3.10	2.14
23	2.33	1.71	2.54	2.00
24	1.50	1.50	3.05	2.50
25	1.86	1.67	1.73	1.42
26	1.00	1.00	2.57	1.75
27			1.00	1.00
28			4.00	4.00
29			1.00	1.00
Average	2.55	2.06	3.24	2.21

number of studies, according to the survey by Blumstein et al. (1986). In this section we will use two measures: the cumulative frequency, that is, the number of infractions committed during adolescence and up to the mid-20s, and the annual frequency, that is, the number of infractions by years of involvement in illicit activities, which Blumstein et al. (1986) denoted by the Greek letter lambda.

The data are reported in Tables 3.1, 3.2, and 3.4. Frequency of hidden delinquency was not calculated for the adolescents, because the self-administered questionnaire proposed only ordinal categories of response, such as never, once or twice, several times, and very often.

Cumulative and Annual Frequency

Among the adolescents, the 229 active individuals, on arriving in their mid-20s, committed an average of 4.9 officially sanctioned infractions (it should be pointed out that the median was 2.5 and the standard deviation was considerable, 8.0). The frequency of official criminal activities increased from adolescence to youth, going from an average of 3.3 infractions between ages 12 and 18 to 4.8

from age 18 to the beginning of the 20s (the median almost doubled from one period to the other but the standard deviation increased relatively little). This large difference in median indicates that individuals who are less active at adolescence tend to commit more infractions when they are adults. The annual frequency is necessarily less than the cumulative frequency, but the gap between them is only about one infraction. Thus, during adolescence the annual (median) frequency is 1.0 versus 1.4 for the cumulative frequency, and during youth it is 1.5 versus 2.5. Thus there is a slight increase in the annual frequency from adolescence to youth.

Regarding the 470 wards of the court, the average frequency of official crimes up to the mid-20s was triple that of the adolescents—15.35 compared with 4.91. This difference was observed as well at the median level, whereas the standard deviation merely doubled. The increase in frequency of criminal activities from adolescence to youth is even more striking among the wards of the court: The average went from 8.09 to 13.94, the standard deviation increased from 10.57 to 16.78, and the median doubled from 4.29 to 8.77. Göppinger (1987), for his delinquent sample in Germany, reported an average cumulative frequency slightly lower, 14; he also noted an increase from adolescence to youth.

As far as the annual frequency is concerned, the differences are less stiking from one age level to the other, but the intensity tended to increase: The annual average was 2.98 versus 8.09 for the cumulative average during adolescence, 3.09 versus 13.94 during the first adult years, and 2.56 versus 15.35 all told. These results indicate that the delinquents were much more active than the adolescents, and this activity tended to increase from adolescence to youth.

It is impossible, unfortunately, to compare these results with those of other studies, because the data reported by Blumstein et al. (1986) concern arrests rather than convictions. We are, however, able to confirm one of Blumstein et al.'s general conclusions concerning variations in the frequency of criminal activities, namely, that the frequency increases substantially as we go further into the justice system. Erickson and Empey (1963), too, reported frequency differences of this kind between nondelinquents, delinquents in the community, and delinquents placed in trained school. Tracy (1987), in a recent analysis of the data of the Philadelphia cohort, also showed that the delinquency status "being a known delinquent," implies major differences in the frequency of hidden offenses, irrespective of race and social class.

Referring now to the frequency of criminal activities as revealed in interviews with the wards of the court (Table 3.2), we can make additional observations. Although Table 3.2 presents the averages and standard deviations of the cumulative and annual frequencies, we limit our comments to the medians, because the averages were affected by a small number of individuals who committed a great many crimes. Thus, 13% of the sample of delinquents reported a total of more than 1,000 crimes up to the average age of 23. The median of the cumulative frequencies was 33.17 during adolescence and 30 after that, to reach a number of 47.6 crimes. The median of the annual frequencies was 16.82 overall. It showed a definite increase between ages 12 and 18; after age 18 until age 25 it went from 8.27 to 16.61.

Again, it is impossible to compare these figures directly with data on adult hidden delinquency reported by Chaiken and Chaiken (1982) and for adolescents by Erickson and Empey (1963), Tracy (1987), or Tolan (1987). The samples were different, the data-gathering methods were not equivalent, and the age at the time of the interview was not the same. However, according to the data we have, the annual number of criminal acts in Quebec seems much less than in the United States; the median reported by the Chaikens was 41.60, against 8.68 for our subjects, and the threshold of the 90th percentile is twice as high–2,126 in Rand's (1987) survey versus 1,166 in our data. Cumulatively, the differences in the average frequency are also very great when we compare Erickson and Empey's, Tolan's, and Tracy's data with our own. The validity of the conclusion that Quebec youth are less criminally active than American young people, based on the comparison between results of these American studies and our results is reinforced by the fact that, in the preceding section, we arrived at a similar conclusion concerning the gap between the indices of participation in the two societies.

Tables 3.1 and 3.2 have enabled us to make a comparison that is rare in the scientific literature, that is, between the frequencies of hidden delinquency and official delinquency. Farrington (1984) made such a comparison for specific types of crimes and showed a great variety of frequencies according to the nature of the crimes. From his data it is evident that the discrepancy decreases with the seriousness of the crime. Since Farrington did not present overall results, we will do so. At adolescence, one infraction in eight leads to a conviction, if we count cumulatively, and one in four, if we use the annual figures. During youth these proportions become reversed. In short, the more crimes that an adolescent commits, the greater the chance of a conviction; the fewer crimes committed, the less the probability of a conviction. This conclusion is also supported by Elliott and Ageton (1980) and Tracy (1987). During youth the situation is reversed, so that the fewer the crimes committed over the entire period, the greater the probability of a conviction, whereas the greater the number of crimes annually, the less the probability of a conviction. There are many possible explanations for this.

One is the justice system's use of plea bargaining, which is much more frequent in the case of adults than in the case of minors. Plea bargaining means that a person accused simultaneously of a number of infractions has a good chance of being convicted for only a few of them. This is what we established with regard to armed robbery (see Gagnon & Le Blanc, 1984). The difference observed could also be a result of the general use of diversion with juveniles, the agents of the system of justice possibly responding more to the quantity and seriousness of the crimes then to each specific crime. Interviews with police officers, judges, lawyers, and social workers have shown that they tend not to take action for the first few crimes, giving a chance to the delinquent (Le Blanc, 1985a).

A second explanation could be the way that crime is accomplished at each phase of life. In chapter 2 we established that crimes become more serious from adolescence to youth. During adolescence the infractions are ill prepared and often triggered by hedonistic motivations, whereas during the young adult years they are often more impulsive, when directed against individuals, or technically more sophisticated, when acquisitively motivated. These changes in the characteristics of perpetration may explain the differences we observe, namely, that at the time of adolescence a concentration of infractions will lead to a conviction, whereas during youth even a scattering of infractions will end in conviction. During adolescence, minor infractions, if they are numerous, will very likely lead to a conviction, whereas after the age of 18, a more serious crime, even a relatively isolated one, will also likely lead to a conviction.

Perhaps both of these explanations are equally valid. However, we must not underestimate the second explanation, which refers to the way the crime is accomplished. In short, analysis of the frequency of criminal activities, just as in the case of participation, has brought to light three facts: an increase in the extent of criminal activities from adolescence to youth; a big difference between the intensity of the criminal commitment of adolescents and delinquents; and a marked disparity between the amount of hidden delinquency and official delinquency, the latter being only 10 to 25% of the former.

Variations in Frequency According to Age

The disparities in official delinquency that we just noted between the adolescents and the delinquents, like those between the averages and the medians, lessen when the frequency of crimes is calculated on an annual basis (Table 3.4). This phenomenon is well illustrated by the general average of the means and annual medians; the delinquents show a general annual average of 3.24 and the adolescents 2.55; at the same time, the gap between the average and the median is narrower among the adolescents and more marked among the delinquents. In short, the annual frequency is relatively constant in each group and the difference between the medians of each group are generally stable.

Furthermore, from one age bracket to the other, the frequency is relatively stable. The median for the delinquents, for example from 8 to 24 years of age, is between two and three crimes. The average is a little more unstable, with variations going from 2.5 to 4. For the adolescents we observe the same phenomenon but at a lower level of frequency, most of the medians are between 1 and 2. With regard to the averages, the peak of the distribution occurs at age eighteen for both the delinquents and the adolescents. The distribution of the frequency of the criminal activities according to age, then, is platykurtic. Blumstein et al. (1986) also came to this conclusion. Thus, although we noted the presence of cycles of participation and a difference in the occurrence of peaks (the peak of participation is at age 15 and of frequency at age 18), in spite of the increase in frequency from adolescence to early youth, the annual frequency remains stable throughout time. These differences between the diverse indices can be explained in two ways: First, they are caused by changes in the crime mix (analyzed in a subsequent section); second, participation and frequency respond to different etiological factors. It is conceivable that frequency is associated primarily with situational factors, with what Cohen and Felson (1979, 1980) called routine activity, whereas participation could depend on structural factors–integration into the job market or school, adequacy of the parents' education, social class, and so on. What is important is the fact that participation and frequency have proven to be relatively independent factors that merit a specific place in the study of criminal behavior.

In concluding, we note that the annual frequency of convictions, with an average of 2.55, is twice the one Farrington, Gallager, Morely, Ledger, and West (1985) observed in their London sample, 1.25. However, it is definitely lower than the estimates calculated by J. Cohen (1986) for crimes leading to an arrest in the United States, just under 10 crimes.

Variety

Variety, diversity, and polymorphism are all terms that appear in the criminological literature; they refer to the cumulative participation in several categories of crime by a particular subject. Ever since the works of Nye, Short and Olson (1957), the ideas of frequency and variety are often confused in studies on hidden delinquency. In fact, many measures, for example, Nye and Short's scale, are actually indices of variety, since they summarize the different crimes that a person admits having committed, even though the summary is presented as a frequency measurement. This difficulty was recognized some time ago, notably by Hindelang et al. (1981); these authors used a measurement of the frequency and one of the variety of hidden delinquency, cumulative and annual, the measurement of the cumulative variety being the most reliable and bearing the strongest associations with the correlates of delinquency. When official delinquency is referred to, the main measure most authors use is frequency, the question of variety using being ignored, as the survey of Blumstein et al. (1986) shows; they do not seem to consider variety a component capable of describing criminal activities.

We propose to make a clear distinction between variety and other operational concepts that describe criminal activities, for two reasons. First, a number of studies (Farrington, 1982; Favard, 1980; Guttridge, Mednick, & Van Deusen, 1982; Le Blanc, 1986b; Loeber, 1982; Robins & Ratcliff, 1979) show that the variety of illicit acts is connected in some way with subsequent chronic delinquency. Second, an experimental basis shows that variety is relatively independent of other descriptive concepts whether we study hidden delinquency (Fréchette, 1980) or official delinquency (Le Blanc, 1986b). Our strict definition of variety is the following: the accumulation of criminal activities of diverse kinds, committed by a person during a given period of time.

Given this accumulation of illicit activities, two questions arise: Is homogeneity versus heterogeneity still a controversial issue? What is the degree of variety? These are two independent questions, but necessarily interrelated. The first concerns the presence of diversity in the criminal activities, that is, participation in one or several forms of criminal behavior; the second concerns the degree of variety present in these activities or the number of types of criminal activities practiced by an individual.

Homogeneity/Heterogeneity

The controversy opposing homogeneity and heterogeneity is still going on. Until only a few years ago, the question had yet to be solved empirically. An analysis of the hidden delinquency among adolescents that we undertook in the 1970s showed a definite preponderance of heterogeneous acts at a given age level, but the persistence of homogeneity from one age level to the other (Caplan & Le Blanc, 1976). In a recent survey of the literature, Klein (1984) confirmed the versatile nature of the illicit activities of adolescents and concluded that there is no specialization. It is unfortunate, however, that Klein and several other authors confused the diversity of delinquent activities with specialization. Specialization is the repetition of the same types of infraction over time, according to the definition adopted by Blumstein et al. (1986), whereas diversity is the simultaneous accumulation of many different kinds of infraction. Thus specialization could occur with heterogeneity at a given moment in time if a delinquent is always committing, for example, two types of crime. The data in Tables 3.1 and 3.2 show that hidden illicit activities are primarily heterogeneous for a majority of the adolescent group, whereas the criminal activities for which they were convicted by the courts appear homogeneous for more than half of them; furthermore, the illicit activities committed by most of the delinquents are heterogeneous, whether hidden or official.

Where the hidden delinquency of the sample of adolescents is concerned, two fifths of the subjects reported homogeneous criminal activities (36% at age 15 and 41% at age 17). According to our analysis (Caplan & Le Blanc, 1976, in most of the cases, they got involved in only one type of infraction. But, a majority (60 to 70%) preferred to commit many different kinds of offense. With infractions that were sanctioned, they seem to have been, for a large majority, of only one type. Thus, the illicit activities, as known by the court, appear to be homogeneous. This difference is evidently due to the selective nature of the justice system; the fact is, criminal activities that lead to a conviction are very often the most serious of all those committed by the adolescent, since the main criterion of diversion is the gravity of the crime [see the survey by Gottfredson & Gottfredson, 1980, for the United States; this is also true in Quebec with regard to the decisions of the police (Le Blanc, 1971) and of the court (Le Blanc & Beaumont, 1985)].

With regard to the sample of delinquents, the picture is clear: Their illicit activities, whether hidden or official, are heterogeneous (at adolescence only 14% of the subjects who reported hidden delinquency and 26% whose delinquency was official engaged in homogeneous activities; during youth the proportions were 23 and 24%). The difference between the two types of conduct is slight, probably because the intensity of the acting out, for this group, overcomes the influence of the justice system. Moreover, the place occupied by homogeneous delinquency is fairly stable from adolescence to youth. The shorter the period of observation, the homogeneous the illict activities appear; for example, at age 17, the delinquency observed covers only 2 years and the homogeneity is 45%, whereas for a much longer period (between ages 7 and 25 years) the degree of homogeneity is much lower, 11% in the case of hidden delinquency and 14% in that of official delinquency. Chaiken and Chaiken (1982) reported similar proportions of homogeneous offending for hidden delinquency in their adult samples, and Göppinger (1987) found only 16% of homogeneous delinquency for German official delinquency.

Finally, it should be noted that in the case of homogeneity, the difference between the adolescents and the delinquents is twice as great for both the hidden and official delinquency. Thus, at the beginning of adolescence the percentage of hidden delinquency is 35% among the adolescents and 19% among the delinquents; similarly, for the entire period of adolescence the percentage of official delinquency is 59% among the former and 26% among the latter.

It appears, then, that variety acts in the same way as frequency and participation. There is a clear difference in scale between the adolescents and the delinquents, the illicit activities of the former displaying much more homogeneity. Moreover, heterogeneity remains quite stable through age in both groups. Finally, official delinquency differs from hidden delinquency in that it is much more homogeneous, due to the selection of only the most serious acts for sanction by the justice system.

Degree of Variety

Since the majority of delinquents and many adolescents clearly exhibit different kinds of activities, it is important to find out the extent of this heterogeneity. Tables 3.1 and 3.2 show that the differences between the averages and the medians are slight, and thus we shall take the former into account. It is remarkable that if we start with hidden delinquency, the averages of variety are in the same range from the beginning to the end of adolescence and from adolescence to young youth, a fact also observed by Petersilia et al. (1978) in their exploratory study (the differences between the adolescents and delinquents are fairly slight). Tolan (1987) presented averages comparable to ours for his normative sample using five categories of crime, the same number of categories we used. Zimmerman and Broder (1980) reported the averages of variety to be a point and a half above our averages, but they used seven categories of infractions rather than five; however, the difference in the degree of variety between their adolescents and delinquents is much more obvious than what we observed, and this same difference is also more pronounced in the study of Hindelang et al. (1981).

Our analysis of official delinquency gives a totally different picture: The average degree of variety increases from adolescence to youth (going from 1.09 to

TABLE 3.5. Median frequency of categories of crimes.

Degree of variety*	Adolescents		Delinquents			
	Official delinquency		Hidden delinquency		Official delinquency	
	Adolescence	Youth	Adolescence	Youth	Adolescence	Youth
1	1.1	1.9	3.1	2.2	1.2	1.9
2	2.1	3.5	10.3	14	2.6	3.4
3	4	5.33	35	70.5	4.6	5.8
4	5	8.5	47	570	8.2	9.1
5	16.5	16.5	121.5	4,004	10	12.5
6	9.5	13.5	144	76.5	14	14.2
7					23	17.5
8					18	17.5
9					18.5	25.5

*Number of types of crimes.

1.94 among the adolescents and from 3.06 to 3.73 among the delinquents) and there is a difference of almost two types of infraction between the adolescents and the delinquents (for example, during adolescence the average degree of variety is 1.09 for the former and 3.06 for the latter).

Why is the degree of variety not the same for the hidden delinquency and the official delinquency? Why does the degree of variety in the hidden delinquency remain quite stable from one stage of life to the other, whereas greater variations are observed in official delinquency? An explanation currently advanced is the trivial nature of the majority of indictable offenses included when hidden delinquency is measured (see Hindelang et al., 1981; Le Blanc, 1983a). It is very possibly the case here, since we used a self-administered questionnaire for the adolescents, which, although it mentioned some serious crimes such as burglary, was largely composed of minor infractions. On the other hand, with the delinquents we relied on an interview in which were gathered all the crimes committed by each subject independent of the crime's seriousness. However, we are inclined to look for another explanation of the difference observed between variety and frequency, on the one hand, and between variety and the nature and/or gravity of the illicit activity, on the other. We shall come back to the relationship between the latter two, but for the moment our concern is the connection between frequency and variety.

Variety can hide very different levels of frequency. Table 3.5 shows, as could be expected, that the median frequency of illicit acts increases with the degree of variety. What is more interesting is the fact that the association is considerably stronger for the hidden delinquency of the delinquent group. This means that frequency is not at the level it should be when we take official figures into account. At the same time we find that the degree of variety affords a better indication of the actual illicit activity of the delinquents than the degree of frequency (taking into account the difference between the median frequencies of their acts when hidden delinquency becomes official delinquency). Furthermore, we must point out the similarity of the medians between the two groups, adolescents and delinquents, for official delinquency. This implies that the justice system selects different types of crimes among the total, without taking into account the actual frequency of the acts. Variety seems to be a more reliable measure than frequency and, at the same time, relatively independent. It is important to consider its value if we are to understand the meaning and justification of society's interventions in reaction to criminal acts.

The data we have analyzed lead us to conclude that variety, when its presence or absence is verified, behaves in the same way as frequency and participation at the three levels of comparison we have used: It differentiates one sample from the other, hidden delinquency from official delinquency, and each phase of life from the two others. When the degree of variety is measured, there is a difference only between the two samples. On the other hand, it appears that variety is a good reflection of what really goes on and is not redundant with frequency.

Gravity

Sellin and Wolfgang, in their classic book *The Measurement of Delinquency* (1964), proposed, as a major innovation, a method for evaluating the qualitative dimension of criminal activities – use of a measure referring to appreciation of the seriousness of a crime by the people of a given social milieu. In many recent studies researchers have used instruments based on the legal gravity of the crimes, more specifically, on the degree of punishment imposed by the Criminal Code. Sellin and Wolfgang, for their part, favored a weighted index based on the results of a survey (the questionnaire they used asked respondents to attribute to each description of a criminal act a subjective value proportionate to its gravity) that offers a graduated scale of seriousness. The damage to the victim of a crime could thus be precisely evaluated on the basis of public opinion.

It is unfortunate that Blumstein et al.'s report "Criminal careers and career criminals" (1986) used the term *seriousness* to designate the pattern of offense types that are committed, something quite different from the "seriousness" to which Sellin and Wolfgang initially referred. The Blumstein report thus creates the same type of confusion it objected to in the case of prevalence, since it attributes a new and comprehensive meaning to an idea that had a specific definition in prior criminological literature. It is to avoid such confusion that we use the term *gravity*.

Akman and Normandeau (1968) have partially replicated Sellin and Wolfgang's study in Canada. Since they obtained a correlation of .96 between the estimates of seriousness for the same criminal acts in Philadelphia and in Montreal, we have assigned to each category of crime the degree of gravity that Wolfgang, Figlio, Tracy, and Singer (1985) furnished in a recent study. By multiplying the frequency of the infractions for each category by the appropriate degree, we have been able to calculate two indices of gravity: the total gravity of a person's illicit activities, that is, the sum of the scores of seriousness for all the crimes that an individual has committed, and the average gravity of the infractions committed by criminally active subjects. These scores enable us once more to compare hidden delinquency and official delinquency, adolescents and delinquents, as well as adolescents and young adults. These comparisons of the seriousness of the illicit activities is based on the data presented in Table 3.1 and 3.2.

Gravity is thus confirmed as a measurement equivalent to those obtained for cumulative participation and frequency; at the same time it offers a qualitative assessment of the illegal activities. It varies in the same way as the measures of participation and frequency between samples, periods of life, and measures of delinquency. Adult crimes have higher scores of central tendency than juvenile crimes, and delinquents have higher scores than adolescents. Wolfgang et al. (1987) observed the same for the variations of official delinquency according to the period of life and the delinquency status.

Gravity by Crime

To facilitate understanding of the results we present on the average gravity of crimes committed, we use the scores assigned by Wolfgang et al. (1985) to a long list of criminal acts, the minimum being .20 and the maximum 79. For the sample of delinquents, the median scores for gravity are between 5 and 7 (we note that there is little disparity between the averages and medians) for both official and hidden delinquency. For the sample of adolescents, the medians in the case of official delinquency are 5 or less. These figures indicate that the crimes are not very serious, considering that the theoretical maximum gravity is 79. They involve such acts as purse snatching, aggravated theft involving $10.00 or more (with a weapon or through intimidation), burglary involving $1,000 or more, common theft of $1,000 or more, the use of heroin, and so on (1985). It turns out, as well, that the median gravity of official infractions shows little variation in the different comparisons, an observation we also made regarding the degree of variety and annual frequency.

Thus, it can be concluded that the gravity of the illicit activities remain at a fairly constant level from one sample to the other and from one age bracket to another. Even though the median gravity tends to increase from adolescence to youth in delinquents and to be greater among delinquents than among adolescents, these trends are not very marked. These data support a position currently held in criminology—that the infractions committed by youngsters are generally of limited gravity, so that the justice system usually has only minor crimes to deal with.

Total Gravity

The other indication of gravity, that of the total gravity of all the criminal activities, shows more marked differences, as noted also by Zimmerman and Broder (1980). The differences between the adolescents and the delinquents are clearly significant, as is the increase from adolescence to early youth. Still more interesting is the difference in scale between hidden delinquency and official delinquency. To go by medians, the differences imply that the gravity is from three to eight times greater in the case of hidden delinquency, thus confirming the selective nature of diversion, which we have already mentioned.

The conclusions we drew from our study of criminal activities by means of these various indices are both clear and agree with our previous findings: (a) There is a definitive aggravation from adolescence to youth; (b) there is a clear disparity between hidden delinquency and official delinquency, in favor of the former; and (c) there is a difference of degree when delinquents are compared with adolescents.

We must point out that, taking into account the construction of the index of total gravity (the frequency of the infraction multiplied by the score of the corresponding gravity) and the almost maximum correlation between the total gravity of the illicit activities and their frequency (.98 among the delinquents), the measure of total gravity can be considered an alternative to frequency but cannot replace it if we want to get a detailed picture of the criminal activities. The average gravity obviously remains an effective measure for assessing the qualitative aspect of current criminal activity.

Violence

The problem of violence has always been in the foreground, publicly and in debates on crime policy. It is in evidence daily in the media and is the subject of many scientific works (Mathias, DeMuro, & Allinson, 1984; Moore, Estrich, McGillis, & Spelman, 1984; Wolfgang & Ferracuti, 1967). In spite of all the attention violence has received, scientists have still not agreed on a definition for it (Marceau, 1985). It is possible, however, to base a minimal definition of violence on the certifiable use of force and intimidation in the perpetration of a criminal act. Our definition of violence applies to infractions against persons (assault, assault and battery, murder, homicide, rape) and infractions against property that involve the use of a weapon (armed robbery, aggravated theft). Tables 3.1 and 3.2 present data on the participation of the subjects in these types of crimes and on their cumulative frequency.

For the adolescents, participation in crimes with violence, as registered at the Office of the Court Clerk, appeared rare. Zero point six percent had been convicted for a crime of this type during adolescence and 2% during youth, for a total of 2.4% between latency and the mid-20s. Thus the cumulative participation in violence was low, even if it increased slightly with age.

Whereas such crimes were rare for the adolescents, they were not for the delinquents. In fact, two fifths of the latter sample declared they had participated in a crime of violence (40% during adolescence and 46% during young youth) and about a third had been convicted for this type of infraction (28% during adolescence and 35% during youth). Moreover, the disparity between hidden and official delinquency was much more pronounced, the differences between medians being about two infractions but the differences between averages and standard deviations being considerable. Obviously, a limited number of delinquents committed violent crimes frequently but only a small proportion of them were convicted. The important finding was that the frequency of illicit acts of violence increased from adolescence to youth. Finally it should be mentioned that participation in and the frequency of personal crimes are much lower in Montreal than in the United States (Visher & Roth, 1986; J. Cohen, 1986).

Evaluation of the Comparisons

Having proceeded with three comparisons (hidden versus official delinquency, adolescents versus delinquents, adolescence versus youth) and having used five descriptive parameters (participation, frequency, variety, gravity, and violence), we will now summarize the main conclusions we have drawn.

First, there is clear evidence that criminal activities intensify from adolescence to youth. Generally speaking, participation, frequency, variety, gravity, and violence increase from one phase of life to the next. This basic observation leads us to the idea of criminal patterns. Since there is an increase in criminal activities continuing through at least two stages, adolescence and youth, the term *process* can be applied to the evolution of illicit activities among delinquents.

Second, the comparison of the illicit activities of a representative sample of the general population with those of a sample of wards of the juvenile court has enabled us to understand a fundamental fact: In spite of a marked difference in scale between the two samples, the consistency of the criminal activities is confirmed. What is more, in both samples we have found the same variations at each phase of life, whether in official or hidden delinquency. The same basic process seems to be involved. However, whereas the adolescent sample is interesting from the point of view of epidemiology, the delinquent sample is more useful for understanding the dynamics of criminal activities. Variations in participation are more extensive among the delinquents, and the largest number of subjects are at the extreme of the scales. For these reasons, chapters 5 and 6 will be limited to the sample of delinquents. Focusing on this sample is like examining the phenomenon with a microscope. In that sense, Cernkovich et al. (1985) were right when they pointed out that persistent delinquents are generally not included in studies of hidden delinquency and when they recommended using samples of officially recognized delinquents to ensure more valid results in regard to chronic delinquency.

Third, comparison between hidden and official delinquency shows clearly the effect of the justice system's selection practice, but this finding is secondary in the study we have undertaken. Furthermore, the difference in extent between the two measures of delinquency leads us to consider that self-reported delinquency provides the more exact description of illicit activities, the one closest to reality. The following chapters, consequently, will be based on the delinquency as reported by the delinquents when interviewed.

4
A Boundary View of Offending

From the study of the five main characteristics of offending (participation, frequency, variety, gravity, and violence) it has been possible to give, in chapter 3, an overall picture of the criminal activity of our subjects. Another approach remains to be explored, a boundary perspective. This approach has appeared fairly recently in criminology. It focuses on continuous criminal activity, particularly between adolescence and youth. It is primarily interested in the appearance, the duration, and the extinction of offending.

This approach means that once more we will be tackling the question of the continuity or the lack of continuity of criminal activity, a question widely debated and studied in psychology and dealt with in criminology by means of specific concepts (such as precocity, duration, and desistance) as well as by study of the dynamics of illegal activity and the processes of escalation and specialization. In the literature, the conceptual framework for this boundary approach has generally remained simplistic, because criminologists have been reluctant to draw useful concepts from the sociology of occupations or from the psychology of development. Blumstein et al. (1986), in their work on the concept of criminal career, made a remarkable effort at systematization in this direction and put forward the proposition of a specific model of career. We will be using the concepts of precocity, duration, and desistance introduced by these authors in their model; furthermore, we will give special attention to persistence throughout the various stages of development.

Lerner (1986) described the continuity/discontinuity opposition in development as follows: "If things stay the same, continuity exists, and if things change, discontinuity exists" (p. 183). Is a person's criminal activity characterized by continuity or discontinuity? In the light of results reported in chapters 2 and 3, it is clear that criminal activity as a particular type of human behavior is not continuous. It seems to be limited to a relatively short period of time, mainly during adolescence and youth, and furthermore, variations emerge from one age level to another in most of the five descriptive parameters used to study the form it takes. The first part of this chapter will be devoted to verifying the accuracy of this finding by using more pertinent measures, such as precocity, duration, and desistance as well as the transition from juvenile to adult crime.

Traditionally, criminologists have analyzed continuity in two ways—by studying precocity and by describing the transition from juvenile delinquency to adult crime. More recently, the ideas of duration and desistance were introduced to describe the persistence of criminal activities. Applying four boundary parameters, we made comparisons between official and hidden delinquency, between adolescents and delinquents, and between adolescence and youth in order to complete the study undertaken in the preceding chapter. We then went on to study the crime mix and, above all, its transformations with age.

Precocity

Going back to the work of Lombrosos (1899) on precocity, the age at which delinquency begins has been confirmed many times by criminologists as a key factor in predicting the continuity of delinquent behavior. Every survey of the literature done over the past 30 years, particularly those of Sellin (1958), Mannhein (1965), Ohlin (1974), Loeber (1982), and Blumstein et al. (1986) have stressed the importance of this factor. Since the works of the Gluecks, there has been a dearth of empirical studies describing the relationship between precocity and the other characteristics of criminal behavior. More recently, numerous studies have also gone into this question, notably those of Farrington (1982, 1983), Hamparian, Schuster, Dinitz, and Conrad (1978), McCord (1979, 1982), Robins and Ratcliff (1979), Rutter, Tizard, and Whitmore (1970), Shannon (1978), Wadsworth (1979), Wolfgang et al. (1972, 1987), and Fréchette and Le Blanc (1987).

On the basis of the data we have gathered, we feel we can make our own contribution to clarification of the role of precocity. Our first step will be an analysis of the distribution of cases according to the age at which hidden delinquency began, taken into consideration both the first offense and the first sequence of consecutive offenses. We will then analyze the information we have concerning the moment at which hidden and official delinquency started among adolescents and wards of the court, as well as variations in the starting age with different types of crimes.

Beginning with hidden delinquency, the delinquent group shows a marked tendency to commit their first offense at an early age. As Table 4.1 shows, 11% of these subjects started their delinquent activities before the age of 7 and 53% before the age of 12. Thus, half the sample can be considered *primary delinquents*, to use the terminology of Cormier, Kennedy, Sangoviz, and Trottier (1959), that is, persons who started delinquency during childhood (4%) or latency (48%). Those who started their delinquent activities during adolescence are called *secondary delinquents* (46% of our sample). Finally, less than 1% of the wards of the court who had not official juvenile delinquency can be classified as *tertiary delinquents*, since their criminal activities started after the age of 18. In a similar study, Petersilia et al. (1978) observed that more than 90% of their sample of 49 adult criminals reported having started criminal activities before the age of 18; they were all primary or secondary delinquents. The same tendency is

TABLE 4.1. Distribution of age of onset of criminal activities: Comparison of adolescents and delinquents and of hidden and official delinquency.

Age (years)	Delinquents: Hidden No.	Delinquents: Hidden %	Delinquents: Official No.	Delinquents: Official %	Adolescents Official No.	Adolescents Official %
3	1	0.2				
4	4	0.9				
5	13	2.9				
6	33	7.3				
7	36	8	3	0.7	0	0
8	40	8.9	6	1.4	1	0.5
9	28	6.2	12	2.8	1	0.5
10	60	13.3	17	4	0	0
11	23	5.1	17	4	2	0.9
12	65	14.4	27	6.3	5	2.4
13	48	10.6	47	10.9	0	0
14	46	10.2	90	20.9	6	4.8
15	30	6.7	86	20	19	9
16	14	3.1	42	9.8	18	8.5
17	6	1.3	21	4.9	17	8
18	1	0.2	17	4	25	11.8
19	1	0.2	17	4	33	15.6
20	0	0	10	2.3	30	14.2
21	1	0.2	4	0.9	22	10.4
22	1	0.2	5	1.2	12	5.7
23			5	1.2	16	7.5
24			3	0.7	2	0.9
25			1	0.2	3	1.4
Mean	10.73		14.61		18.58	
SD	3.23		3.02		3	
Median	10.96		14.46		18.86	

SD, standard deviation.

reported by Göppinger (1987). It should also be noted that Tolan (1987) reported a median age of 12 for his sample of adolescents taken from the general popultion; the median age is 11 for our sample of delinquents.

A stricter way of establishing the start of criminal activities, and one that reduces the distorting effect of fortuitous acts and memory lapses, is to use the age at which the first sequence of crimes began. Interestingly enough, this does not change the foregoing proportions in any significant way. In a preceding work (Fréchette & Le Blanc, 1978), we showed that 48% of delinquents commit their first series of crimes before the age of 12. These data demonstrate the ability to engage in illicit activities at a very young age (even before puberty for a large number of delinquents).

With regard to the official delinquency of the wards of the court, a totally different picture of precocity emerges, one similar to that reported in all the criminological studies on the subject. No longer are half the cases primary delinquents, but only 3%. Tertiary delinquency goes from 1 to 14%, while secondary delinquency increases from 46 to 73%. Table 4.1 also shows that most of the subjects of the adolescent group (68%) can be characterized as tertiary delinquents and that very few of them (2%) are primaries. With delinquents, the difference between the distribution of precocity in hidden and official delinquency may be due to the tolerance accorded to very young offenders and to the practice of diversion introduced and reinforced over the past 10 years in Montreal, as explained in the preceding chapter. It should be noted that this difference is likely to increase because, at the time we recruited our sample of delinquents, the minimum age of criminal responsibility in Canada was 7 years whereas since 1984, with the new Young Offenders Act, it is 12 years.

It would be interesting to compare these results with those of other studies. This is possible only with official delinquency, although four factors may interfere: the age of legal responsibility, which changes from one legal system to another; the origin and nature of the samples; the type of information chosen to measure precocity (actual perpetration, arrest, conviction); and the availability of data to calculate equivalent statistics. It has been possible, however, with regard to the starting age of offending, to compare Montreal (Table 4.1) with Philadelphia (Wolfgang et al., 1972), England (Wadsworth, 1979), Stockholm (Wikström, 1987), and Copenhagen (Teilman, Van Deusen, & Mednick, 1984). Thus, the average age when criminal activities began during adolescence is distributed in the following way: Among the delinquents in Montreal it is 13.7 years (conviction), in Philadelphia 13.9 years (arrest), in England 14.5 years (conviction), in Stockholm 14.76 years (arrest) and in Copenhagen 14.9 years (conviction); for the Montreal adolescent sample it is 15 years (conviction). Wolfgang et al. (1987) reported age 16 for arrests when the period covered was not just adolescence but up to age 30, and Wikström (1987) reported age 17.3 when the period covered went to age 25. If we use a comparable period, the averages are 14.6 years for delinquents and 18.6 years for adolescents (convictions, Montreal).

These data call for some clarification. First, the age of entry into delinquent activities seems relatively stable from one country to the other when the samples are directly comparable and when the parameter is conviction; there is a difference of only half a year between England and the cities of Copenhagen and Montreal. Second, the variations in precocity appear to be quite consistent, for in the case of hidden delinquency of the wards of the court, the average age of first crime is 10.6 (official delinquency occurs later, at an average age of 13.7); for the adolescents it was much later, the average being age 15 (see Tables 4.2 and 4.3). Thus, youngsters who become deeply involved in delinquency begin their illicit activities much earlier.

These findings indicate that there is a gap of about 3 years between the commission of the first offense and the appearance of the adolescent in the justice system and of 4 years between the first offense and the first official sanction by a court. In effect, the average age at which the first offense occurs is 10.8 years and the average age for the first conviction is 14.6 years, taking into account all criminal activities up to the mid-20s.

TABLE 4.2. Hidden male offending: Boundary parameters.

Parameter	Adolescence	Youth	Total
Precocity*			
Mean	10.62	18.18	10.78
SD	3.02	1.91	3.23
Median	10.83	17.85	10.95
Duration†			
Mean	5.33	4.32	10.76
SD	3.03	2.03	3.98
Median	4.89	4.56	10.9
Termination‡			
Mean	15.48		18.93
SD	1.06		3.56
Median	15.44		18.7

SD, standard deviation.
*Age at first crime.
† Interval in years between first and last crime.
‡ Age at which last crime was committed.

This brings back the question of the diversion practices that have been introduced into our justice system, as they have into judicial systems in most other Western countries. These figures show a large number of youngsters between the ages of 10 and 14, who are at high risk of persisting in delinquent activities without preventive or curative support during a crucial phase of their development. Their offenses may not be very serious, but the precocity of their

TABLE 4.3. Official male offending: Boundary parameters.

	Adolescents			Delinquents		
Parameters	Adolescence	Youth	Total	Adolescence	Youth	Total
Precocity*						
Mean	15.03	20.09	18.58	13.7	19.36	14.61
SD	1.93	1.83	3	2.12	1.88	3.02
Median	15.42	19.78	18.86	14.1	18.89	14.56
Duration†						
Mean	1.53	2.51	2.5	2.45	3.93	5.23
SD	0.88	1.23	1.6	1.52	1.83	3.24
Median	1.27	2.21	2.12	2.1	3.6	4.84
Termination‡						
Mean	15.39	20.85	19.76	14.51	21.4	19.93
SD	1.83	1.81	2.9	2.08	2	3.43
Median	15.81	20.67	20.13	14.9	21.41	20.54

SD, standard deviation.
*Age at first crime.
† Number of years of criminal activity.
‡ Age at which last crime was committed.

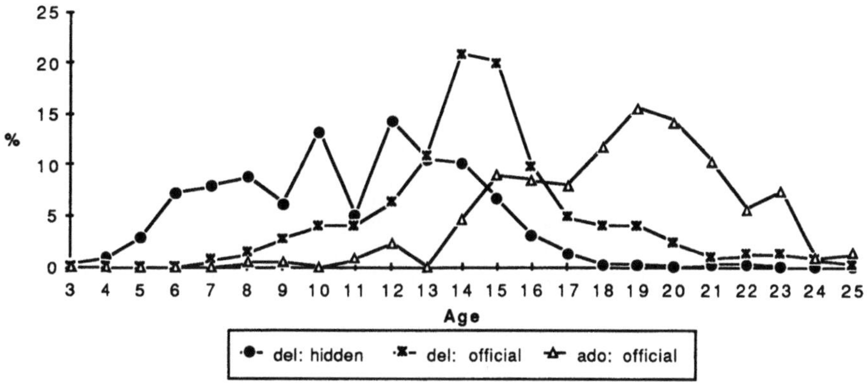

FIGURE 4.1. Age of onset of criminal activities, hidden and official delinquency, adolescents and delinquents.

illicit activities alone should prompt a second look by the court before proceeding with diversion. Present practices of the police, of centers for delinquent youths, and of social services support diversion, with the result that youngsters in early adolescence are very likely to be diverted from the the system. This tendency is also reported in the survey of Gottfredson and Gottfredson (1980); it is the case in Quebec at the police level (Le Blanc, 1971), at the prosecuting level (Trépanier & Gagnon, 1984) and at the court level (Le Blanc & Beaumont, 1986; Le Blanc & Brousseau, 1974).

Figure 4.1 presents another important finding. Regardless of the fact that 18 years is the legal age at which juvenile delinquents are considered adult, there seems to be a similar time cycle for delinquents and adolescents. Among the former, the average starting age for juvenile delinquency is 13.7 years and for adult criminality it is 19.4 years; among the latter, these ages are 15 and 20 years, respectively. Thus, criminal activities seem to be reactivated at the beginning of adulthood, with a respite between the two times for both many adolescents and delinquents. This was also shown to be the case in the study of participation and annual frequency.

To sum up, having established that the age at which the first offense occurs is a good measure of precocity, it it clear that delinquent activity begins at an early age. For a little more than half the group of delinquents, it started before age 12, whereas for most of the others it began at the beginning of adolescence. This proves, rather surprisingly considering the data published on official delinquency, that only an infinitesimal proportion of delinquents commit their first crime after mid-adolescence. Thus, the period of life during which criminal activity is most likely to begin is between ages 10 and 14, with a sort of peak between the 10th and 12th years, at which time a child has to establish his independence, his own frame of reference, and his own values vis-à-vis the adult world. The child quite often joins a group of peers, which offers new confidence

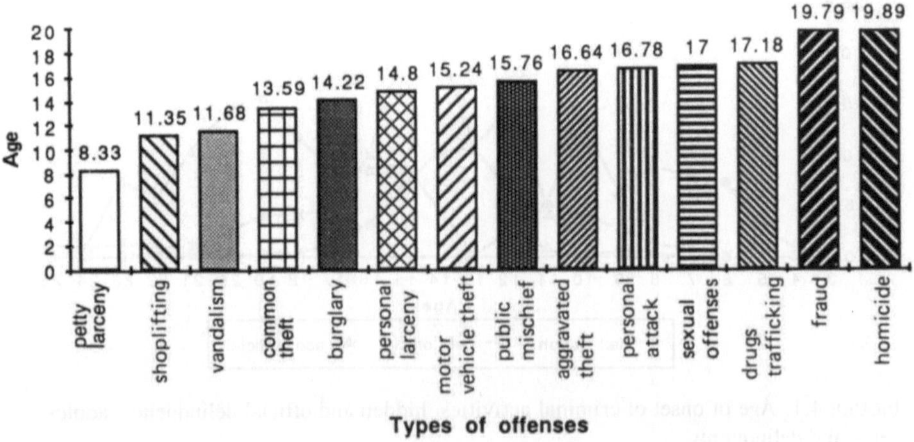

FIGURE 4.2. Average age of onset of types of offenses.

and the security that is crucial at this stage. This could account for the definite tendency of delinquency to emerge and expand during this phase, as the expression of both a form of rebellion toward adults and conformity toward companions. Furthermore, 13 appears to be the age when delinquent activity, having been tried during latency, appears again in certain categories of crime, such as burglary; it seems as though this age represents a critical threshold past which criminal activity will increase and stabilize for 2 or 3 years before subsiding, only to return in full force at the beginning of adulthood. The discontinuous nature of criminal activity is again confirmed.

Are these conclusions about criminal activity in general valid for each of the crime categories we are using? The results reported by Fréchette (1980) concerning the age of appearance of each type of crime during adolescence, as illustrated in Figure 4.2 (we use the averages because they differ very little from the medians), demonstrate four facts: (a) The starting age differs from one form of crime to another. (b) While they are different, the ages marking the onset of illicit activity are concentrated, for most crime categories, within a relatively short span of time, that is, during a period of 5 to 6 years between ages 11 and 17, which brings to light the very important fact that at mid-adolescence, most of the crime categories have already appeared (except fraud and homicidal acts). (c) These various categories of crime, succeeding one another, increase in objective gravity, from minor delinquent acts during latency (petty larceny, vandalism, shoplifing) to decidedly antisocial and technical equivalents of serious adult crimes at mid-adolescence (assault, armed robbery, and so on), with an interim of truly adolescent infractions (such as furtive thefts, breaking and entering, possession of drugs, and so on). (d) Finally, by grouping certain categories of crime according to the time of their appearance, four stages emerge: the stage of nuisance offenses (petty larceny, shoplifting, and vandalism), that of medium-gravity offenses (common theft, burglary, personal larceny, and motor vehicle theft), that of serious crimes (armed robbery, personal attack, sex-related crimes), and that of adult crime (fraud and violent acts).

It thus can be emphasized that various manifestations of criminal activity do not start indiscriminately at just any age. There seem to be chronological thresholds. It appears also that the production of criminal acts, so marked at ages 12, 13, 14, and 15 years, slows down in the second half of adolescence, even if gravity increases up to adulthood, with the emergence of homicidal and fraudulent crimes. The important fact is that criminal activity is apt to expand significantly between latency and adolescence. This comes as no surprise, since this period is characterized at the same time by drastic physical changes, with the beginning of puberty; by marked psychological changes, tied to the development of the personality; and by significant social changes, in particular those brought about by the presence of the peer group.

Persistence

Probably the best way to get an accurate picture of the evolution of offending is through the study of persistence of illicit acts over time. This question of duration has been examined by several others (Green, 1977; Greenberg, 1975; Shinnar & Shinnar, 1975; Petersilia et al., 1978). Using the data we have, we will first analyze persistence in terms of the connection between juvenile delinquency and adult criminality. Even if this distinction is totally arbitrary and due to the fact that justice is dispensed by two independent systems, one for minors and one for adults, a study of the transition from one to the other is crucial in accounting for the evolution of antisocial behavior.

From Juvenile Delinquency to Adult Criminality

Surveys of the literature on this transition (Langan & Farrington, 1983; Blumstein et al., 1986) are unanimous in reporting that, with samples of different nature and origin, from 30 to 60% of adolescents arrested by the police or convicted by a court will have a criminal record as adults: These youngsters are called *persistent delinquents*. The proportion increases with the length of the subsequent control period and usually reflects the base rate of the sample's participation in criminal activities. In other respects, it has been said that new offenders, with no past record as juvenile delinquents, represent around 40% of adult criminals, while 10 to 20% of adolescents who are not identified as delinquents become criminals in their 20s.

Our own data, based on convictions, clearly confirm the connection that exists between juvenile delinquency and adult crime. Table 4.4 presents both the delinquent and adolescent samples. Looking at these figures, it is evident first that those who have a juvenile record are more likely to become involved in adult criminality. Thus, we find that in the sample of adolescents where only 4.1% had

TABLE 4.4. Transfer from juvenile delinquency to adult criminality.

Juvenile delinquency		Adolescents: Adult criminality No	Adolescents: Adult criminality Yes	Adolescents: Total	Delinquents: Adult criminality No	Delinquents: Adult criminality Yes	Delinquents: Total
				Official delinquency			
No	*n*	1,389	147	1,545	36	51	87
	H	90.5%	9.5%		41.4%	58.6%	
	V	97.2%	85.5%	95.9	27.5%	15%	18.5%
	T	86.8%	9.1%		7.7%	10.9%	
Yes	n	41	25	66	95	288	383
	H	62.1%	37.9%		24.8%	75.2%	
	V	2.8%	14.5%	4.1%	72.5%	85%	81.5%
	T	2.5%	1.6%		20.2%	61.3%	
Total		1,439	172	1,611	131	339	470
		89.3	10.7%	100%	27.9%	72.1%	100%
				Hidden delinquency			
No	n				1	27	28
	H				3.6%	96.4%	
	V				5.3%	15.2%	14.3%
	T				0.5%	13.8%	
Yes	n				18	150	168
	H				10.7%	89.3%	
	V				94.7%	84.9%	83.7%
	T				9.2%	76.5%	
Total					19	177	196
					9.7%	90.3%	

H, horizontal; % calculated over the raw total. V, vertical; calculated over the column total. T, total; calculated over all cases. *n*: number of cases.

been officially termed delinquents, 38% of these became identified as adult criminals (this proportion although important is lower than that in the American and British studies), while the proportion of those who, although never convicted by a juvenile court, were later convicted as adults was only 10%. By contrast, it is to be noted that, of the total number of subjects who were convicted by an adult court (11% of the total group of adolescents) a small group of 14.5% had a record as a minor. It is possible, then, to be officially involved in adult crime without having been recorded as a juvenile delinquent, but those who have been convicted as minors have a greater probability of committing crimes as adult.

In the delinquent sample, with subjects who became wards of the court whether as delinquent or as children requiring protection, the figures are much more striking; 75% of those who had been convicted as minor are convicted as adults, and it is to be noted that they represent 85% of those who became adult criminals. It is also interesting to observe that in the subgroups with no recorded delinquency at adolescence but who had been brought to court for protection the proportion of those who got involved as adults was 59%. It is once more evident that an uncertain future lies in store for those youngsters taken in charge by the juvenile court.

Still referring to Table 4.4, perhaps an easier way to describe that transition would be to use the percentage that each entry of the table represents regarding the total number of subjects making up the sample. When we proceed this way, we obtain four types of individuals: abstainers, those who never engage in delinquency or crime; desisters, those who don't persist; recruits, those who start at the adult crime level; and persistents, those who practice both juvenile delinquency and adult crime. Among the delinquents, we find 61% who are persistents, 8% abstainers, 20% desisters, and 11% recruits. By contrast, among the adolescents, 20% are persisters, 87% are abstainers, 2% are desisters, and 9% are recruits. With this method of calculating percentages, the data on the transition from juvenile delinquency to adult crime make it possible to eliminate the confusion that often results from the use of the procedures previously mentioned.

Additional information is furnished by the data on hidden delinquency reported to us by our sample of delinquents. Table 4.4 shows that less than 1% of delinquents are abstainers on reaching adulthood, 76% are persisters, 9% are desisters and 14% are recruits. Here the proportion of persisters increases substantially compared with that of the official delinquency.

Whereas persistence clearly is the rule from adolescence to the beginning of adulthood, it does not show the same strength during adolescence. In fact, our analysis (Fréchette & Le Blanc, 1979) indicates that from the first to the second half of adolescence, among delinquents the proportion of persisters is 26%, the percentage of desisters is 57%, the abstainers remain few at 5%, and the recruits account for 12% (these results are obtained when street time is controlled). These data lead to the conclusion that there is a resorption of activity during the second part of adolescence. This observation has been corroborated in studies done during the same period by Elliott and Huizinga (1980) in the United States, Favard (1980) in France, and Farrington (1973–1982) in England. Thus, the validity of our conclusion in chapter 3 on the cycles of participation in illicit activities becomes strengthened.

To sum up, it cannot be concluded, in the case of either the adolescents or the wards of the court, that criminal activity contains the seeds of an assured stability. Following the first half of adolescence, persistence seems to be problematical for quite a few cases. What is more evident is the fact that illicit activities are carried out intermittently, although a minority of offenders continue diligently throughout adolescence and drift into adult crime. What is also clear is that involvement in serious criminal activity tends to extend over a period of several years, as we shall see in the following section.

Duration of Criminal Activity

A second way of dealing with the question of persistence is to include duration. Few studies have tackled this question, but among those that have (we discovered seven: Blumstein & Cohen, 1982b; Farrington, 1983; Fréchette & Le Blanc,

1987; Green, 1977; Greenberg, 1975; Petersilia et al., 1978; Shinnar & Shinnar, 1975), only three are based on estimates drawn from sources other than the official data—those of Farrington, Petersilia et al., and Fréchette and Le Blanc. These three measure duration on the basis of a prospective or retrospective longitudinal research design, but only the last one reports the duration of hidden criminal activities during adolescence. Although the estimates of duration, measured by the interval between the first and last known crime, vary between 5 and 15 years, an average duration of about 5 years seems to be applicable for the total population of individuals who engage in illicit activities. Farrington (1983), however, reported 8.2 years for those who are active for the longest time and start before the age of 12 (convictions); Petersilia et al. (1978) calculated 8.3 years between the average age at which the first hidden crime is committed and the average age at incarceration, and 10.6 years if the whole period from childhood to adulthood is considered; Fréchette and Le Blanc (1987) calculated a duration of 5 years on the average for the duration of hidden delinquency during adolescence.

These statistics give us the interval betwen the first and last crime. This type of measurement, however, can distort the actual duration due to the fact that some individuals commit few crimes over an extended period, for example, two crimes at an interval of 10 years; they would obtain a high score for duration, but in fact their criminal activities were distributed over a very brief period. For this reason the data given in Table 4.3, describing the number of years of criminal activity, include only the years when at least one crime was committed. In the sample of adolescents, counting only convictions, the average duration of delinquent activities is 2.5 years whereas it is twice as long (5.2 years) in the delinquent group, the standard deviation indicating that the interval between the first and last conviction extends from 1 to 9 years. The average of 5 years that we obtained agrees with those of other authors who use interval measurement to determine duration. It is worth noting that if we calculate the interval between the first and last crime, the average would be 6.7 years; the average number of years of activity thus seems to be a more exact estimate of the duration than the interval between the first and last crime. It is probably justified, then, to conclude that an individual would be in danger of committing a crime during an almost 7-year period, but would actually be active for 5 years.

Concerning the hidden delinquency of the group of delinquents, the only measure we have is the interval between the first and last crime (Table 4.2). What is interesting to note is that the figures are twice as high as those obtained with official delinquency, even though the period covered is shorter. The final interview with regard to hidden delinquency took place around the age of 23, on the average, whereas official delinquency had been followed to the end of the 20s. The duration of criminal activity for the adolescent period is 2.45 years (convictions) and 5.33 years (reported delinquency) and for the entire period of the study 5.23 years against 10.76 years, respectively (10% of the delinquents showed 15 years and more of hidden criminal activity). Persistence thus seems to be very important, since there is an interval of 10 years between the first and last crime,

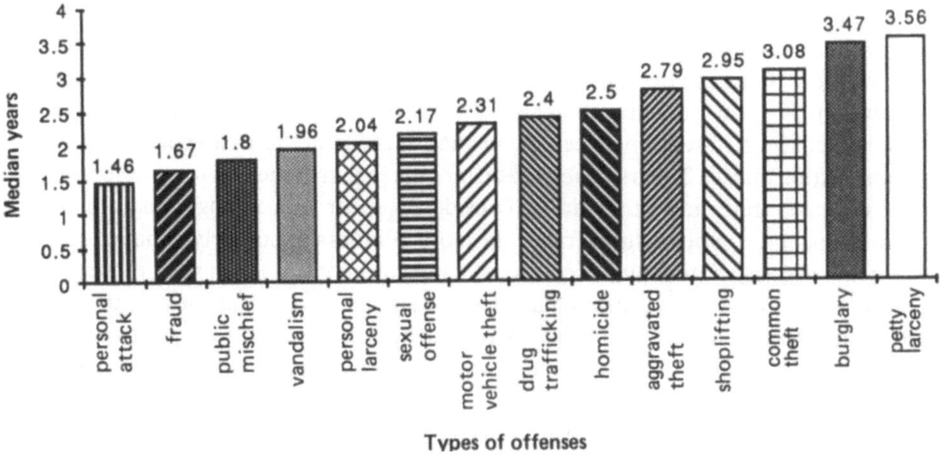

FIGURE 4.3. Median duration of each type of offense.

whereas the danger period, or the number of years during which a person potentially will commit crimes, is a little more than 20 years.

With these measures we were able to build a new index of duration, by which the duration of criminal activities was related to the period at risk. The main advantage of this measure lies in the fact that it allows direct comparisons between samples, between persons of different age groups, and between studies. It had an additional advantage of simplicity—it varies from 0 to 1. For hidden delinquency in the sample of delinquents, the active period was an average of 0.59, that is 59% of the period at risk. It appeared that half of the delinquents were active for a little more than half their period of risk, a third were continually active and had an index of 1, and less than a third were active for a duration of no more than a third of the period at risk. In spite of this persistence, the illicit activities do not necessarily last beyond a single phase; for a good many subjects, criminal activity is limited either to adolescence or to the early 20s. Thus, although persistence is common, it does not necessarily extend over more than one of these important periods of life.

Does the duration of each of our 14 categories of crime differ one from the other? Figure 4.3 gives the median duration of each type of crime (the differences between the averages and the medians are too great to keep on referring to the averages). We note that the duration of two categories is longer than that of the others by about half a year. These are larceny and burglary, which are most likely to figure largely in criminal activity for the longest period of time and to contribute to escalation. Larceny, as we have seen, appears very early, and a third of the delinquents practice it for more than 4 years, whereas burglary marks the transition between minor and serious delinquency with perpetration lasting 5 years and over for more than a third of the delinquents. These two types of crime are accompanied by two others, petty theft, and shoplifting, which have an average duration of 3 years. These four categories make up the bulk of criminal activities, as we will find on analyzing the combinations of types of crime later on in this chapter.

Whereas thefts are the most long-lasting categories of crime, those of shortest duration, 1.5 years, are attacks against the person, fraud, and disorderly conduct in public. The difference between the median duration of these categories and the most lasting ones is 2 years. They are crimes that begin at the end of adolescence, as we have seen, and they can be considered either more dangerous (attacks against people), more astute (fraud), or more pointless (disorderly conduct; this is generally associated with excessive alcohol consumption). Between these two groups are categories with a median of about 2 years; they are crimes committed by only a limited number of offenders and can be quite serious, such as homicidal acts and sex-related crimes, or not so serious, such as vandalism and the sale of illicit drugs.

Thus, not only does each form of criminal activity appear at a specific age, but each can also be said to last for a more or less definite period. As for precocity, four different time periods emerge, and what is the most noteworthy is the fact that serious crimes tend to last the shortest time and least serious ones the longest.

Termination

Our last parameter to describe the development of criminal activities is the age at which they stop. Quetelet (1835), Glueck and Glueck (1943), and Robins (1966) pointed out that beyond 25 years of age there is a substantial reduction in the number of people who remain criminally active. But as Farrington et al. aptly noted (1986), we know very little about the moment at which illicit activities usually stop. Polk et al. (1981) showed that most individuals stop at the age of 17, whereas Barnett and Lofaso (1985), on the basis of the Philadelphia cohort, could find no subjects who stopped before the age of 18. Although quantitative studies are extremely rare, qualitative studies are not much more numerous, and they are concerned only with the reasons for desistance (Brown & Gable, 1980; Cusson & Pinsonneault, 1986; Mulvey & LaRosa 1986; Shover, 1983, 1985). With such meager and contradictory facts, any new finding is welcome. Tables 4.2 and 4.3 show the age at which the last crime was committed, for the delinquent and adolescent samples and for hidden and official delinquency.

Let us start with official delinquency. It is remarkable that the average age of the last crime is almost identical for both adolescents and delinquents – 19.8 for the former and 19.9 for the latter – when the follow-up period extends to an average age of 25 years (the standard deviation is greater among the delinquents).

There are, however, interesting observations to be made when we look at the two main periods of life. For one thing, the delinquents commit their last crime as adults slightly later than the adolescents (at 21.4 years of age on the average as against 20.9). Just the reverse is true, however, for the last crime committed during adolescence (average of 14.5 years for the delinquents versus 15.4 for the

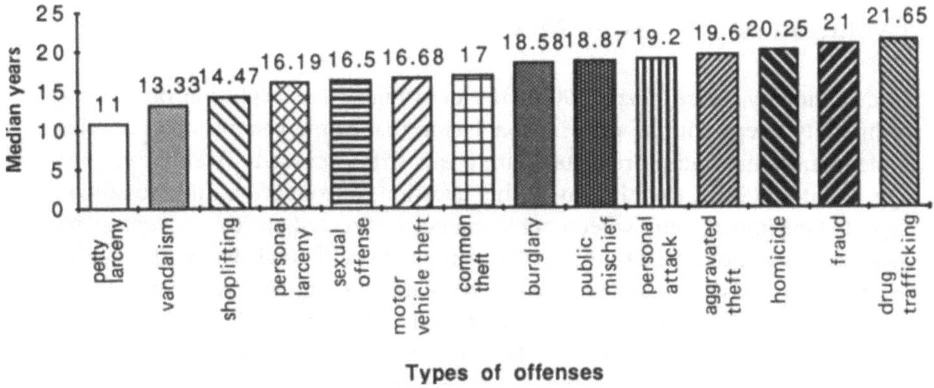

FIGURE 4.4. Median age of termination of each type of offense.

adolescents). What is more interesting is the fact that among adolescents, the gap between the average age at which the criminal activities started and were interrupted is less than 1 year; this means that most of them are involved in temporary delinquency, probably of one type, whereas the gap is much greater for the delinquents, up to 5 years, thus confirming their persistence in criminal activity with the risk that it will become more versatile. As for hidden delinquency, the delinquents, who were interviewed as adults at an averge age of 23, said that they had committed their last crime at age 19 on the average (the standard deviation being 3.5 years for the group).

These data on the age of the offender's last crime would not be complete without an analysis of variations according to the type of crime. Presented in Figure 4.4 is the median age at which the last crime was committed for each of the 14 categories of crime. Two findings are important. First, when placed in order according to the age at which they stopped, the types of crime fall into a sequence reproducing the relative gravity order; the most serious crimes (aggravated theft, homicidal conduct) stop at the most advanced median age, whereas the minor offenses (petty larceny, vandalism) tend to disappear at the other extreme. Second, certain crime categories are grouped according to phase of development: Petty larceny is typical of the latency period and tends to stop before the age of 12; after that, six categories of crime whose gravity is not excessive (vandalism, shoplifting, personal larceny, theft of a motor vehicle, and common theft) are lived through during adolescence; and finally, seven types of crime, most of which are among the most serious ones (burglary, personal attack, public disorder, aggravated theft, homicidal behavior, fraud, drug trafficking), are typical of crimes ending during youth. The median age at the last crime is over 18 and even up to 21.5 years. Each form of criminal activity, then, appears to be dropped at a specific moment. This conclusion, however, should be considered simply as an hypothesis, since the follow-up period is not long enough to guarantee that the criminal activity had actually stopped.

Evolution of the Crime Mix

In criminology, since Ferri (1905), the question of the evolution of forms of criminality keeps coming up. His conclusion that crime becomes less and less violent and more and more astute with age is still discussed. Twenty-five years ago, Pinatel (1963), to help clarify this question, introduced a directional concept, to take into account whether delinquency is directed more against property, against persons, or against mores. Our criminological knowledge on this subject is not very precise; it dates back about 40 years, but studies have been rare and have focused almost exclusively on official delinquency. Thus the Gluecks (1940), with a sample of wards of the court, and the McCords (1959), with the aid of a list of convictions, clearly established that crimes against property were dominant during adolescence where crimes of violence were proportionately more numerous during adulthood. Some fairly recent studies (Moitra, 1981; Wolfgang et al., 1972, 1987) have confirmed these observations. The data on the perpetration of crime that we presented in chapter 2 also show that criminal activities take on a more violent form as age increases. In a recent U.S. report, Blumstein et al. (1986) introduced the idea of a crime mix to account for the combination of different types of infractions that individuals commit.

It can be particularly interesting, then, to describe illicit activities in terms of their orientation, as was done in the studies just cited, and also in terms of their combined structures, as we have done with the delinquency reported by the adolescents (Caplan & Le Blanc, 1976) and with that reported by the wards of the court (Fréchette, 1980). To focus on these combined structures means analyzing the different combinations of crime categories and looking for consistent links between the types of infraction. Crime mix can be studied in two complementary ways: The first one describes the directional profile of criminal activity at a given age and the second one describes the combined structures that emerge from the illicit activities taken as a whole.

Changes in the Directional Profile of Criminal Activities

Figure 4.5 presents the distribution of participation for each category of illicit activities at three different periods, in decreasing order of the percentage of participation for each of them: before the middle of adolescence, during the second half of adolescence, and during youth. Figure 4.6 presents data concerning the average frequency of perpetration for each of the categories.

Regarding Participation

In the analysis of participation for each of the crime categories (Fig. 4.5), let us note first that after age 18 two new categories emerge, fraud, with a prevalence of 15%, and homicidal acts (murder and attempted murder), with participation of 5% for the ex-wards of the juvenile court.

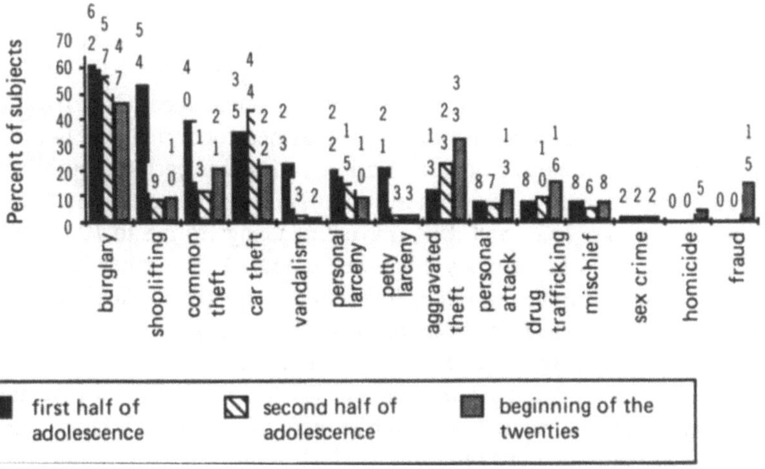

FIGURE 4.5. Participation of wards of the court in each category of crime: first and second half of adolescence, beginning of the 20s.

Considering the 14 crime categories, it appears that, during youth, burglary is by far the most dominant crime, followed by aggravated theft, with theft of a motor vehicle and common theft almost exactly in third rank. A little behind these come personal attack and homicidal act and possession of or trafficking in drugs, followed by offenses that were much widespread during adolescence:

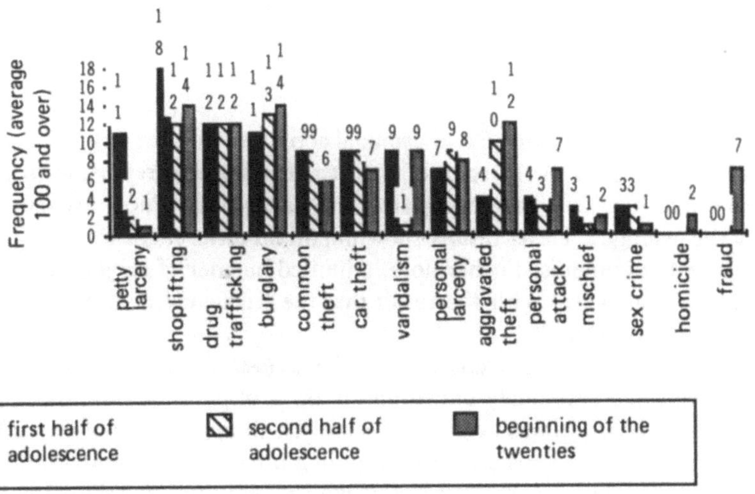

FIGURE 4.6. Average frequency of perpetration for each crime category among wards of the court: first and second half of adolescence, beginning of the 20s. Averages were calculated without the few subjects who reported frequencies of 100 or more.

shoplifting, personal larceny, and public mischief (disturbing the peace). It comes out clearly again that minor forms have almost disappeared and that more serious crimes (armed robbery, for example) are gaining ground. At the same time, a new astute type of delinquency, fraud, is introduced. Of particular note is the increase in crimes against the person, armed robberies, and homicides.

The comparative analysis of participation during this period (youth) with the two preceding periods is very interesting. The gradual appearance of astute delinquency (fraud, 15%, and drug trafficking going from 8 to 10 to 16%) and homicidal acts (5%) has already been mentioned. On the other hand, there is almost total disappearance of minor forms of delinquency, such as petty larceny (from 21 to 3%), shoplifting (from 54 to 10%) and vandalism (from 23 to 2%). With regard to acquisitive delinquency, certain categories diminish, such as burglary (62 to 57 to 47%) and personal larceny (22 to 15 to 10%) and some increase only to finally decline, such as automobile theft (35 to 44 to 22%) or to increase again, such as common theft (40 to 13 to 21%). Aggravated theft, however, (particularly armed robbery) progresses systematically, going from 13 to 23 to 33%. These two-way movements, combined with the almost total disappearance of minor crimes against property, clearly show a significant escalation in the gravity of criminality.

In brief, the intensified gravity of the acquisitive delinquency, accompanied by increased participation in crimes against the person (personal attacks going from 8 to 13%, and homicidal acts, nonexistent during adolescence, rising to 5% after the age of 18) lead to the conclusion that a definite intensification of criminal power occurs in early youth, involving both physical and psychological destructiveness. It must be remembered, however, that this increase in gravity is already present at adolescence or is demonstrated, for instance, by participation in illicit activities during the second and even the first halves of adolescence.

Regarding Frequency

Let us look now at the profile of criminal activities with the help of frequencies of offenses (Fig. 4.6). In spite of the fact that subjects reporting frequencies greater than 100 have been eliminated, the standard deviations are much higher than the averages. These results show important differences between the minimums and maximums; furthermore, a limited number of subjects report astronomical frequencies, with the result that the frequency distributions take the form of an extended "L."

Comparison of average frequencies of the various categories of crime confirms the conclusions previously drawn on the basis of participation, especially the preponderance of crimes against property, the disappearance of less important acquisitive and malicious crimes in favor of more serious or more astute crimes, and finally the general escalation of delinquent activities, based on the fact that crimes against the person gain more ground than crimes against property.

It is interesting, incidentally, to note the resemblances and differences between Figure 4.5, illustrating participation, and 4.6 illustrating frequency. Where crimes against the person are concerned, both participation and frequency reveal the same thing, whether it concerns the order of crime categories or the evolution of each of them over time. In the case of victimless crimes, we note that possession of and trafficking in drugs shows little participation but a high rate of frequency; it is one of the categories whose frequency is in the lead and remains there whatever the period of life.

With regard to crimes against property, the comparison between participation and frequency is much more complex. It must be pointed out first that in both cases petty larceny disappears with time, whereas aggravated theft and fraud remain fully active. On the other hand, what we might call "hedonistic" crimes, such as shoplifting and vandalism, show substantially less participation, but a very high rate of frequency among those who still practice them at the end of adolescence or the beginning of adulthood. It is difficult to know if this high frequency reflects specialization or a late escalation of delinquency; the first hypothesis seems the more plausible. The comparison between participation and frequency in the case of common theft, theft of motor vehicles, and personal larceny shows that, here again, participation diminishes and frequency stays high and relatively stable, probably indicating an accumulation of crimes against property that were successful and became reinforced, with more diversification and versatility and at the same time more abundance. Finally, burglary seems to constitute a particular case, since participation in it decreases but its frequency keeps on increasing. It is to be noted that for those who persist, this kind of offense is the mainstay of their illicit activity, especially in view of the fact that it is dominant at every stage of life under study, from the first half of adolescence to youth.

From Adolescence to Youth, Aggravation of Forms

From the data illustrated in Figures 4.5 and 4.6, it is possible to obtain a good picture of the direction of delinquency, as it was reported by the wards of the court. The most common form of delinquency is, without question, theft for the purpose of acquiring material goods. Almost all delinquents during their adolescence and early 20s engage in theft. At the same time, more astute delinquency is developing, as shown by the increase in drug trafficking and the emergence of fraud. Similarly, there is more and more "interpersonal" delinquency, involving direct coercion of the victim as the adolescent grows older, so that acts of violence (aggravated theft, particularly armed robbery, and personal attack), already present at the beginning of adolescence, constantly gain ground during the three periods studied and culminate in adulthood with the appearance of homicidal acts. On the other hand, spiteful delinquency (vandalism and public mischief), which concerns vindictive acts or simple pranks, diminishes considerably and becomes stabilized at a very low level of frequency later on.

Thus it must be pointed out, first, that the most frequent forms of delinquency are burglary and motor vehicle theft, regardless of the period under consideration. Second, material destructiveness, so widespread during the first half of adolescence, becomes minimal during the 20s. Third, destructive acts of violence against the person, although minor during adolescence, become widespread on reaching adulthood. From an evolutionary perspective, violent acts aimed at persons deserve special attention, since gratuitous destruction is eliminated on reaching mid-adolescence whereas utilitarian violence becomes more and more evident. It is clear that criminal activity becomes progressively more serious and reaches a peak past the age of 17 or 18.

Changes in the Crime Mix

With this knowledge about the directional profile of illicit activities at each phase of life and the evolution through these same phases, it is time to make a thorough analysis of the composition of the crime-mix characteristics for each phase and to scrutinize the various combinations of the categories of crime. Furthermore, such an analysis of the crime mix will show what type of crime is repeatedly associated with another; it is a reliable way to acquire new significance and scope. Obviously, in such a perspective the crime mix is defined as a structure, as an organized set of crime categories.

To accomplish the analysis it is necessary to refer once again to the list of 12 crime categories described in chapter 1: petty larceny, shoplifting, common theft, burglary, vandalism, motor vehicle theft, personal attack, public mischief, personal larceny, drug and sex-related crimes, aggravated theft (with the addition at the beginning of adulthood of fraud and homicide). Table 4.5 presents the combinations practiced by a minimum of 3% of subjects at the beginning of adolescence. This table lists the most frequent configurations for each degree of diversity, using the self-reported delinquency described by the wards of the court. As we established previously, about three quarters of these youngsters said they were involved in several of the 12 categories of adolescent crime.

There is no point in discussing Table 4.5 in detail because of the large number of combinations listed; overall comment will suffice. First, burglary is universal in the manifestations of heterogeneous activity, no matter what the degree of variety or the phase of life concerned. Even the combinations least often repeated include this type of theft. This means that for every delinquent who is truly inclined to crime, this type of offense appears as a basic activity, as a kind of criterion capable of revealing true delinquency.

Second, when the degree of diversity increases, automobile theft appears to be the category of infraction most often associated with all the others, and in particular with burglary. The complementary nature of this activity, especially as the subjects grow older, leads to the belief that it is a reinforcing element capable of consolidating the criminal orientation, and it shows strong affinities with other categories. When we look at the modus operandi, it appears also that it is an offense committed to facilitate the commission of other crimes, to increase, for instance, the offender's mobility. The data presented in chapter 2 already pointed to the secondary nature, so to speak, of this type of crime.

TABLE 4.5. Crime mix, self-reported delinquency of the delinquent sample.

Categories of crime (variety)	Beginning of adolescence			Middle of adolescence			Youth		
	Com.	*n*	%	Com.	*n*	%	Com.	*n*	%
Two	SB	18	15.4	BM	25	35.7	BTh	12	27.9
	TB	18	15.4	BTh	8	11.4	BM	4	9.3
	TV	15	12.8	BP	5	7.1	TB	4	9.3
	ST	11	9.4	SB	3	4.3	ST	2	4.6
	BV	7	6	LM	2	2.9	TTh	2	4.6
	BM	7	6	SM	2	2.9	BP	2	4.6
	LB	5	4.3	TM	2	2.9			
	SM	4	3.4						
	LT	3	2.6						
	SD	3	2.6						
	BP	3	2.6						
	Other	23	19.7		23	32.6		27	62.8
	Total	117	35.2		70	53		43	34.9
Three	STB	12	12.9	BMTh	8	19.1	BMTh	7	17.1
	SBM	9	9.3	MPM	5	11.9	BThD	3	7.3
	TBM	5	5.2	SBM	3	7.1	TBM	2	4.9
	LSB	5	5.2	TBM	2	4.8	BPM	2	4.9
	LBM	4	4.1	BPTh	2	4.8			
	SBP	4	4.1						
	SBV	4	4.1						
	LST	3	3.1						
	STM	3	3.1						
	BPM	3	3.1						
	SPM	3	3.1						
	Other	42	43.3		22	52.4		25	61
	Total	97	29.2		42	31.8		41	33.4
Four	SBMV	4	6.6	BPMTh	2	12.5	ThADF	2	10
	STBM	4	6.2						
	SBPM	3	4.6						
	LSTM	2	3.1						
	BPMTh	2	3.1						
	BPMTh	2	3.1						
	SBPM	2	3.1						
	Other	49	75.4		14	87.5		18	90
	Total	65	19.5		16	12.1		20	16.3
Five	LTBPM	2	5.9				TBThDF	2	16.7
	STBPTh	2	5.9						
	Other	30	88.2		4	100		10	83.3
	Total	34	10.2		4	3		12	9.8
Six	Other	14	100					5	100
	Total	14	4.2					5	4.1
Seven	Other	5	100					2	100
	Total	5	1.5					2	1.6

C, combinations of types of crimes:
L, petty larceny; S, shoplifting; T, common theft; B, burglary; P, personal larceny; M, Motor vehicle theft; Th, aggravated theft; V, vandalism; A, personal attack; D, drugs; F, fraud.

Third, the escalation in illicit activities as the subjects grow older, noted in chapter 2, is clearly confirmed when we look at the dominant configurations. The combinations of minor crime categories (petty larceny, shoplifting, common theft) gradually disappear with age. The configurations including personal theft and aggravated theft (armed robbery) are much more numerous by the end of adolescence and at the beginning of adulthood than they were to the middle of adolescence. Of particular significance is the recurrence of crimes against persons when the criminal activities start to become heterogeneous, and persistent, to such a point that, for many subjects, any kind of diversification of criminal activities has to be through perpetration of serious offenses.

Fourth, as might be expected (see the increasing percentage under "Other" in Table 4.5), the greater the number of crime categories, the more subjects there are with individualized configurations. Similarly, the proportion of exclusive combinations rises considerably from the beginning of adolescence and to the mid-20s. It is important to point out that even when there is this double increase in individualization of the configurations, burglary remains a core activity. This type of crime appears to feed any kind of significant criminal involvement, thus becoming what can be called the main axis of the criminal orientation, around which gravitate secondary manifestations of antisociality.

Fifth, when we compare the dominant configurations from one phase to the next, we note a tendency toward specialization. In fact, as age increases, a more homogeneous configuration emerges and dominates for each degree of diversity. The trend is such that from the beginning of adolescence, when a dominant configuration is present in only 15% of the subjects, at the end of adolescence and the beginning of the 20s, the presence of such a configuration is at least twice what it was. Furthermore, examination of these prevalent combinations shows that before mid-adolescence criminal activity mostly consists of minor crimes (petty larceny, shoplifting, common theft) or marginal ones (vandalism), whereas in the second half of adolescence, it is predominantly composed of serious crimes (motor vehicle theft, personal theft, armed robbery), the orientation being even more accentuated at the beginning of the 20s. With time, there is a move away from the relatively minor infractions in such a way that, in the end, there is a concentration of more significant crimes (involving more serious forms of illicit activity) and more homogeneous ones (limitation to one form of acquisitive criminal activity).

Retrospectively, it can be said that delinquency takes at first the form of a heterogeneous activity combining various types of theft. This was also our conclusion when we analyzed configurations of the illicit activities reported by the adolescent sample (Caplan & Le Blanc, 1976). However, among the delinquents, burglary is definitely dominant, as Fréchette (1980) found after completing an in-depth study of theft and of the configuration formed by the categories of theft. Burglary emerges as the heart of all illicit activities, increasing even when heterogeneity becomes greater and also as the subjects grow older. To this crime are added what might be called secondary infractions, the most prevalent being armed robbery. Furthermore, burglary is fully compatible with the various categories of crime, its extensive use in combination with other infractions making it the most prevalent of all, regardless of age. This type of theft seems to be associated, with particularly significant frequency, with the most dangerous forms of illicit activities and can be considered a good barometer of a person's criminal potential.

One particular configuration seems to be favorable for the development of criminal activity, namely, burglary associated with automobile theft. It seems to constitute the core of serious delinquency and eventually becomes a component of the most dangerous forms of theft. No other configuration, through the degrees of variety and the three phases of life, is able to play the same role. This typical configuration becoming stronger as heterogeneity increases, it is possible to say that diversification of crimes is accompanied, paradoxically, by reinforcement of a specific group of offenses, acquisitive by nature, impersonal and crafty. This configuration can thus be called a structuring configuration, for it generates and supports all sorts of criminal activities.

In short, among the wards of the court, burglary appears as a crucial form of criminal activity. It can be qualified as a *common activity*, for it involves a much greater number of subjects than the other categories of crime; as a *polyvalent activity*, capable not only of being associated with any other category of crime, but also of maintaining a very strong affinity for all of them; and as a *catalyzing activity*—while tied with certain categories of favorite crime categories, it seems the most capable of being associated with the most dangerous forms of criminal activity. It lies at the heart of the process of amplification and escalation, as we will see in the next chapter. Consequently it can be considered the center of gravity of criminal activity.

Longevity, Persistence, Discontinuity

At the end of this analysis some major conclusions are obvious. First, on the basis of what we have observed in a representative sample of the adolescent population, it is clear that criminal activity is very widespread and can even be considered a common occurrence during adolescence. It is also clear that it starts very early: Half the sample of wards of the court had committed offenses before adolescence. It appears that for this group it tends to persist, covering a relatively long period of about 5 years on the average, and thus extends into a good part of the crucial phase of adolescence. Finally, it turns out that each form of criminal activity has a distinct age for its emergence, a specific duration, and a particular age when it ceases. These characteristics seem to depend on the gravity of the crimes: Minor crimes begin early, before the age of 12, and extend over a relatively long period of 3 years or more, stopping by mid-adolescence at the latest. The most serious crimes begin later, in the second half of adolescence or at the beginning of adulthood, and extend over a shorter period, often less than 2 years. Nonetheless they are the last to disappear during the 20s.

These results lead us to conclude that the diverse manifestations of criminal activity are of an intermittent nature when taken individually; at the same time they generate continuity when considered in relation to one another, particularly if we recognize the very real probability of juvenile delinquency turning into adult crime. Moreover, criminal activity proves intermittent on another count—the fact that no one continually commits crimes. There are periods of remission followed by periods of great activity, and vice versa. All in all, criminal orientation is characterized by two main ingredients: relative longevity and intermittent persistence.

Such relative continuity can also be observed by using changes in the crime mix at each stage. The analyses we conducted on crime combinations and the resulting conclusions show the steps by which forms of criminal activities become aggravated. We believe that, through our comparative analysis of the directional profiles of illicit activities from one phase of life to another, we have furthered our present knowledge and understanding. Escalation begins with burglary, is increased with theft of a vehicle, and becomes consolidated with armed robbery. Crimes against property, then, are a sort of preparation for crimes against individuals. Acquisitive delinquency, and burglary in particular, has been insufficiently studied by theoreticians and researchers. The criminological literature is far from recognizing the importance of its role in the process of criminalization. The description of this aggravation of illicit activities furnishes an excellent introduction to the questions we deal with in our next chapter, the presence of a developmental process in offending.

While the description of criminal activities based on boundary parameters has made it possible to establish both the intermittent and persistent nature of such activities, further study is called for of the mechanisms responsible for the development of illicit activity, particularly the mechanisms that allow such activity to begin in the first place, and the mechanisms that cause it to escalate and that guarantee its consolidation, or conversely, foster its elimination.

5
A Process View of Offending

In chapter 4 we proposed an analysis that would delineate the frontiers of the evolution of criminal activity—the beginning, the duration, and the end. Another approach, rarely used in criminology but current in psychology, is the developmental approach, which is mainly interested in the processes underlying the continuity of behavior. Applied to criminal activity, it would study the changes in a person's illegal activities with age, particularly the changes within the person himself, and would seek to identify the mechanisms that support the persistence of such activities.

Some Definitions

This approach means taking up once more the question of the dynamics of the illegal activity with the processes of escalation and diversification. In the literature, the conceptual framework of the developmental approach has generally remained simplistic because criminologists have never drawn on the concepts of the sociology of occupations or the psychology of development. This chapter is meant to fill that gap by adapting the theoretical and methodological framework of the psychology of development, so admirably presented by Lerner (1986), to the analysis of criminal activities.

Lerner proposed studying development in terms of continuity/discontinuity, but he also showed that it is important, in conformity with the requirements of the psychology of development, to analyze the quantitative and qualitative changes that occur in behavior. Certain principles established by developmental specialists give us a theoretical base that can serve as a foundation for our analyses. We use the orthogenetic principle of Werner (1957), according to which "whenever development occurs, it proceeds from a state of relative globality and lack of differentiation to a state of increasing differentiation, articulation and hierarchic integration" (p. 126). This principle is recognized as a general rule of development: As well as specifying the nature of developmental changes, it represents an enlightening frame of reference for the analysis of continuity/ discontinuity. The application of this principle to the study of the development of criminal behavior will make it possible to detect three dynamic processes that support this type of conduct: activation, escalation, and desistance. Each of these processes will be illustrated on the basis of relationships between the various descriptive and developmental parameters we have put forward and described in the preceding chapters.

Up to now we have approached the development of criminal activity on the basis of unidimensional characteristics – its duration, the age the first crime was committed, and so on. We now propose to combine the main descriptive and developmental parameters. We want to illustrate how characteristics are combined to constitute processes that make the development of criminal activity not a matter of chance. Over the past 15 years, since research done by Wolfgang et al. (1972), longitudinal studies have furnished data on the relationship between several of the parameters we are using, and syntheses, such as those of Loeber (1982, 1987) and Blumstein et al. (1986), have led to clarification of the conceptualization of certain processes. All this work, however, is intuitive, because it is not based on a well-thought-out procedure for reconstructing the natural dynamics of the development of criminal activity.

The procedure we prefer for the construction of these mechanisms of development is the one used to work out measurements in the natural sciences, particularly in physics. Duncan (1984) described it as follows: A list of fundamental elements, physical quantities, for example, is compiled, then the variables are defined according to the combinations of these basic elements, in such a way that the variables are represented mathematically by the product of the fundamental elements adjusted by integral calculus. By way of analogy, we propose to define the processes that encourage the development of criminal activity as the result of the relationship between two or more descriptive and developmental parameters that are the basic elements of criminal activity. The advantage of this procedure is twofold. First, it affords clarity concerning the elements in question in the operative definition of concepts such as escalation, desistance, and activation. Second, it can be reproduced, that is, it is possible for another researcher to reconstruct the same measurements and verify the validity of our results.

By applying this procedure, we find three basic processes that support the development of criminal activity, particularly of persistent offending – activation, escalation, and desistance. These three are perhaps not the only processes, but they seem to be the most important if we review the literature. Little is known about the first, activation; there are references to it in the literature surveyed by Loeber, and he conceptualized it as the variety hypothesis (1982) and progression or innovation rate (1987). The second, escalation, is the subject of numerous controversies in the criminological literature, as shown in the surveys done by Klein (1984) on whether a large number of persons concentrate on certain forms of crime, and by Loeber (1985a, 1987) and Blumstein et al. (1986) on the progression from one type of criminal activity to another. We shall return to this further on, since these processes emerge clearly from our data and most particularly because we propose a conceptual clarification and a new strategy of analysis.

The last process, desistance, is a subject whose importance is recognized by criminologists, for example Farrington et al. (1986c), although few have studied it. At the operational level, all these processes, as we will demonstrate, stem from the combination of two or more of the descriptive and developmental parameters used until now.

The *activation* process refers to the way the development of criminal activities is stimulated as soon as it has begun and the way its persistence is assured. Once this process has begun, the delinquent activity is marked by a high level of frequency, duration, and variety, as well as precocity. We find that the process of activation is based on three separate but closely interrelated mechanisms—acceleration, stabilization, and diversification. *Acceleration* refers to the relationship between precocity and frequency; *stabilization* is inferred from the connection between precocity and duration; *diversification* is measured by the degree of variety in the criminal activity, taking precocity into account. These mechanisms mean that if the delinquency starts early, it is likely to be abundant, lasting, and varied. We also submit that the fundamental process of activation is the combined effect of acceleration, stabilization, and diversification; the second of these mechanisms, stabilization, is postulated to be the main support of the other two.

Stabilization more directly refers to the way in which the delinquent activity becomes persistent, resulting in its longevity. This presumes an inverse relationship between precocity and duration, so that the earlier the delinquent activities begin, the longer they will continue. To the best of our knowledge, this mechanism has never been adequately described in the criminological literature.

The mechanism of acceleration is better known. Recent studies that persons who are arrested early on have a higher rate of frequency than those arrested later on (J. Cohen, 1986; Farrington, 1983); on the other hand, those who start early commit more serious crimes later on (Shannon, 1978). It has similarly been established that early starters are more likely to become chronic delinquents and recidivists, according to the results of Glueck (1937) for the first case and of Mannheim and Wilkins (1955) for the second. These findings have been confirmed many times. In addition, Fréchette and Le Blanc (1979) were the first to describe the exact relationship between precocity and frequency on the basis of self-reported delinquency; Loeber (1982), on the basis of data on official delinquency reported by Farrington (1982) and Hamparian, Schuster, Dinitz, and Conrad (1978), called this relationship the early-onset hypothesis.

Finally, for its part, the mechanism of diversification refers to the way the criminal activity quickly becomes heterogeneous in relation to precocity, variety being the more accentuated the earlier the illicit activities begin.

In describing the processes of *escalation* and specialization, we propose to clarify two questions fiercely debated in criminological circles. Blumstein et al. (1986) made a clear distinction between the two: "Escalation is the tendency for offenders to move to more serious offense types as offending continues" (p. 84) and "specialization is the tendency to repeat the same offense type on successive arrests" (p. 81). In terms of the descriptive and developmental parameters we are using, we propose the following definitions: Escalation refers to the appearance of a sequence of diverse forms of delinquent activities that go from minor infractions to the most serious crimes against the person as the subject increases in age. This sequence represents a more or less standard pattern of development of offending among subjects that are heading for significant delinquency (the different parameters—nature of the crimes, gravity, age of onset, duration, age of termination—are obviously contributing factors in the definition of this process).

Specialization can be manifested in at least three ways. First, as described by Chaiken and Rolph (1985), the person, during a limited period of time, concentrates on a particular form of crime and produces a string of offenses. Second, the subject shows a certain degree of specialization over a given period, and it is this degree of specialization that should be evaluated. This has been done in numerous studies, including that of Wolfgang et al. (1972), of Farrington (1986a) and Farrington and Snyder (1988), and of Klein (1984) and Kempf (1987). Third, with the passage of time, the person concentrates more and more on certain crimes or specific forms of criminal activity; this concentration, according to Blumstein et al. (1986), is sufficient to be called specialization. Since specialization involves relinquishing a versatile criminal activity for a more homogeneous type of crime, we included specialization in the process of desistance. Thus specialization is seen as a step toward final desistance.

This process of *desistance* is the last to be included in our study. It is a process that depends on the variety, gravity, and frequency of the criminal activity. This means that the longer the duration, the higher the frequency, and the greater the variety and gravity, the greater the chance of desistance due to saturation. Obviously the process of desistance can be studied only among persons whose delinquency is recurrent; one cannot speak of desistance in the case of the occasional delinquent. This process of gradual withdrawal from criminal activity will be approached through three mechanisms: deceleration, specialization, and reaching a ceiling. *Deceleration* assumes that the annual frequency of offending diminishes in the years preceding desistance. It can be inferred from the relationship between frequency and the age of termination. *Specialization* implies a reduction in the variety of criminal activities. It can be observed through the relationship between the age of termination and variety, particularly in the form of a decrease in the degree of variety in the years preceding termination. *Culmination* refers to the situation of the delinquent who has reached his highest level of seriousness in crime, and that level remains stable for a period before desistance.

The study of these three processes enables us to verify the extent to which the development of criminal activities obeys the orthogenetic principle, that is, evolves from a state of relative globality marked by the absence of differentiation to a state of greater differentiation with articulation and hierarchic integration. If we see the processes of activation, escalation, and desistance brought to completion among a significant group of individuals, we can conclude that the orthogenetic principle applies to criminal activity as well.

Activation

The process of the activation of illicit activity is measured by three specific mechanisms: acceleration, stabilization, and diversification.

Acceleration

The surveys on precocity (Blumstein et al., 1986; Farrington et al., 1986c; Loeber, 1982) all point to the fact that the earlier the illicit activity begins, the greater the probability that it will become chronic. We believe that acceleration is the basic mechanism underlying criminalization, the connection between precocity and intensity having emerged very clearly. The perpetration of crimes at an early age would be a sort of behavior matrix necessary for the appearance of an intense subsequent commitment to crime. With this mechanism, it is the influence of precocity on the capacity to commit offenses that is in question. More specifically, it is the connection between the age at the time the first crime was committed and the subsequent frequency of the criminal activities that is measured. Table 5.1 shows that there is such a connection, since Spearman's correlations are all statistically significant at $p < .001$ (we used Spearman's rather than Pearson's r because our frequency distributions are biased due to a limited number of subjects with very high frequencies). Another way to verify if the distributions of the medians across the ages of onset are random or specific, indicating a reduction of the frequency as the age of onset increases, is to calculate the one-sample-runs test for each distribution (see Siegle, 1956). Table 5.1 shows that they are all statistically significant, which means that the frequency of offending is dependent on the age of onset. The median frequencies are not randomly associated with precocity.

The connection between precocity and criminal productivity during adolescence was described by Hamparian et al. (1978) using arrests and by Farrington (1982) using convictions. Fréchette and Le Blanc (1979) and Tolan and Lorion (1987) did the same regarding self-reported delinquency. All of these authors calculated the average frequency of the crimes committed according to the age level at which they started or some similar measures of frequency. Loeber (1982) compared the distribution obtained from the data gathered by Hamparian et al. and Farrington; the graph he constructed clearly shows that the average frequency of the crimes committed diminishes as the starting age of the criminal behavior increases. It is interesting to note that the data compiled by Hamparian et al. are in an almost monotone form, whereas those of Farrington show major fluctuations around the age of 15. For their part, Fréchette and Le Blanc (1979) established that the average frequency of the crimes reported by the adolescents at each interview diminishes as the starting age of the illicit activities increases, latency and puberty being the ages most conducive to subsequent criminal productivity. In their study of a sample of adolescents, Tolan and Lorion showed that the best predictor of the frequency of self-reported offending is precocity (1987) and, as in the preceding studies, that those who start early,

TABLE 5.1. Acceleration: Median cumulative frequency of offending by age of onset.

Age of onset (yrs)	Median number of crimes committed: Official delinquency: Juvenile	Official delinquency: Adult	Official delinquency: Total	Hidden delinquency: Juvenile	Hidden delinquency: Adult	Hidden delinquency: Total
3				12		
4				92.5		
5				131		
6				75		
7	16		26	57		46.5
8	14.5		26.5	61.5		41
9	6.5		22.5	74.5		82.5
10	5.33		17.25	40.5		18
11	4		6	22.25		4.5
12	4.33		8	33		12
13	7.35		11	21		11.5
14	4		9.5	6.17		18.5
15	3.61		9.5	5.17		12.75
16	3.14	11.5	8	9.5		17
17	1.9	15.25	9.25	1		13.5
18		11.1	10		45.5	11.5
19		7.67	6		22	7.5
20		4.5	6.83		16	3.33
21		5.83	2.5		2.5	2
22		3.87	3		1.29	4
23		2.12	2		1.75	
24		2.12	2			
25		2.25	3			
r_{-s}*	−.24	−.47	−.2	−.40	−.42	−.25
One sample run test						
n1	6	3	9	7	1	2
n2	5	7	10	8	5	14
runs	4	2	6	3	2	3
p†	.05	.05	.1	.05	.05	.05

*Spearman's rank correlation.
†Probability.

at the beginning of adolescence, reach a frequency four times higher than late starters (1987). Furthermore, Fréchette (1980) observed a similar connection between precocity and frequency for the great majority of crime categories studied individually.

The mechanism of acceleration is in operation during the period of adolescence, if we are to accept our results and the conclusions of other studies. If this is the case, the question arises, Does acceleration stand out if we consider a wider range of ages? Table 5.1 furnishes some additional information on the mechanism of acceleration (medians are shown, since there is often a considerable gap between the average and the median). First, as shown by our study and other studies using arrest data (Wikström, 1987; Wolfgang et al., 1987) and conviction data (Farrington et al., 1987; Göppinger, 1987) distributed well into the 20s, the decrease in incidence of criminal acts that occurs with increased starting age is also true of adult crime, official and hidden. Since the Young Offenders Act applies in Canada up to eighteen years of age, but several adolescents in our sample had been transferred to the adult courts before their 18th year, it is for this reason that the medians of frequency for the sixteen- and seventeen-year olds are given at the level of official adult crime.

Second, the median frequencies fluctuate much more in the case of hidden delinquency; they decrease more consistently then they do in official delinquency. The difference observed between hidden and official delinquency can probably be explained by the fact that the first includes a tremendous variety of acts, from the most minor to the most serious, whereas the second very likely includes more of the most serious crimes. According to the data presented in the preceding chapter, the frequency of minor crimes is much higher than that of very serious ones.

Third, if we examine the distribution of the median frequencies of hidden delinquency between the age of 7 and the beginning of the 20s, we see that there are two starting periods that have a particularly stimulating effect on subsequent offending. The first period, before the age of 10, signifies that the subjects who begin that early engage in the greatest activity later on, with a median of about 40 crimes, a median that rises to 82 crimes when only 9-year-olds are taken into consideration. The second period is mid-adolescence, between 14 and 16 years, with a median of about 18 crimes. Thus, there are two determinant periods that trigger criminal activity, the first illustrating the theory of precocity and the second the disturbing influence of the end of compulsory schooling. In Quebec the end of compulsory schooling occurs at the 15th birthday; the great majority of our subjects dropped out of school at this age (see Fréchette & Le Blanc, 1987).

There are two other, less accelerating periods with about a dozen offenses each—puberty, on the frontiers of adolescence, and the border between adolescence and youth, age 17 to 18. Finally, when the starting age approaches the early 20s, very little offending ensues. Data on convictions handed down between the ages of 7 and 25 confirm the existence of similar periods, but with a difference due to delay in convictions for official delinquency compared with hidden delinquency, a delay we discussed amply in the preceding chapter.

Finally, as precocity diminishes, the average output of subsequent offenses decreases. It can be pointed out that this process, by which the increase in frequency is in an inverse relationship to the degree of precocity, can be described in a more complex manner. In a recent study (Fréchette and Le Blanc, 1987) comparing 11 categories of crime, three models for the differential effect of precocity were found. First, for certain crimes there is a direct specific influence, which means that the earlier the first of these crimes is committed, the more illicit activity there is later on. Thus, for armed robbery, personal larceny, and theft of a motor vehicle, almost half the perpetrators show both precocity and abundance. The connection is such that, if these crimes are abundant at the end of adolescence, there "must" have been early involvement. Second, for other criminal manifestations the influence is strong but not specific, in the sense that even if precocity signifies an abundance of crimes, the inverse is not true: A late start in mid-adolescence can also show great abundance. Burglary, drug trafficking, and shoplifting correspond to this model; at whatever age they have begun they consistently reach a high level of perpetration. Finally, for some crimes precocity has no specific influence, for example, common theft and personal attack. Precocity does not result in greater frequency later on; these crimes are largely unaffected by an early start and seem to be of a more incidental nature.

Stabilization

Since the criminal activities of our delinquents generally extend over more than 5 years, one can ask whether precocity might be the principal source of this stabilization. Table 5.2 clearly shows that the earlier children begin criminal activities they tend to continue. On the one hand, the Spearman correlations are negative and greater than .40 and are all statistically significant at $p < .001$; on the other hand, the one-sample-runs tests are also highly statistically significant and indicate that the medians of duration are far from randomly distributed. Table 5.2 also shows the monotonicity of the decrease in duration.

These observations are true for adolescence, youth, and the entire period under study and for both hidden and official delinquency. Dunford, Elliott, and Huizinga (1983), for their part, observed no connection between precocity and duration in their national study on the evolution of hidden delinquency among American adolescents. In the light of our data, we believe their results are not valid for two reasons: They used a sample of the general population that included very few really active offenders and they dichotomized the variable duration, 2 years and less versus more than 2 years, making it insensitive to the most significant variations (as seen in our data), those that go beyond 5 years. Contrary to the data of these authors, Wikström's (1987) data on the persistence of arrests, calculated in number of years for a standard follow-up period of 5 years, agree with our data on conviction – the persistence of crime tends to decrease when age of onset increases. Farrington et al. (1987) also reported diminution of the average career length with increase in the age of onset.

According to our data, early practice of criminal activities fosters their stabilization in a person's behavior pattern. What is remarkable in the distribution of the medians of duration is their consistent decrease at two periods of acceleration for medians of frequency. Thus, with official delinquency, those who start at 7 or 8 years of age will be active for more than 10 years, whereas those who begin in their 20s will be active for about 2 years. In the case of hidden delinquency, these figures increase: Those who start before the age of 6 will persist for more than 12 years, whereas those who begin in their 20s will continue for only 1 or 2 years. Some would argue that the results concerning latecomers to crime could reflect underestimations of the duration of their criminal activity. This is unlikely, because even if seriousness increases with age, participation and frequency are very low in the late 20s and desistance is high (see Farrington et al., 1987;

TABLE 5.2. Stabilization: Median frequency of duration by age of onset.

Age of onset	Median frequency of duration (years) Official delinquency Juvenile	Official delinquency Adult	Official delinquency Total	Hidden delinquency Juvenile	Hidden delinquency Adult	Hidden delinquency Total
3				13		
4				12.5		18
5				11.12		14.5
6				9.25		13
7	6.75		11.67	8.29		11.75
8	6.5		10	7.57		11.75
9	4		9.33	6.37		9.37
10	3.4		7.59	5.84		9
11	3.33		5.94	3.29		5.5
12	2.45		5.89	3.72		8.5
13	2.87		5.55	2.85		7
14	2.09		5.24	2.17		6.33
15	1.84		5.01	1.75		6
16	1.43	4.12	4.59	2		6.75
17	1.27	5.2	4.62			2.5
18		4.72	4.76		4.6	5
19		4.08	3.41		3.17	3
20		3.34	3.3		2.5	
21		3.15	2.5		1.5	
22		2.63	2.6			
23		2.06	2.8		4.5	
24		1.86	1.67			
25		1.67	2			
r_s*	−.50	−.45	−.40	−.87	−.43	−.63
One sample run test						
n1	7	4	9	8	2	5
n2	4	6	10	6	3	11
runs	2	2	2	2	3	2
$p^{\dagger}$	.05	.05	.05	.05	.1	.05

*Spearman's.
† Probability.

Wolfgang et al., 1987); Cormier et al. (1959) have also shown that the recidivist rate for latecomers is low.

From our data it can be concluded that latency is a crucial period of acceleration and stabilization, whereas mid-adolescence can be a period of acceleration but not one of great stabilization. We have already established that the duration of the criminal activity varies according to its nature (chap. 4), the most serious lasting the shortest time and the least serious extending over a longer period. Burglary, because of its long duration and its association with other types of theft, is an omnipresent type of crime. Since precocity and frequency also vary with the type of crime (chaps. 3 and 4), it is possible to conceive stabilization as a double-action mechanism. First, persons who start their criminal activity early could

TABLE 5.3. Diversification: Median amount of variety of offending by age of onset.

Age of onset	Median number of different crimes					
	Official delinquency			Hidden delinquency		
	Juvenile	Adult	Total	Juvenile	Adult	Total
3				3		
4				4.33		7
5				5.25		7.5
6				3.56		6.5
7	4		7	3.14		4.37
8	3.5		4.5	3.64		6.33
9	4		7.83	3.5		6
10	4.2		6.25	3.68		6.25
11	2.75		3.29	2.79		4.5
12	2.87		4.67	3.53		6.17
13	3.55		4.8	2.83		5.5
14	2.55		4.17	2.17		4.75
15	2.48		4.67	2.08		3.75
16	2.22	3.5	3.94	1.75		4
17	1.75	5.67	5	1		2.5
18		4.45	5		2.5	2
19		3.3	2.12		3.08	4
20		2.64	3.17		1.4	
21		2.7	1.5		1.5	1
22		1.87	2		1.25	1
23		1.17	1.33		1.37	
24		1.37	1.25			
25		1.75	3			
r*	−.24	−.44	−.23	−.34	−.31	−.29
n1	9	3	10	9	2	13
n2	2	7	9	6	4	5
runs	2	2	6	4	2	2
p†	.05	.05	.05	.05	.05	.05

*Spearman's.
†Probability.

stabilize it by successively accumulating several types of more and more serious crimes, a process of escalation that we shall examine subsequently. Second, they could persist because of the long duration of burglary, which accompanies other types of theft depending on the circumstances. The duration of the criminal activity would stem from precocity, and stabilization would occur in these two major ways.

Diversification

Whereas acceleration and stabilization seem to be important mechanisms in the development of criminal activity, it is interesting to find that they are sustained by diversification. Diversification is defined here as the result of the relationship between precocity and the degree of variety of the crimes. Table 5.3 presents these data.

An examination of the table shows that the earlier the illicit activities begin, the greater their variety later on. However, the relationship here is less significant than with acceleration and stabilization. Two observations can be made. First, the coefficients of correlation of Spearman, while statistically significant $p < .001$, are slightly weaker than the ones observed for acceleration and stabilization. Second, the distributions of the medians (the median number of crime categories) are affected by some fluctuations, but the one-sample-runs tests are statistically significant, which means that the median degrees of variety are not distributed at random across the ages of onset.

Furthermore, whether in the case of hidden delinquency or official delinquency, whether during adolescence, youth, or the two together, the differences between the medians when criminal activity starts very early or begins much later are sufficiently great for us to recognize the influence of the mechanism of diversification. Thus, the degree of variety goes from seven to three for official delinquency and from seven to one for hidden delinquency, a substantial difference. Similarly, Tolan and Lorion (1987), on studying the self-reported delinquency of a sample adolescents, showed that precocity is the best predictor of variety and that the latter is significantly less if the illicit activities start at mid-adolescence. Wikström (1987), using arrest data, also showed that specialization diminishes from the first part of adolescence to the second, which means that diversification increases.

The Effect of Activation

The data analyzed so far support the fact that the earlier a person starts criminal activities, the more numerous, the more lasting, and the more varied they will be. The mechanisms of acceleration, stabilization, and diversification, then, help us to understand how criminal activities develop. We have postulated that these mechanisms are autonomous but also closely interrelated and that their combination is necessary if the illicit activity is to persist and increase. To confirm this, we did an analysis of the correlations between precocity, frequency, duration, and variety (we use Spearman correlations because certain distributions have very few subjects with scores that differ vastly from the general tendency). The simple and partial correlations displayed in Figures 5.1 and 5.2 will assist us in discussing the process of activation; the simple correlations are statistically significant at $p < .001$.

It must be pointed out that onset is by definition an antecedent variable and the other three parameters are necessarily consequential variables; furthermore, the variables duration, frequency, and variety are necessarily concurrent characteristics of offending. The one-directional light arrows in Figures 5.1 and 5.2 show the antecedent relations, whereas the two-directional light arrows show that the concurrent variables are mutually influential. Let us start with the self-reported delinquency of the subjects interviewed during adolescence and adulthood (Fig. 5.1).

The correlation between onset (precocity) and duration (stabilization) is much higher ($-.62$) than that between onset and frequency (acceleration) ($-.25$) or

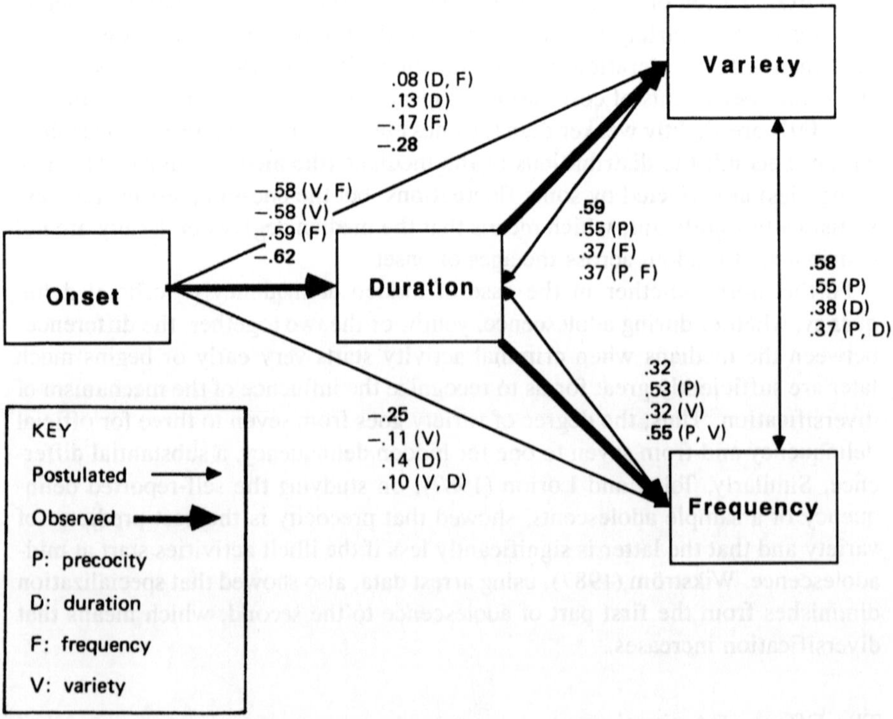

FIGURE 5.1. Correlations between onset, frequency, duration, and variety of criminal activities in self-reported delinquency: Effect of activation.

between onset and variety (diversification) (−.28). The major effect of precocity would be on persistence, the mechanism of stabilization seeming more fundamental than acceleration and diversification in fostering offending. This conclusion is confirmed by the partial correlations. The partial correlation between precocity and duration does not change significantly if frequency, variety, or both of these variables are controlled: It moves from −.62 to −.58. However, the partial correlation between onset and variety virtually disappears, going from −.28 to .08, and the correlation between onset and frequency is much reduced, from −.25 to .10. There are drastic changes if duration is controlled.

Incidentally, the very strong connection between frequency and variety that our correlations point to had already been observed by Dunford et al. (1983) in their national study on the evolution of hidden adolescence among American adolescents. Tolan and Lorion (1987) also reported high correlations between precocity, frequency, and variety in the hidden delinquency of the adolescents in their sample. But these authors, as our partial correlations show, should have controlled for these variables before inferring redundancy between these parameters of offending.

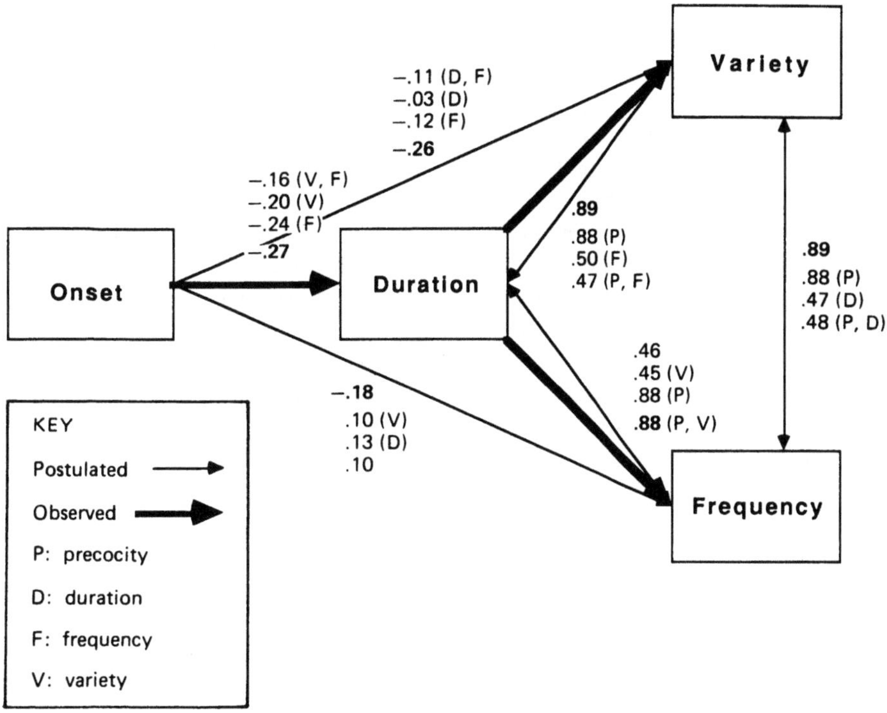

FIGURE 5.2. Correlations between onset, frequency, duration, and variety of criminal activities in official delinquency: Effect of activation.

Figure 5.1 shows that the correlations between variety and onset and frequency and onset tend to be fallacious because they diminish to .10 when duration and the other variables are controlled, while the correlations between duration and variety and duration and frequency are still in the .30s if the other two variables are controlled. It should also be noted that when precocity is controlled these relations are hardly modified, a result that indicates that the age of onset affects variety and frequency through duration. As shown in Figure 5.1, with the large arrows, the effect of precocity is first in terms of duration, then it manifests itself with variety and frequency. The effect of activation depends on the stabilization of offending in the behavioral pattern of the subject; it is then amplified through acceleration and diversification which are reinforcing each other.

Are these conclusions valid for official delinquency? Looking now at the data for the whole sample of delinquents (Fig. 5.2), the correlation between precocity and duration is higher (−.27) than that between precocity and frequency (−.18) or variety (−.26). The major effect of precocity would be on persistence, the mechanism of stabilization seeming more fundamental than acceleration and diversification. However, the dynamics of development depend on the interaction between frequency, duration, and variety; the correlations are around .88

between these three parameters of the illicit activity and after controlling for the other variables, they are still high, around .47. There is interaction among them but it is very much influenced by duration, since the partial correlations are much lowered when this variable is controlled compared with the situation when frequency or variety is controlled. The high correlations among these parameters is even independent of precocity, since the control of this variable does not affect them. However, the effect of precocity is through duration, since the initial correlation between onset and duration (−.27) is not significantly altered by the control of either frequency or variety or both (respectively −.24, −.20 and −.16) and since the correlations between onset and variety (−.26 to −.11) and onset and frequency (.18 to .10) are brought to the .10 threshold by the control of duration. The effect of precocity is then clearly in terms of stabilization of offending; it has an indirect impact on frequency and variety, meaning that acceleration and diversification support the mechanism of stabilization when persistent offending is developing.

It is also interesting to compare Figures 5.1 and 5.2, even if they support the same conclusions. There are two major differences in the correlations. The correlation between precocity and duration is much higher for self-reported delinquency than for official delinquency, and the reverse is observed for the correlations between duration, frequency, and variety. Conversely, the attenuating effect of the control of duration when we are concerned with the correlations between onset and frequency and onset and variety is much smaller for official delinquency than for self-reported delinquency. These differences are a reflection of the functioning of the justice system, as we have explained previously. Because of diversion, delinquents enter the justice system late, the consequence is a shorter range for the variable duration, which implies smaller correlations. Fundamentally, however, the two sets of correlations support the same general conclusion: Offending is activated through stabilization and amplified through acceleration and diversification. Criminal activity must last before it will become abundant and varied.

These results support a new definition of the mechanisms of activation. Stabilization must be conceived as the direct effect of precocity on duration, whereas acceleration and diversification have to be redefined as the indirect effects of precocity on frequency and variety through duration.

In short, activation has a number of effects. The first is stabilization; here precocity is confirmed as a strong source of duration. The illicit activities are persistent but not necessarily abundant and/or varied. The second is acceleration, when criminal behavior is reiterated over time. This leads to a high frequency: The offenses are numerous and lasting but not necessarily varied. The third effect is diversification, precocity fostering a high degree of diversity. The criminal activities are then lasting and heterogeneous but not necessarily abundant. Finally, the fourth effect, the most criminogenic of all, depends on the interactions among duration, frequency, and variety on a foundation of precocity, with criminal activities that start early and later become abundant, varied and long lasting due to the dynamic effect of these three mechanisms on one another. This is how chronic delinquency is created. The development of criminal activities is not a matter of chance – such development is predictable because it is determined by the four effects of activation just enumerated.

Escalation

This mechanism will be studied by means of two conceptual frameworks. The first, centered on the illicit acts themselves, tries to discover a series or a specific sequence of criminal manifestations in the development of the illegal activity. The second, focused on the individual who contravenes the Criminal Code, attempts to show a gradual increase in involvement in illicit behavior. This view questions the position that stages of evolution in offending do not exist. As we shall see, a good part of the confusion in the criminological literature is due to the lack of differentiation between these two complementary perspectives.

Gibbons (1965, 1975) described the criminal career as a sequential model composed of stages through which the offender evolved, but current studies have not shown interest in this approach of escalation. When investigating whether the development of criminal activity conforms to a criminalization model, one can determine at the same time whether the activity is marked by a regular increase in the gravity of the crimes. What we think we will observe is a string of crimes that become more and more serious as time goes on. This postulated sequence is evidenced by data on the variations in the crime mix according to age and on the variations in the age when delinquency started and stopped, as well as the duration of each type of criminal activity (reported in chap. 4). In fact, each age period has a dominant crime mix, and crime can be ordered in a specific sequence according to age of onset, duration, and age of termination. Farrington et al. (1987) have also observed this.

This progression from minor crimes to major ones as the subject's age increases shows that the development of criminal activities is not due to chance but is organized according to the principles of predictability or is even an invariant sequence over time. Robins and Wish (1977) showed that maximum precision in predicting behavior can be attained only on condition that the first behavior is constantly adjacent to another in the pattern of development and that a particular sequence of behavior manifests itself over time.

To state that people who are involved in delinquency go through specific stages of development is to suggest a standard pattern of criminalization. This pattern obviously involves an increasing capacity to commit crimes, but also the appearance of phenomena that criminologists have called regression or retention. *Regression* is a backsliding, meaning that after the subject has reached an advanced age of serious crime, he goes back to committing crimes of less gravity. *Retention*, the term used by Loeber (1986) and which we feel is more appropriate than that of Patterson (1982), arrested socialization, or that of Robins (1980), accretion, is characterized by the fact that an individual who has reached an advanced stage of gravity still continues to practice crimes of lesser gravity. Our hypothesis asserts that the evolution of a person's criminal conduct is a matter of development by stage. There are two models according to the distinction made by Loevinger (1966). The hierarchic model does not imply that all individuals go through the same stages of delinquency, but that most start or stop at different stages and only a certain number go through all the stages of gravity. The embryonic model, on the other hand, states that all individuals go through the same stages in the same manner. Although many personal development theories put forward the embryonic model, the hierarchic model is predominant, as shown by Lerner (1986).

The two approaches to escalation we referred to, the one concerned with the sequence of delinquent conduct, the other with the evolution of the individual, are firmly rooted in numerous psychological theories and are supported by a great many studies (see Lerner, 1986). Not only do these two approaches to development apply to the evolution of the psychological functioning of the person, but the surveys made by Loeber (1982, 1985a, 1987) show that the same conceptions of development seem to be found in behavior problems and the licit and illicit use of drugs.

With reference to these last types of conduct, Loeber (1987) reported a number of studies that establish the existence of an unvarying sequence regarding the consumption of licit and illicit drugs. It starts with use of beer and wine, cigarettes and alcoholic beverages, especially gin, followed by the consumption of mild drugs (hashish and marijuana), to end in experimentation with stronger drugs. This unvarying sequence is based on a progression between adjacent types of behavior (we also observed this course among our samples of adolescents and delinquents; Le Blanc & Tremblay, 1987). People engaged in this process go through it partially or wholly at a personal rhythm and in conformity with the hierarchic model of development. With regard to behavioral problems that are different from delinquency, Loeber (1985a, 1985b, 1987) reported studies that support the fact that they, too, occur in sequences: Oppositional behaviors (disobeying parents and so on) would be followed by offensive acts (fighting, lying, recalcitrance in school, etc.), the next stage being acts of aggression (personal attack and so on).

In criminology, as Blumstein et al. (1986) stated, "A belief in escalation is probably the most widely held view of the pattern of criminal careers" (p. 84). In fact, a century ago Worsley described the progression "from petty delinquencies to greater and more heinous crimes" (1949, p. 12; cited by Morris & Giller, 1987). In spite of all the similar assertions since this distant era and even after numerous empirical studies, criminologists are far from being unanimous on this question, as evidenced in the recent surveys of J. Cohen (1986) and Loeber (1987). There seem to be two reasons for this disagreement. First, the studies often suffer from confusion due to the use of escalation to account for research results that were obtained to clarify a different question, namely, offense switching; they neglect the question of progression in the criminal activity. The second reason is the excessive empiricism and lack of conceptualization in these studies. .

The first of these two problems is general in the social sciences and is particularly evident in research on escalation. Two well-known studies are good illustrations of the problems confronting researchers who undertake to study the escalation process – those of Nye and Short (1957) and of Wolfgang et al. (1972). The former investigators were interested in grading of the illegal activities as reported by the adolescents themselves; the Guttman technique was used to construct a scale of delinquency that represented a continuum of gravity. In spite of its initial success and several replications, this method proved inefficient as the questionnaires of self-confessed delinquency became more complex (see Hindelang et al., 1981, and Le Blanc 1983a). Wolfgang et al. (1972) were concerned with patterns of offensive behavior, and more specifically, with specialization, offense switching, and changes in the qualitative content of the offense conduct. To clarify these questions they used transition probabilities by trying to model crimes with the Markov chain technique. None of their studies used the idea of escalation to guide the analysis and interpretation of results. Despite this omission, subsequent research works were constantly referring to the study of Wolfgang et al. to deal with the question of escalation or to support opposing positions, bypassing the work by Nye and Short, which had the merit of dealing directly with the problem of the gradation of delinquent activities.

The second difficulty is more insidious. It consists of setting up a procedure of analysis, such as the technique of transition matrices (which is most effective in the study of offense switching), to deal with the entire question of progression in delinquent activities, from the most minor to the most serious. This approach often does not respect the basic conditions of this analysis (it should be a longitudinal study with measurements taken at several points and should be concerned with a very large sample) and does not have adequate conceptualization. We examined about 20 studies that deal directly or indirectly with this question (Bursik, 1980; Chaiken & Chaiken, 1982; Collins, 1981; Datesman & Aikin, 1094; Dunford et al., 1983; Fréchette & Le Blanc, 1979; Frum, 1958; Kobrin & Klein, 1983; Lab, 1984; Moitra, 1981; Rankin & Wells, 1985; Rojek & Erickson, 1981; Shannon, 1978, 1982; Smith, Smith, & Noma, 1984; Soothil & Gibbons, 1978; Thomas, 1976; Weis, 1979; Wolfgang et al., 1972, 1987). Various difficulties and limitations mark these studies:

Some are not directly concerned with the subject, for they analyze the progression from statutory to criminal offenses rather than the progression in the criminal activities themselves. Most use a simplistic definition of the gravity of crimes, referring, for example, to categories such as crimes against property, crimes against persons, and other infractions. Thus they omit the possibility that there may be as many variations in the gravity of crimes belonging to a category that is too general as there are differences among the categories themselves.

Other studies use such a large number of categories that it becomes mathematically impossible to detect some kind of structure among occurrences that are fairly rare.

Some of the samples are too small to allow the use of the transition matrices procedure with any confidence.

Some studies use transition matrices almost exclusively whereas other techniques would be as pertinent, if not more so.

In most of the studies the results show the well-known bias that results from the use of official data, because very few of them refer to self-reported delinquency.

All of these studies take only one of the possible describers of the activities directly into account, that, the type of crime, generally at two different times, and consider their gravity only indirectly.

Finally, they generally confuse the gradation of the criminal activities with progression within the criminal activity itself.

Despite all these difficulties, one of the main results of the study by Wolfgang et al. (1972), namely, that gravity increases linearly with successive arrests, still holds true. It is even replicated in their most recent study (Wolfgang et al., 1987). A reanalysis of previous studies done by J. Cohen (1986) shows that some authors who got negative results on that question had not interpreted their data correctly. The theory of progression, whether in terms of escalation within criminal activity as time goes on or in terms of a sequence among the categories of crime, is more pertinent than ever.

The Gradation of Criminal Activities

Our analysis of hidden delinquency, reported above, shows that, on the one hand, types of crime seem to be linked in a specific way according to the starting age, duration, and age when they stopped, and that the types of crime committed (including combinations of crimes or crime mixes) and their frequency, gravity and violence change as age increases. To better illustrate this sequence (always keeping in mind the possible interactions among all these aspects of the criminal activity), we constructed Figure 5.3 concerning criminal activities during adolescence (Fréchette & Le Blanc, 1979, 1987). The order of the crimes in this figure is determined by the average age at which each type of crime began. On examining this graph, the obvious conclusion is that a specific sequence of crimes exists in the development of criminal activity, taking into account that the length of each bar represents duration.

Three other conclusions, of major importance, are also evident. The first concerns the spectacular acceleration of the process of change or increase in the forms of delinquent activity, especially after the age of 12 and up to about 14, as if the polymorphous nature of the activity intensified at this time to culminate in a diversity of acts, whereas previously it had been limited to a few categories of minor crimes. The second refers to the early discarding of a number of minor infractions (petty larceny and shoplifting) and the concentration on the most serious crimes at mid-adolescence.

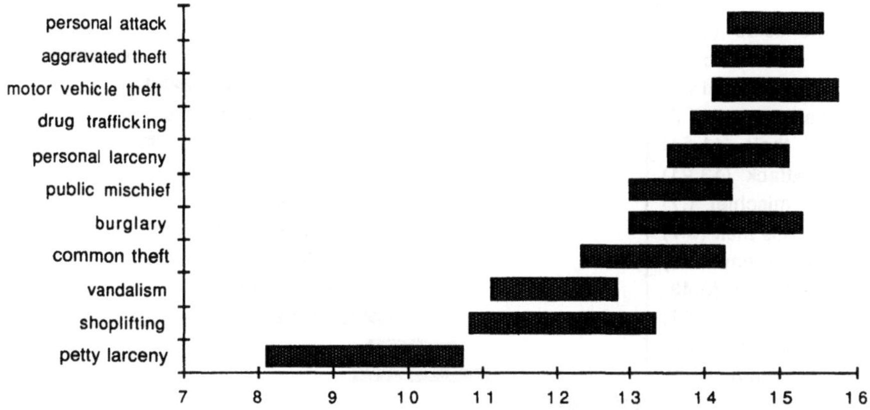

FIGURE 5.3. Gradation of criminal activity during adolescence, average age of onset, and duration by type of crime.

The third is that not only are all forms of crime, from the most benign to the most serious, set in motion from the age of 14, but they tend definitely to decline by about age 16. Thus the general phenomenon observed previously, where the criminal activity was abandoned at the end of adolescence, is confirmed for each particular form. It is clear, on the basis of these three conclusions, that delinquency is primarily a problem of the first part of adolescence; it tends to have only a limited duration and to mid-adolescence appears to be essentially heterogeneous. This means that each age level has one or several particular forms of criminal activity. At the same time it is evident that from one level to another there is a constant increase in the gravity of the acts.

Reading these data once again, we find that there are four stages in the development of criminal activity and that they form an unvarying sequence. They are, in the following order, emergence, exploration, explosion, and conflagration. At first, usually between the ages of 8 and 10, the delinquent activities are homogeneous and benign, almost always expressed in the form of petty larceny; this is the stage of *emergence*. After that, the testing period, generally between ages 10 and 12, is characterized by a diversification and an aggravation of the offenses. Essentially a matter of shoplifting and vandalism, this stage is one of *exploration*. Later, at about age 13, there is a substantial increase in the variety and gravity of the crimes, and four new types of crime develop—common theft, public mischief, burglary, and personal larceny. This is the *explosion* stage. Its mainstay, burglary, constitutes the major component of this escalation, because of its longevity (average duration 2.29 years). Finally, around the age of 15, the heterogeneity, variety, and gravity increase further and, at the same time, four more types of crime are added—drug trafficking, motor vehicle theft, armed robbery, and personal attack. This is the stage of *conflagration*. Thus, starting from mid-adolescence, with the exception of homicidal acts and fraud, the entire gamut of crimes has been experienced. In addition, the overlapping of the

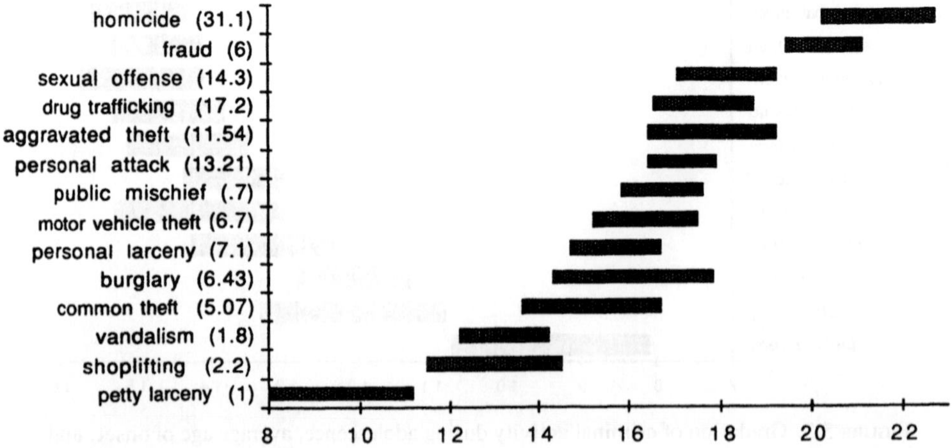

FIGURE 5.4. Gradation of criminal activity: Median age of onset and duration by age and seriousness of the crime (grades are in parentheses; see chap. 3 for explanation of grading).

duration clearly shows that the same crimes are committed from one stage to another, particularly those of the exploration and explosion stages and the explosion and conflagration stages.

Once it had been established that there is a sequence of delinquent activities throughout adolescence, the question arose whether there is a similar sequence during adolescence and adulthood. J. Cohen (1986), in a survey of the literature, was unable to find one specific sequence for official delinquency, but was able to conclude that seriousness increased from adolescence to adulthood. It occurred to us, however, that perhaps these results were negative because they referred only to official delinquency. In a subsequent analysis we therefore used all our data on hidden crime, from childhood to an average age of 23, for the 219 subjects of the sample of delinquents who were interviewed again as adults. In addition to data on starting age and duration (we used the medians because the differences between the averages and medians of duration were substantial), we added the average degree of gravity for each category of crime, based on the scale designed by Sellin and Wolfgang (1964) (the procedure for attributing the scores of gravity is described in chap. 3). Figure 5.4 presents these data.

The order of the crimes having been established on the basis of mean age when each began to be perpetrated, it is remarkable to find the concurrence between this order and that furnished by average score of gravity (these scores are in parentheses after each crime in Fig. 5.4). Furthermore, the gravity scores confirm the existence of the stages described previously: The categories of crime during the exploration stage are more serious than those that precede this stage (that is, during emergence), but less serious than those during the following stage (explosion), and so on. Thus the average gravity for each stage, respectively, is 1 for emergence, about 2 for exploration, between 5 and 7 for explosion, and between 11 and 17 for conflagration. Only two crime categories depart from this progression—public mischief between the ages of 16 and 19, whose gravity does not conform at all to that of the crime categories surrounding it, and fraud, which is more an adult infraction, committed between ages 19 and 21 and whose gravity is at the same level as that of stage three, explosion. Despite these exceptions, we come to the conclusion that the four stages described are confirmed and that the dynamics of progression also seem to operate at the adult level, at least up to the mid-20s. Figure 5.4 also shows a fifth stage that occurs only in adulthood; it is a progression toward more astute and more violent forms of criminal behavior. It will be called *outburst*.

This demonstration of the sequence of criminal activities is based solely on main tendencies with regard to gravity, duration, and precocity according to age and types of crime. There is a technique for constructing a cumulative scale with items of increasing difficulty; it is Guttman's scalogram technique (Goodenough, 1944). This technique compares a perfect scale with the data gathered. A perfect scale of four items would produce five models of answers—0000, 0001, 0011, 0111, and 1111; for the scale to be adequate, the coefficient of reproducibility should be greater than .90 and the coefficient of scalability greater than .60. A scale of this type uses the embryonic model of development, which means that every individual goes through the same stages in the same order, as well as a predictability that extends to all the stages. In other words, behavior during the first stage can predict not only that of the next stage but of all the other stages. The authors of several recent studies, cited previously, favor the hierarchic model of development, which affords predictability that extends only to the next stage. We applied Guttman's technique to confirm, in an indirect way, that the hierarchic model gives the best account of the development of criminal activities. If, in applying the Guttman technique, we can construct an adequate scale, the embryonic model will be validated; if a quasiscale of criminal activities is consistent with the data, the hierarchic model can be sustained; and, if the statistics are very bad, we have to conclude that criminal activities cannot be ordered in a sequence.

First, we used this type of analysis on our data concerning the subjects who recounted their criminal activities in three separate interviews from adolescence to adulthood. This was done by using the five stages described earlier and by operationalizing them in the following way: A subject was given a score of 1 if he had committed at least one crime among the categories belonging to a specific stage. With the results we obtained, it was impossible to reproduce adequately the model underlying the Guttman technique. It was, however, possible to approach the situation of a quasiscale because the coefficient of reproducibility was .56. This result can be attributed to the fact that participation in the categories of crime constituting stages of emergence and of outburst was low, 17 and 23%, respectively, and because only two subjects had committed crimes belonging to all five stages. In short, over the period from childhood to the mid-20s, it is impossible to confirm an embryonic model of the development of delinquent activities. The coefficients of the Guttman technique, as well as the correlation between the stages, show that it is a partly hierarchic model with predictability such that each stage predicts the next stage but not the later ones. It is still possible, however, that with a longer period of time and a larger number of subjects, the results might correspond more to the embryonic model.

Second, we concentrated on the period from the beginning of childhood to the end of adolescence and conducted the Guttman analysis on 396 delinquents regarding the four stages that seem to characterize the development of delinquent activities during adolescence. The results are disappointing but convincing. They are disappointing because, whereas precocity seemed to be the force activating delinquency, the emergence stage, in which petty larceny is dominant between the ages of 8 and 11, does not actually trigger the escalation. In fact, the coefficients from the application of the Guttman technique are at the same level as those previously reported for the five stages. If there is a progression among types of criminal activities, it is mainly limited to only one subsequent stage. These results are convincing because, if we take only the three central stages exploration, explosion, and conflagration, the coefficients obtained by means of the Guttman technique come close to the threshold that characterizes a perfectly cumulative scale, the coefficient of reproducibility being .75. At the same time, it is a hierarchic model because the coefficients of association between the adjacent stages (the Q of Yule) is significant (.52 between exploration and explosion and .47 between explosion and conflagration) and is less so between the extremes (.09 between exploration and conflagration).

We can also confirm the existence of a sequence or gradation of the crimes by means of an analysis of official delinquency. In Figure 5.5 two stages emerge, property offenses between the average ages of 15 and 18 (particularly larceny, burglary, car theft, personal larceny, and public mischief) and crimes against the person later on (robbery, assault, homicide, sex crimes, drug trafficking, and fraud). We could even say that homicide and drug trafficking constitute a separate set of offenses because they tend to appear later than the other offenses in this stage. Each stage is not much less homogeneous than the stages of self-reported delinquency, and there are major similarities of content. The first stage in official delinquency tends to group types of crime similar to those in the third stage in self-reported delinquency, explosion; and crimes in the second stage in official delinquency correspond grossly to those in the fourth stage in self-reported delinquency, conflagration, and in the fifth stage, deepening. If the contents correspond generally, the ages are somewhat dissimilar, due to the delayed effect of the system of justice.

However, these results are not as convincing as those obtained in the case of hidden delinquency, for several obvious reasons. In the first place, minor crimes rarely come to the knowledge of the justice system; and second, official criminal activity is usually of short duration (not oftem more than 2 years) and is sanctioned (taken into account) by the justice system only after mid-adolescence. Our

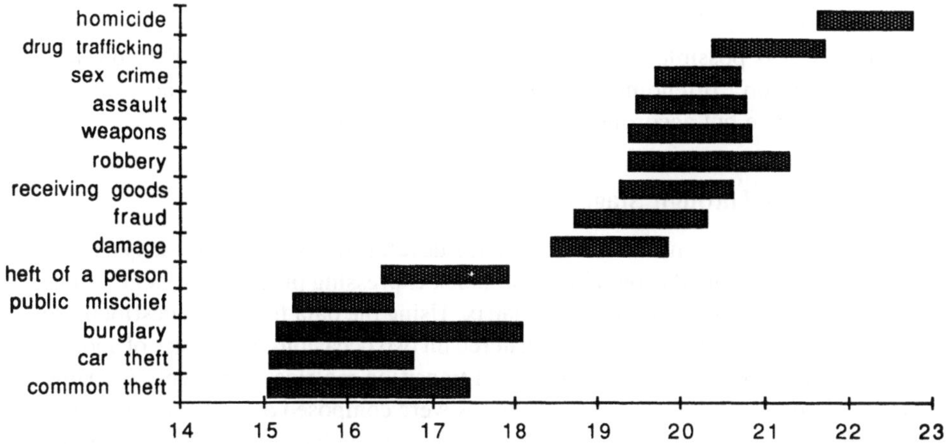

FIGURE 5.5. Gradation of official delinquency: Average age of onset duration by age, and types of crime.

results, in terms of an increase in seriousness of offending from adolescence to youth, are in accordance with J. Cohen's (1986) survey of the literature.

All our results concerning the gradation of the crimes lead to three conclusions.

1. The gradation of crime categories should not be conceived of as a certain ordering of all crimes, but as a sequence of three specific groups of crimes. The basic sequence is shoplifting and vandalism between the ages of 11 and 14; four types of theft—common theft, burglary, personal larceny, and/or motor vehicle theft—between 14 and 17; and more serious categories of crime such as personal attack, armed robbery, drug trafficking, and/or sex-related crimes between 16 and 19. In this perspective, the crimes at the two extremities of the continuum of seriousness, petty larceny versus fraud and homicidal conduct, do not fit in any evolutive pattern of criminal activity.
2. The hypothesis supported by Robins and Wish (1977) is confirmed, namely, that behavior involving a less serious category of crime is the best predictor of the next more serious category of crime (e.g., personal larceny predicts aggression or robbery better than vandalism) and that the sequences appear invariable, among both adolescents and delinquents. Our study was unable to confirm a strict sequential order between the five stages. However, a questionnaire on hidden delinquency, administered to a national sample of young Americans on a number of different occasions by Dunford et al. (1983), established, with the probabilities of transition, at least three stages that they called exploratory delinquency, patterned nonserious delinquency, and patterned serious delinquency.
3. Even though precocity emerged as the driving force activating the criminal behavior, the sequence of the crimes found in the three stages, exploration,

explosion, and conflagration, constitutes the true process of escalation. Hence it is possible to say that, thanks to stabilization, diversification, and acceleration, offending can develop with increasing seriousness during adolescence but according to a sequence that is hierarchic.

Progression Through Stages

Le Blanc, Loeber, and Côté (1988) have developed a strategy of analysis that makes possible calculation of a global index expressing progression, regression, or stability in terms of a transition matrix. Using the data from the questionnaire on self-reported delinquency administered on two occasions to samples of adolescents and delinquents, they constructed transition matrices with types of crime placed in order of gravity. These matrices were composed of coefficients of predictability, RIOC (Loeber & Dishion, 1983). On the basis of these coefficients, a global index of progression was deduced. Over a period of 2 years, 34% of the adolescents had progressed from one type of minor crime to a more serious type, whereas 31% were practicing less serious crimes and 29% kept to the same type of crime. Among the delinquents, 24% had progressed during a 2-year period, 20% had regressed, and 48% kept to crimes of the same level of gravity. It should be noted that these two groups of subjects were on average 14 and 15 years old, respectively, during the first inteviews (unpublished data, Le Blanc & Loeber). The percentage of 34% adolescents who have progressed was composed of 11% pure progression, which means adopting more serious crimes later on, and 21% retention, that is, committing more serious crimes while continuing to commit minor ones. Among the delinquents these proportions were 3 and 21%, respectively. Considering the short interval (2 years) between administrations of the questionnaire and the homogeneity of the age of the samples, the reported level of progression seems remarkable.

Looking at data gathered from the three interviews with our group of delinquents and considering the stages of gradation of crime, we observe a progression for 92% of the delinquents when the five stages are taken into account (31% by one level of gravity, 43% by two, 25% by three, and 3% by four). This level of progression is lower when only adolescence is considered: it goes to 74% over the four stages emergence, exploration, explosion, and conflagration (44% by one level, 27% by two, and 3% by three).

If we limit ourselves to the three fundamental stages that foster the process of escalation (exploration, explosion, and conflagration) and if we consider the period from childhood to youth (Fig. 5.6), it is interesting to note that 84% of delinquents change the level of criminal gravity over time, whereas 15% limit themselves to a single stage of criminal activity (1% at exploration, 11% at explosion, and 3% at conflagration). Figure 5.6 also shows that 13% of the delinquents regress (11% to explosion and 2% to exploration) whereas 72% progress to the higher stage. In this case, there are progressions of one step, from exploration to explosion, 17%, from explosion to conflagration, 19%, from exploration to conflagration, 2%, and through the three stages, 34%. The percentages are highest

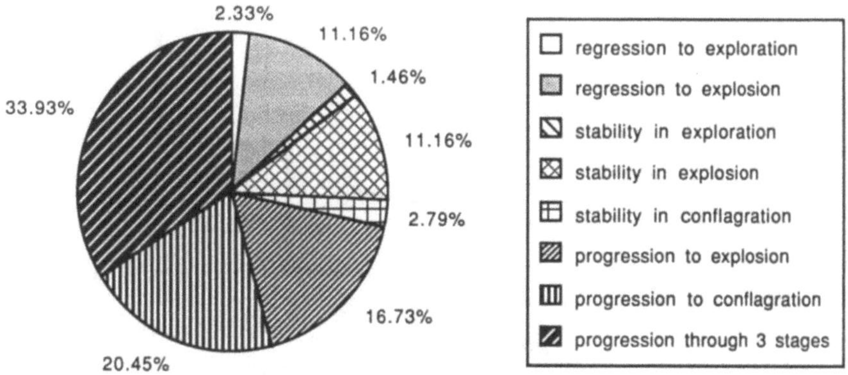

FIGURE 5.6. Development of self-reported delinquency (delinquent group).

in terms of progression and reflects the hierarchic model of the development of offending that we have proposed.

Cases of regression and of stability are rare. Among subjects who change the level of their illicit activities, 84% do so according to the hierarchic model, moving up one or two steps in seriousness, whereas 16% deviate from this model, starting their criminal activity with a more serious category of crime and then committing a less serious offense. These observations again confirm the developmental model that we have put forward.

This type of evolution is also evident with official delinquency, but the proportions are different and there is no regression, only progression and stability. About 40% of subjects have moved from property offenses to offenses against persons; the level of criminal seriousness thus increases from the middle of adolescence to the beginning of adulthood. The rest of the subjects are stable in terms of the nature and crime mix of the crimes they were convicted for. About 30% committed one type of crime during a particular period, as follows:

23% of subjects committed property crimes only during adolescence and 3% only during adulthood
1% of subjects committed crimes against persons only during adolescence and 4% only during adulthood
6% of subjects repeated the same category of crime, property
29% of subjects committed a combination of the more and the less serious crimes (9% before age 18, 7% after this age, and 7% during the two periods)

To sum up, illicit activities progress from minor crimes to more serious ones and for the large majority of delinquents they progress in sequence. Many delinquents go from exploration to explosion, many from exploration to explosion and then to conflagration, and some from exploration to conflagration or explosion to conflagration (Fig. 5.7), and some from exploration to conflagration or explosion to conflagration (Fig. 5.7). Although fewer than 15% of subjects limit

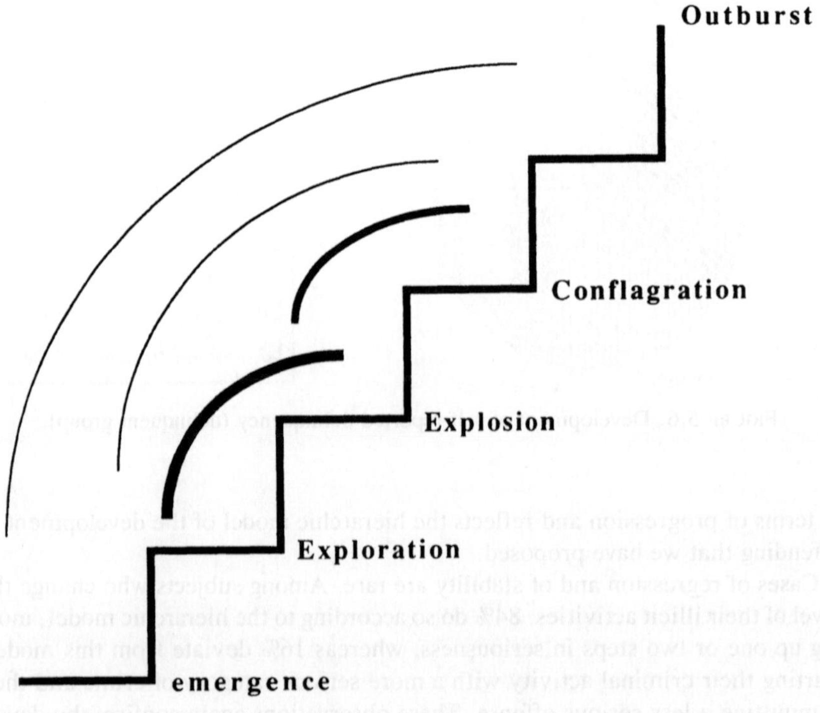

FIGURE 5.7. Progression of criminal activity through stages of offending.

themselves to crimes common to a single stage (usually explosion), which is mainly due to their preference for burglary, others, in keeping with the rules of the hierarchic model, go through several stages. They do not all start with the same type of crime nor end with the same one, and their transition from one to the other is not always standard, but they follow the direction stipulated by the sequential progression of the stages. The most common sequence is exploration to explosion and conflagration; however, two other sequences are frequent—exploration to explosion or explosion to conflagration.

The Escalation Process

Our study of the gradation of crime categories over time and the offenders' passage through these same categories has shed light on the escalation process that marks the development of criminal activity. In a first step, it was possible to show the gradation of crime categories by means of several analyses done with different descriptive and evolutive parameters of criminal activity (gravity, types of crime, precocity, age of termination, duration, and so on). There were five stages—emergence, exploration, explosion, conflagration, and outburst—each occurring at a given age, each being characterized by specific crime categories, each having a particular level of gravity.

In short, delinquency emerging during latency does so almost exclusively with petty theft. Then comes exploration at the beginning of adolescence with shoplifting and vandalism, followed by explosion at mid-adolescence with much more serious crimes, such as automobile theft, personal larceny, common theft, and particularly burglary. Because of its duration, burglary is the backbone of the developing criminal activity. By the end of adolescence, criminal activity has escalated into conflagration with still more serious crimes, such as personal attack, armed robbery, sex-related crime, and drug trafficking; to end finally in adulthood with astute crime, such as fraud, or crimes of violence and homicidal acts. Not only have we been able to identify these stages in the development of criminal activity, but we have succeeded in detecting three consecutive stages—exploration, explosion, and conflagration—that typify the pattern of its evolution. A sequence of this kind had already been discovered by Robins and Wish (1977) in the case of behavior problems, by Dunford and Elliott (1983) concerning delinquency, and Loeber (1987) maintained that it can be extended to all antisocial behavior. Our data unequivocally confirm the positions of these authors.

Next we followed the evolution of the delinquents through these stages and found that more than one third of them go through all three; and in the order described—exploration, then explosion, then conflagration. Another third of the sample go through two adjacent stages, and very few skip a stage. This confirms the fact that delinquent conduct follows a hierarchic model of development.

In the light of all these findings, and by simplifying the stages, it turns out that the process of escalation starts at the onset of adolescence with theft and vandalism, is accelerated with the addition of burglary, and is consolidated at the end of adolescence by more serious crimes against persons and property. According to works cited by J. Cohen (1986) as well as our own, this explains why there is no sequential progression in the crimes committed in adulthood: Persistent delinquents have already covered the entire gamut of delinquency before reaching adulthood, and there is nothing left for them to do but specialize or choose those crimes in their repertoire that offer the best opportunities. Finally, we can say with conviction that the development of criminal conduct is not a matter of chance, as studies using transition matrices and the Markov chain technique have mentioned. On the contrary, this development is organized according to a precise sequence, and once firmly established it continues in a relatively consistent way with predictable manifestations. Not all delinquents go through each stage, even though they conform to the general trend of the evolutionary pattern.

Desistance

In the various studies of desistance from criminal activity, authors have adopted two different positions. The first group sees desistance as a process of involution that extends over a more or less long period, and they focus only on the factors that encourage it, not on describing it (Cusson & Pinsonneault, 1986;

Jolin & Gibbons, 1988; Meisenhelder, 1977; Mulvey & LaRosa, 1986; Shover, 1983, 1985; West, 1982). The second group is interested only in the criminal activity itself, the first aspect studied being the particular moment the activity stops (Farrington et al., 1986c, referred to a number of studies that report data on the age at which the offending stops, data that we have previously used with our own samples). The second aspect studied is the question of specialization. This is perceived of as a sort of desistance, since the subject relinquishes many diverse types of criminal activity to specialize (we cite only a few studies on the subject and some recent surveys: J. Cohen, 1986; Farrington, Snyder, & Finnegan, 1988; Klein, 1984).

Both these ways of presenting desistance describe a basic process; that is, a gradual withdrawal from criminal activity. The curves of participation, like those presented in chapter 3, leave no doubt that the criminal activity of most individuals disappears during their 20s—a fact documented in criminology time and again since the work of Quetelet (1835). The crucial question is, How does desistance occur? According to the method we have proposed and applied, desistance can be analyzed only through the combination of descriptive and developmental parameters, the point of departure being the age at which the criminal activity stopped. In line with the principles of this method, we can speak of three mechanisms—deceleration, specialization, and culmination.

Deceleration refers to the relationship between the frequency of offending and the moment the criminal activity stops; we can assume that during the years preceding total desistance the annual frequency tends to diminish gradually. *Specialization* is the adoption of criminal activities that with time become increasingly less heterogeneous, so that the closer to the age of desistance the more the degree of variety is curtailed. *Culmination* refers to reaching the highest level of serious criminal activity, after which offending continues for a certain period before stopping. This ceiling acts as a sign that desistance is imminent.

These mechanisms cannot be studied in the same way as the mechanisms of acceleration, diversification, and stabilization, that is, having in view the entire gamut of criminal activity. It is obviously impossible to speak of desistance in the case of the occasional criminal; the process of desistance can be studied properly only with chronic offenders whose level of activity is sufficiently high to show gradual withdrawal. We therefore will use the duration of criminal activity as a sign of chronic delinquency, for the following two reasons. First, it has previously been shown that the key to the process of activation is stabilization, that is, the connection between precocity and duration. Consequently, it is logical to use duration to operationalize chronic delinquency, since it is the main effect of precocity as well as being central to activation. Second, it is important to make sure of the operational purity of the variables; since the mechanism of deceleration is defined by reduction in frequency as the moment approaches for the illicit activity to stop, there is no question that frequency would characterize both chronic delinquency and the mechanism of deceleration. To avoid this overlaping we will use duration as our indicator of chronic delinquency.

Deceleration

If acceleration is one of the mechanisms that supports the consolidation of illicit activity, deceleration would logically be a process that favors desistance. Offenders are not going to stop their criminal activities suddenly; they will begin by reducing the number of crimes they commit, a significant lessening in frequency occurring prior to the time they cease altogether. To demonstrate this process conclusively, we would need to show that our subjects had terminated their criminal activities for a period of several years. We cannot demonstrate this, because our subjects were only in their mid-20s when we last collected data on their self-reported and official delinquency. Nonetheless, we can present some facts that support the theory that the deceleration of criminal activities is a sign of imminent desistance.

To verify the presence of deceleration, we used two criteria for the selection of subjects. First, their criminal activities had lasted longer than the average duration among the sample – more than 5 years for reported crime and more than 3 years for official delinquency. Second, they had stopped illegal activities at adulthood. We eliminated, however, those subjects whose offenses began only during adolescence and whose activities could thus be too closely associated with the hazards attached to this phase of life. Table 5.4 shows the annual frequency of crimes committed in the years preceding desistance for the subjects answering these two criteria (the average is used for official delinquency because the distribution of the frequencies does not include extremes; this is not the case for reported delinquency, hence we use the median).

Whether hidden delinquency or official delinquency, the conclusion is the same: The frequency of occurrence of illicit activities diminishes as the time of desistance approaches, and the last year of activity is characterized by a significant drop in frequency. In short, the frequency reaches a maximum plateau 2 or 3 years before cessation, then diminishes, and finally the crimes are stopped. For example, among those who stop their official delinquency at age 18, a peak of 8.6 crimes a year is reached at age 16, diminishes to 7 at age 17, and reduces to 3.4 at age 18, the year the criminal activity is discontinued. In the case of hidden delinquency, the peak is 58.5 offenses at age 16, dropping to 28 crimes at age 17 and decreasing to 15 at age 18.

Looking at the total period of offending, the reduction among our sample of delinquents is such that the annual frequency during the year criminal activity stops is lower than the general trend, which is 2.5 in five cases out of seven for official delinquency, and is less than the median, which is 16 for reported delinquency. This is all the more significant in that at the peak that precedes this slowing down, the frequency is much greater than the general trend. The findings regarding official delinquency seem more convincing than those concerning reported crime. In the former, the year the activity stops is followed by at least 2 years without any new crimes, whereas in the latter, the year of desistance is simply the last year during which the illicit activities are reported to have occurred.

TABLE 5.4. Annual frequency of offending before the age of termination: Hidden and official delinquency.*

	Age of termination, hidden delinquency (5 years duration or more)							
	16	17	18	19	20	21	22	23
Annual	0	5						
median	58.5	28	15.5					
frequency	750.3	11.5	11	10				
	15	10.5	16	9.5	9			
	505	21	12	30.5	25.5	9		
	624.5	624.5	16	15	11	9	8.5	
	11	11.5	12.5	16	10.5	17	11.5	10.5

	Age of termination, official delinquency (2 years duration or more)															
	8	9	10	11	12	13	14	15	16	17	18	19	20	21	22	23
Annual	9	4	0	5	13	4.5	5.5	12	7.5	0.75						
mean	0	0	0	0	0	0.5	1	5	8.6	7	3.4					
frequency	1.3	1	1.3	7	10	5	2.6	2.7	4.2	7	4	3.8				
	2	1.6	3.6	1.3	1.3	1.2	3.1	3.5	4	2.6	3	3.9	1.7			
	5	2	2.6	1.5	4.8	2.5	5.8	3.3	4	3.2	2.2	2.3	1	1.2		
	0	1	2.5	3.2	4	3.1	3.3	4.5	2.4	3.4	8.4	3	1.5	2.6	2.3	
	5	2.5	2.6	1.3	1.5	2.5	1.2	2.7	3.1	3	5	8.7	2.3	1.7	2.7	1.2

*Data on hidden delinquency were obtained yearly only from age 16 on.

Criminal activity, then, after a period of acceleration is characterized by a deceleration among delinquents who commit crimes continuously throughout their adolescence. Loeber (1987), on the subject of desistance, spoke of a regression toward the mean. It is much more than that, however, since the annual frequency is definitely less than the central tendency, even before the year the crimes cease. We believe it is a question of deescalation, that is, a process of desistance that extends gradually over several years. Let us now see whether specialization has anything to do with desistance.

Specialization

Confusion concerning specialization will not be dispelled by considering it as one of the mechanisms of desistance. It should be remembered, first, that the development of criminal activity is marked by gradual diversification of crimes committed, and second, that consolidated illicit activity can only be versatile. To consider specialization as a process of desistance could minimize the confusion. In this perspective, specialization would be characteristic only of those delinquents who had been active for a long time. According to this definition, half of our sample of adolescents and a quarter of our sample of delinquents showing homogeneous but infrequent delinquency would not be specializing, since in their case there would be no question of gradual desistance. Wikström (1987), contrary to most researchers who assess specialization, measured it only among subjects who showed a certain level of frequency.

In fact, as we pointed out at the beginning of this chapter, the idea of specialization is open to confusion because of varying operational definitions. Even if we adopt the definition of Blumstein et al. (1986), whose restrictive formulation (the tendency to repeat the same type of crime over and over) facilitates measurement, the difficulty is not completely resolved. On the contrary, there is a risk of confusing several phenomena—the appearance of a series of similar crimes over a relatively short period of time, the degree of specialization among delinquents in a particular group, the potential of each type of crime for repetition, and the stability of delinquent conduct in general. In our opinion, specialization, strictly speaking, is the concentration of criminal activity, which has previously been expressed in a variety of forms, into a limited number of crime categories.

Criminologists familiar with police practices have often noted arrests for several crimes of the same kind committed within a relatively short period; for example a series of burglaries on adjacent streets within the same day. Furthermore, when we conducted our follow-up interviews with our group of delinquents, they frequently reported a series of crimes committed over relatively short periods of time, 20 burglaries in 2 weeks, for example, or 75 thefts of pension checks from mailboxes in 1 day. Clearly, what Chaiken and Rolph (1985) called spurts of offending are not signs of specialization. Series of crimes such as these do not necessarily mean that the criminal activity has become restricted or specialized; they are often preceded and followed by other kinds of crimes and are generally not carried out with any greater degree of sophistication.

The studies based on transition matrices that J. Cohen (1986) reported throw little light on specialization because, by referring to the matrix diagonal, it is possible to account for only two adjacent categories of crime. Such reference thus gives a necessarily limited view of the criminal activities as a whole. These studies conclude that specialization is minimal (Blumstein et al., 1986). Also, the works surveyed by Klein (1984), which use different data sources and various methods of analysis, arrive at the same conclusion. It must be pointed out, however, that most of these recent studies, because they are generally transverse rather than longitudinal, often confuse occasional delinquency, which comprises one or two crimes of the same nature, with specialization.

Other works reported by J. Cohen (1986) calculate the potential for specialization of various forms of crimes, that is to say, the relationship between the degree of specialization shown by the diagonal of the transition matrix and the prevalence of each category of crime as furnished by the marginals of this same matrix. This procedure makes it possible to arrive at a more precise measurement of the degree of specialization. It is quite similar to the one proposed by Farrington (1986a) and used in recent works by Kempf (1987) and by Farrington et al. (1988) (it is even more exact because of the adjustment through expected frequencies). However, only adjacent crimes are taken into consideration, and again the whole set of illegal activities is unrecorded.

Finally, the stability of delinquent conduct, defined operationally by the diagonal of transition matrices in the large majority of studies from Wolfgang et al. (1972) to Farrington (1986a), should not be considered specialization. In fact, analyses of the data we acquired from the administration of our questionnaire on hidden delinquency at a 2-year interval show that there are three kinds of stability: (a) the repetition of the same type of crime, (b) the repetition of the same combination of crimes, and (c) the repetition of the same type of crimes along with varied combinations of other crimes. Among adolescents these forms of stability are characteristic of 4, 14, and 15% of subjects, respectively, whereas among delinquents, the proportions are 0, 17, and 31%. The diagonal of the transition matrix covers all of these subjects and could give the impression that all of them specialize. Strictly speaking, however, only the first form of stability, where the same type of crime is repeated many times, would correspond to specialization as most criminologists theoretically define it. The second form, repetition of a specific combination of crimes, could be defined as specialization if there were only a limited number of crimes, but our observations show that this is not the case for the majority of subjects. This third form of stability, repetition of the same kinds of crimes but accompanied by different combinations of acts each time, is definitely not specialization.

With all this confusion about the definition of specialization, we thought it would be useful at this point to come back to the basic parameters that have guided us from the beginning of this study. The parameter that seems closest to the idea of specialization is variety, and so we began to look at the changes in variety over time. Then, in accordance with the method proposed earlier, we studied the chronic delinquents who, after having been involved in many different forms of delinquent conduct, settled for a smaller number of categories of crime or only one.

Degree of Specialization

Since the survey of the literature by J. Cohen (1986) shows that specialization among adults is higher than among minors, we undertook to ascertain whether variety diminishes from adolescence to youth. Table 3.1 clearly shows that the proportion of offenders who commit only one type of crime, as well as the median degree of variety, are relatively stable from one period to the other for both adolescents and delinquents and for hidden delinquency and official delinquency. Table 3.5 establishes that the proportions of subjects committing combinations of two, three, four, or five types of crime are much the same during adolescence and youth, and even at the beginning and the end of adolescence.

These facts show that there is no validity to the theory that there is a good deal of specialization among our subjects, even among a group of delinquents whose activities are numerous and long lasting. Even dealing with the question more directly, by counting the number of persons who commit the same kind of infraction as an adolescent and as an adult, or how many reduce the variety of their crimes, we get results that are not very convincing. Regarding the reported offenses of the group of delinquents, only 3% repeated the same type and few more than 19% repeated the same combination of more than two categories of crime. There were 54%, however, who reduced the degree of variety from adolescence to the beginning of adulthood, but only a little less than half confined themselves to one type of crime. Only a quarter of the initial group, then, specialized between adolescence and youth in the sense that they tended to adopt a specific type of infraction either because they had decidedly reduced the variety of their crimes or because they had always committed the same type of crime.

On analyzing the evolution of official delinquency between adolescence and youth, we find that only 16% repeat either the same crime (5%) or the same combination of crimes (11%), 37% lessen the degree of variety, while a minority of 14%, after having practiced several kinds of infraction, finally choose one particular type of crime. These proportions would probably diminish if we were to eliminate the occasional offenders hidden among the specialists, those who commit a single crime at adolescence and the same crime as an adult (this subgroup is estimated at 3% of offenders who persist; Le Blanc, 1986b).

Wikström (1987) approached the question of specialization in a new way. He calculated the proportion of crimes belonging to a particular category of crime. If two thirds of them were of a specific type, he considered the criminal activity of the subject specialized. Also, to exclude occasional delinquents who are necessarily specialized, he calculated the degree of specialization only for subjects who had committed three or more crimes. According to his data on arrests of offenders born in Stockholm in 1953, 27% of those who had committed at least three infractions before their mid-20s were specialists, particularly in theft. Our sample of Montreal adolescents, which is directly comparable to Wikström's birth cohort, shows a proportion of 38%. This difference is no doubt due to the fact that in Stockholm the infractions were those known to the police, whereas in Montreal the infractions has led to convictions. Using this method, only 14% of wards of the court had specialized.

Specialization exists, but it seems to be true of only a small proportion of delinquents, especially when subjects who commit only one or two crimes have been eliminated. It is sufficiently widespread, however, in terms of the developmental perspective we have adopted to be of interest in clarifying the evolutionary process that governs specialization and leads to the gradual lessening of diversity as the criminal career continues.

Mechanism of Specialization

To trace evolution toward more and more specialized criminal activity, we defined specialization strictly in terms of reduction in the number of categories of crime the subject commits after have been involved in a variety of offenses. Table 5.5 shows the median degree of variety in official delinquency according to the duration of active offending, but taking into account only subjects who had practiced more than one category of criminal activity during the preceding year. Although we have said earlier that the degree of variety is relatively stable over time, it turns out that the subjects who had practiced more than one category of crime in a given year (no matter which) showed less variety during subsequent years. For all the subjects, the median degree of variety, which usually varied around 1.6, became more than 2 among those practicing multiple forms of crime, but generally fell below 1.6 as they continued their activities. For example, subjects who continued their illicit activities for at least 3 years showed a median variety of 2.6; those who persisted showed decreasing medians of variety – 1.8 for 4 years of activity, 1.5 for 5.

To sum up, multiform criminal activities are consistently followed by a much more restricted range of crimes. It is not specialization in the strict sense of the term, since few subjects ever concentrate on a single type of crime. Looking at what happens from adolescence to adulthood, we see the same thing: Offenders gradually limit the variety of their crimes. Older delinquents vary their activities less and less, become more selective after a certain period of maximum versatility. They never specialize, however, in the sense of limiting themselves to one type of crime. The best way to describe the reality would be to conclude, as Klein (1984) did using a cross-sectional approach, that criminal conduct is essentially versatile. It is initiated by a process of behavioral activation that causes the individual to venture into many forms of illicit activity. This quickly subsides, so that whereas at adolescence offenders are capable of trying very type of crime, on reaching adulthood they restrict the range of their criminal activities, which tend to become more serious, however.

TABLE 5.5. Variety of criminal activities (median number) by number of years of active offending.*

Years active	Global	Juvenile period					Global	Adult period				
1	1.98	2.56					1.46	2.49				
2	1.61	1.53	2.3				1.48	1.44	2.39			
3	1.6	1.67	1.71	2.46			1.68	1.75	1.71	2.61		
4	1.68	1.58	1.8	1.93	2.35		1.7	1.65	2	1.82	2.53	
5	1.61	1.5	1.75	1.9	1.83	2.28	1.35	1.38	1.36	1.54	1.17	2.31
6	1.5	2.25	2	2	1.5	1.5	1.64	1.75	1.57	1.67	1.44	1.33

*All subjects had committed more than one crime during the preceding year.

TABLE 5.6. Age of termination and attained stage of seriousness (%)

Age of termination (yrs)	Stage of seriousness		
	Regressing	Stable	Progressing
17		100	
18		83.3	16.7
19		60	40
20		33.3	66.7
21		70.6	29.4
22		64.3	35.7
23	5.9	47.1	47.1
Total	1	61.4	37.6

Culmination

We have shown previously that not only is there a gradation of crimes but that the offender deeply involved in criminal activities goes through a consistent sequence of stages. In the case of self-reported delinquency, more than 85% of subjects in the sample went through at least one stage. Among those who followed the typical sequence, four fifths reached the threshold of intensity that we have called explosion, and more than three fifths reached conflagration, that is, were capable of committing the most serious crimes, with the exception of homicide.

Although, in our definition, culmination refers to reaching the point where criminal activity is maintained at a certain level of gravity, we were able to evaluate it between the first and second half of adolescence and between adolescence and youth. By cross-tabulating the level reached during the first part of adolescence and that reached during the second half, it was possible to conclude that 58% of delinquents reached their maximum level, or ceiling, during adolescence; this means that they maintained the same level of gravity before and after the age of 15½. Furthermore, 27% went on to a higher level of gravity, whereas 15% returned to a lower level. Between adolescence and youth, 61% reached a ceiling whereas 38% increased the level of gravity and 1% reduced it. On the whole, the standard process starts with minor illicit activity followed by a diversity of crimes that become more and more serious, to stop finally at a certain level of gravity. This level is reached fairly quickly during adolescence and tends to become stabilized. If the level changes during adulthood, it is because of the addition of the new crimes fraud or homicide.

Table 5.6 compares the level of gravity reached and the age when criminal activities stop . It turns out that for the majority of subjects who terminate their illicit activities, the maximum level of gravity is reached during adolescence, with the exception of those who stop only at age 20 to 23 and whose crimes increase in gravity during those years. For the entire group, arrival at the maximum level of gravity should not only precede termination of the criminal activities but be accompanied by a drop in frequency.

Table 5.7 shows the annual frequency of criminal activities according to the level of gravity reached. We found that those who maintained the same level of

TABLE 5.7. Frequency of criminal activities (median number) at each age by attained stage of seriousness (%)

Age (yrs)	Stage of seriousness Regressing	Stable	Progressing
16		0.17	0.13
17		0.32	0.33
18		2.17	5.50
19		1.50	9.50
20		0.75	5.50
21		0.83	7.83
22		0.50	3.00
23	2.00	0.21	0.36
24		0.13	0.16
25		0.03	1.49
Total	21.00	172.50	200.50

gravity between adolescence and youth showed medians that were definitely lower than those who went on a higher level of gravity. What is more, the annual frequency decreased significantly between ages 18 and 25, going from 2.17 to 0.03. Culmination meant both a reduction in frequency and a stabilization at a given level of criminal gravity.

The Saturation Point

During our analysis of desistance we explored the possibility that criminal activity slows before coming to an end. We thought that this slowing process would become apparent in three ways: deceleration, specialization, and culmination.

The data we have presented support this hypothesis. Deceleration is observable and significant; specialization is evident although limited; and the large majority of subjects reach a ceiling. These conclusions, however, are provisional because they do not yet offer all the necessary guarantees of validity. First, it is possible that many subjects did not stop their illicit activity completely, since the oldest were only in their mid-20s when our research ended. Second, we do not always have information on hidden delinquency and, as we have shown in the preceding chapters, it is essential to consider more than just official delinquency. These conclusions, therefore, can be considered plausible, but not definitive.

The effect of saturation can be deduced from Figures 5.8 and 5.9. These figures extend Figures 5.1 and 5.2, in which the process of activation was studied through the relationships between precocity, duration, variety and frequency. They present an analysis of the correlations between these five variables (we always use Spearman's correlations because certain distributions have a few subjects whose scores differ vastly from the central tendency). The simple and partial correlations displayed in Figures 5.8 and 5.9 will assist us in dis-

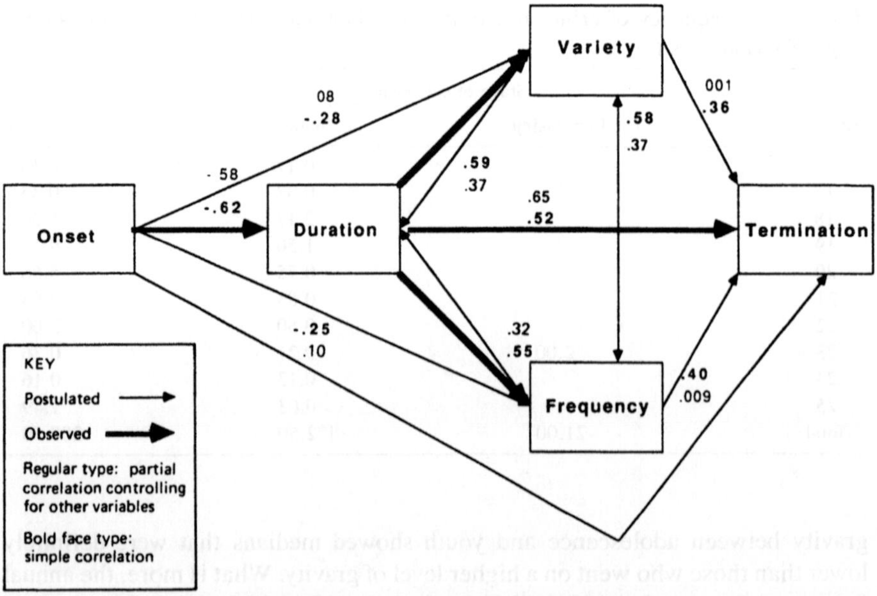

FIGURE 5.8. Correlations between onset, duration, frequency, variety, and termination of criminal activities in self-reported delinquency: Effect of saturation.

cussing the process of desistance. The simple correlations are statistically significant at $p \leq .001$, except for the correlation between age of onset and age of termination.

We will point out again that onset is by definition an antecedent variable and the variables duration, frequency, and variety are necessarily concurrent characteristics of offending. They are also intervening variables in relation to termination. Furthermore, the variable age of termination is necessarily a consequential variable with regard to the others. The one-directional light arrows in Figures 5.8 and 5.9 show the antecedent relations, whereas the two-directional light arrows show that the concurrent variables are mutually influential. Let us start with the analysis of the self-reported delinquency of subjects interviewed during adolescence and adulthood and give our main attention to the correlations with age of termination, because the other correlations have been analyzed earlier.

The correlations between age of termination and the other variables are somewhat at the same level, except for onset, which is not statistically significant. Since these correlations are positive we can infer saturation, because later termination is associated with longer duration, higher frequency, and a more diversified set of crimes. Desistance seems, however, more dependent on duration than on the other parameters of offending. This conclusion is confirmed by the partial correlations. The partial correlation between duration and termination does not

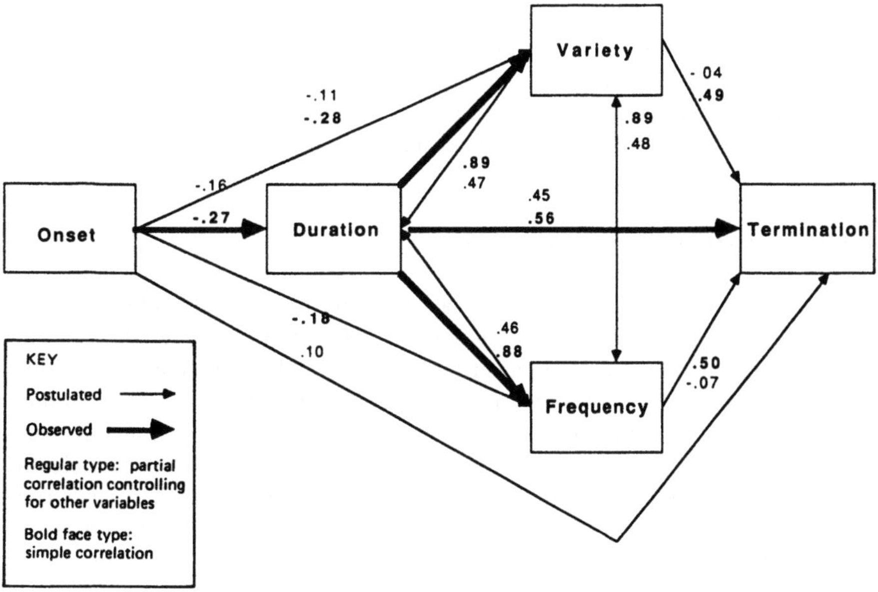

FIGURE 5.9. Correlations between onset, duration, frequency, variety, and termination of criminal activities in official delinquency: Effect of saturation.

change significantly, it moves from .65 to .52, if all of these variables combined are controlled. However, the partial correlations between variety and termination and frequency and termination are disappearing; when the other parameters of offending are controlled, they become virtually zero. These correlations are then fallacious. As shown in Figure 5.8 with the heavy arrows, the effect of precocity is first in terms of duration, then manifests itself with variety and frequency, and later termination takes place as a consequence of the stabilization of criminal activities in the behavioral pattern of an individual.

Are these conclusions valid for official delinquency? Looking now at the data for the whole sample of delinquents (Fig. 5.9), the correlations that we have just described behave in the same way and are virtually at the same level. Fundamentally, the two sets of correlations support the same general conclusion—offending is activated through stabilization, amplified through acceleration and diversification, and terminated if some saturation occurs. We can conclude, then, that desistance is principally supported by the mechanism of stabilization. Criminal activity must endure before it will be terminated.

In short, among subjects whose involvement in crime is significant, the termination of illicit activities would be preceded by a point of saturation. Desistance occurs after a period of active offending and escalation that leads to a peak of criminal activity. It does not happen suddenly, but is fairly gradual, as if the mechanism of desistance meant a winding down little by little. It is a change that mainly involves deceleration and culmination at a given level of gravity, but for a limited number of offenders it involves also specialization. It is preceded by a lessening of frequency, a maintained level of gravity, and reduction in variety. The entire process of the development of persistent offending is one of progression and regression, not necessarily constant, but with invariable linking.

Criminal Activity–A Process

In view of the foregoing, we can now say that three processes are at the heart of all continuous criminal activity–activation, escalation, and desistance. The complementarity of these forms a veritable process of development, whose components are so closely connected that it is possible to say that the earlier criminal activity begins the greater the chance that it will persist, diversify, and accelerate. Once it is well entrenched, it tends to spread and escalate into a series of crimes of various levels of gravity. This process leads to a peak when saturation is reached; this is a sign of imminent desistance. The deescalation that follows is reinforced by a reduction of frequency, a ceiling with regard to gravity, and a decrease in variety.

This is a brief summary of the entire process. The data we have presented confirms that it is a real and consistent process. It is still necessary, before coming to any firm conclusion, to replicate the same analytic procedure, or one that is even more rigorous, to guarantee the validity of our observations.

Our results confirm the importance and pertinence of the longitudinal approach. We wanted to go beyond the usual analyses in criminology–those limited to a description of the synthetic parameters of criminal activity (frequency, gravity, variety, and so on) and those that consider the frontiers of its development (duration, age at onset, and termination). We wanted to study its dynamic development in depth. This approach shows that if the ideas and customary methods of sociology are supplemented by those of psychology, it is possible to push back the frontiers of criminological knowledge much further. It is legitimate to recognize, as Gottfredson and Hirschi (1987, 1988) did, that those who use the longitudinal approach have not always known how to profit from the kind of data at their disposal. Too often they have been content to apply the same concepts and the same procedures as those who use the transverse. We trust that this chapter has demonstrated that the longitudinal approach is a coherent and appropriate way of studying the development of criminal activity.

6
Offending Patterns

The present chapter further pursues the study of criminal behavior using a different type of data. What we deal with in this chapter is what we referred to earlier as the level of analyses of criminal activity–offending patterns. Having first studied the methods used in perpetrating crimes, applied descriptive and evolutive parameters to examine the illicit activity, and finally reconstituted the course of its development, we are now at a more abstract level, the identification of behavior patterns. Our analysis starts with the construction of a typology of the various patterns of criminal activities observed, taking into account the two major mechanisms that govern their evolution, activation, and escalation. In this way we get an overall picture of the spectrum of configurations.

The configurations of illicit activities will be found by again bringing into play our two major criteria of differentiation, the first distinguishing between reported delinquency and official delinquency and the second between adolescents and delinquents. The typology will be based on diverse components of the reported delinquency of the adolescents. It will then be carefully assessed against the reported delinquency of the delinquents. Finally, after verifying its internal consistency, we will validate it by comparing it with official delinquency. This last step will enable us to complete the study of what might be considered the key dependent variable in criminology, which has been our main preoccupation throughout this book.

Perspectives

Before working out a typology of criminal activity, and in keeping with the continuation of our preceding analyses based on descriptive, evolutive, and developmental perspectives, we wish to discuss two questions that support this step. Since a typology cannot be constructed without referring to a specific concept, let us explain why we chose that of offending patterns rather than career, which is the more current terminology used in criminology today. Since classification has been a strongly criticized approach in criminology, we must also look at other pertinent studies to find a specific procedure for the construction of our typology.

Pattern of Offending Instead of Criminal Career

Criminological history teaches that every 10 years or so a certain theoretical and practical model becomes dominant. Before the Second World War it was ecology and community development. During the 1950s it was criminal personality and treatment. Next it was delinquent subcultures and prevention programs based on opportunities. Soon after, during the 1970s, social control took priority while at the same time the theory of stigmatization suggested nonintervention. Finally, the 1980s will no doubt be identified with the idea of criminal career and selective incapacitation. Although it is not new, the idea of the criminal career has acquired a certain notoriety over the past few years.

As early as 1917, Von Mayr, the German criminologist, was already using the term criminal career; Shaw (1931) and Sutherland (1937) gave it a certain vogue on the basis of autobiographies of criminals; 30 years later, typologies on delinquent roles came to the fore (Clinard & Quinney, 1967; Gibbons, 1965; and others). It was again used in the longitudinal study by Wolfgang et al. (1972), which showed that a small minority of criminals were responsible for most crimes. It was not until the report of the American National Academy of Sciences (Blumstein et al., 1986) that the criminal career was recognized as an essential concept of criminology. It has even become fashionable, as evidenced in the numerous articles that have used the term recently and in the many discussions it has generated.

We have abstained from using the term criminal career for two reasons: (a) Its use helps to maintain a confusion that is already too general in the social sciences, and (b) its use increases the methodological ambiguities that we have already criticized. To apply the term to any prolonged criminal activity seemed an unjustified, excessive extrapolation.

It is an unjustified extrapolation because a career, in the strict meaning of the term given by the sociology of occupations, has a much broader application than simply the activity of working. Becker (1970) defined a career as sequential adjustments to the system of institutions and formal and informal organizations in which a person's work is accomplished when the person occupies a post. Criminal activities, however, are far from being the same as having a job; they do not involve the investment of as much time and continuity as an occupation, and our data on their duration, frequency, and so on show that these activities are intermittent, even among the most active criminals. Even by a stretch of the imagination the career concept is inappropriate, since it implies the presence of regular mechanisms of adjustment to formal and informal organizations. To speak of a criminal career there must be formal and informal supports consistently underlying any activities directly or indirectly connected with the commission of crimes. If such supports existed, and if one were to undertake the task of showing them, which neither Blumstein et al. (1986) nor most recent studies do, it would then perhaps be possible to use the concept of a criminal career.

It is exactly this, interestingly enough, that specialists in the criminal role, such as Clinard and Quinney (1967), Gibbons (1965), Lemert (1972), and Schur

(1971), have been trying to do a few years ago. In speaking of a criminal career or type of career, however, they include so many elements, such as behavior, relations with official institutions (social reaction, etc.), ties with unofficial organizations (the crime world, etc.), explanatory factors (peers, family, etc.), and even personal characteristics (attitudes, self-image, etc.), that, as Sparks, Greer, and Manning (1982) pointed out, the concept becomes a sort of ragbag of criminological information and goes far beyond the question of the formal and informal adjustments that mark the evolution of someone in a given occupation or even in his or her role as worker.

Some authors have wanted to avoid accepting criminal activities as a job as well as encompassing too many aspects of a person's lifestyle. Dunford and Elliott (1984) and Elliott, Dunford, and Huizinga (1987) suggested a typology of criminal activity limited to delinquency reported over a certain number of years. This, in fact, is in line with the behavior profiles we would like to establish, but these authors used the career concept without any justification, unless it is a question of current practice. Smith et al. (1984), on the other hand, did not go along with the career concept and suggested using career line to metaphorically refer to behavior profiles. To avoid such acrobatics, we have chosen the term *offending patterns*.

There is another reason that prompts us to avoid the career concept. We believe that the methodological rule of levels of interpretation and analysis is fundamental in any criminological approach. This rule means that the three levels of interpretation—criminality, criminal, and crime—call for methodologies, theories, and specific constructs adapted to each level. We avoid the career idea because it fosters confusion between two levels of interpretation, the crime and the criminal. For example, Blumstein et al. (1986) defined the criminal career as the sequence of crimes committed by an offender. It follows that everyone who commits more than a few crimes is a career criminal, since each satisfies the criterion of crime sequence. In our opinion, this problem as such is a sufficient methodological reason to avoid the concept, particularly since our book deals with only one level of interpretation, crime itself.

This concept further is of limited use in criminology. It does not touch on all aspects of delinquency, only repetitive delinquency. It does not consider occasional offending, even though such offending constitutes the major part of criminal activity among the general population. It is therefore a difficult concept to integrate in criminological theories because, for the most part, they apply to all aspects of offending. Finally, as Gottfredson and Hirschi (1986) pointed out, it is a concept that offers few practical benefits, since the selective incapacitation policy that it engenders is contrary to ideas of "just deserts" and its applicability is uncertain.

In view of all these methodological and conceptual problems, the term offending patterns seems most appropriate. We shall try, then, with the aid of typologies, to discover the different patterns of criminal activity. This variable will enable us to typify the data derived from our descriptive and developmental parameters and incorporated in the three mechanisms responsible for the development of illicit behavior.

A Typological Approach

Chapters 3, 4, and 5 undertook an analytical type of scientific approach, using descriptive (participation, frequency, etc.) and developmental (duration, starting age, etc.) parameters. When these parameters were combined by two or more, the mechanisms for the development of illicit activity became clear and could be described in precise terms. Following this analytical phase, we still have to come to grips with a large number of criminal activities. The question is, How are we to get beyond the analysis level and arrive at a higher level of understanding and at a synthesis? A synthesis is necessary in order to transform the data on the various components of criminal activity into a single dimension. It means constructing what Stinchcombe (1987) called a concept type, the result of the convergence of different variables that make up the essential aspect of criminal activity.

There are two ways of doing this. One method is to construct this synthetic variable mathematically by taking into account all the measures used in the preceding chapters; to this end, scaling techniques are usual in criminology such as factorial analysis (see the surveys of Hindelang et al., 1981; Klein, 1984; Loeber & Waller, 1988), or the centroid variance analysis (Smith et al., 1984). These techniques afford a relatively effective way of constructing a variable of this kind, but they tend to obscure the substantive significance of the construct obtained (for a review of the results and criticisms of this strategy in criminology, see Brennan, 1987). Another method is to construct a theoretical-empirical typology as stipulated by Hempel (1952) or Stinchcombe (1987), that is, not a classification of a number of logically possible combinations, such as that of Chaiken and Chaiken (1984), but a typology that specifies the manner in which the variables interact. The most recent examples of the use of this method can be found in Fréchette and Le Blanc (1980, 1987) or in Dunford and Elliott (1984) (for a review of the result and criticisms of this method, see Brennan, 1987, once again).

We have chosen this second strategy for three reasons. First, it is in the interest of consistency with the method used for the analysis of the development of criminal activity; next because we give absolute priority to the theoretical significance of the variables we are constructing; and finally because we believe that a construct of this kind is technically feasible considering the concept of criminal activity that we have advanced so far. Following the principle proposed by Duncan (1984), by analogy with the natural sciences, namely, the need to identify the basic elements and construct variables by combining the basic elements, we succeeded in finding three mechanisms and six submechanisms instrumental in the development of illicit activity. It is in conformity with this finding that a typological approach, as described above, is necessary in order to construct the profiles of criminal activities.

Consistency is no doubt important here, but it is not enough to justify the choice of a typological strategy. Brennan (1987) found that this type of approach has three failings—oversimplification, measures that are weak, and definitions of concepts that are imprecise. The first risk brings a dangerous disregard for reality. We believe we have avoided this by including a large number of variables to describe all aspects of illicit activity—around 20, in fact, counting the descriptive and evolutive parameters and mechanisms. As for the definitions of concepts, to avoid their vagueness, we tried to work them out carefully on the basis of numerous facts. Finally, an effort was made to take the operationalization as far as possible, as has been shown in Tables 1.2 and 1.3. In short, the bases of our typological approach appear sufficiently solid to be considered logically and technically sound and to meet the most demanding scientific criteria.

The final reason why we opted for a strategy of this type is the prime importance we accord to theory as the guide for any empirical approach. According to the Albany Conference (1987) and the latest issue of *Criminology*, it seems that this orientation is becoming more and more prevalent in criminology. It is a matter of submitting technical and analytical refinements to theoretical reflection, something the most eminent methodologists have always recommended (Blalock, 1970). The combination of variables in the construction of a typology, then, should be based on conceptual thinking that takes advantage of existing empirical knowledge. We might point out, as an illustration, that there are numerous terms in criminology that refer to patterns of offending, such as occasional delinquency, persistent delinquency, chronic delinquency, late delinquency, and so on, and these should inspire the construction of our offending patterns, on the one hand, and be revalidated by our construction of a typology, on the other. A theoretical-empirical strategy makes it possible to meet this condition, one that we feel is indispensable to the advancement of criminology.

Construction of a Typology of Criminal Activity

Brennan (1987) proposes that a typology be constructed taking into account four elements: choice of content domain, construction of the classification, internal validation, and external validation. Our content domain was limited to criminal activity as specified by the descriptive and evolutive parameters and mechanisms of development that we explained previously. With such a basis, we feel that conceptual clarity, consistency, and pertinence of the components have been ensured, as recommended by Brennan (1987). However, some of our variables are redundant, such as gravity, which is almost entirely correlated with frequency, or are of limited scope, such as those concerning desistance, since the data do not go beyond the end of the 20s. Consequently, these variables will not constitute part of our typology.

Since the method of construction will be described later on, we will limit ourselves here to the last two requirements, internal and external validation. Brennan (1987) set forth four types of criteria for internal validation: (a) homogeneity of classes, (b) coverage of the sample, (c) reliability and consistency, and (d) information loss and distortion. The question of homogeneity of the pattern is the most difficult when classifying variables are used, since their limited scope threatens to produce artificial divisions. To limit this disadvantage, the cutoff points were given particular attention and were chosen according to marked discontinuities in frequency distributions. In this way all the offenders were included in very contrasting groups, which limited the danger of overlap and confusion. As to the need for covering the entire class of infractions, it was accomplished in the following way: With the sample of adolescents, we constructed a general typology including a limited number of common types; with the sample of delinquents, these types were refined thanks to the identification of more specific patterns, making it possible to give greater variety to the basic parameters.

The last stage in the construction of a typology, according to Brennan (1987), is its predictive validation. This was done with the help of other variables that normally discriminate between the diverse manifestations of criminal activity. Considering our original decision to limit ourselves to this aspect of delinquency we had two options – to use the measure of official delinquency or other measures of deviance. Hindelang et al. (1981) had shown in their study on validation procedures that the validity of self-reported delinquency had proved excellent according to the criteria usually used in the social sciences. For this reason, and also in trying to avoid the difficulties involved in distinguishing intermediary styles of career, which Elliott et al. (1987) met when they validated their typology, we proceeded differently. We first constructed a typology of hidden delinquency and then a typology of reported delinquency based on the same principles; we then cross-tabulated the two. Finding no difference in degree between reported delinquency and official delinquency would mean that the two classifications of subjects tend to be isomorphic.

Offending Patterns Among the General Population

A study of offending patterns characteristic of the population in general was carried out on our sample of adolescents, who represented the total male population of Montreal between the ages of 12 and 16 at the time of recruitment. Since this was a random sample, it is possible to generalize the conclusions to the entire adolescent population of that metropolitan region.

The youngsters answered a self-administered questionnaire on hidden delinquency, which was repeated after an interval of 2 years. On each occasion, the illicit activities of the previous year were reported. These two sets of data can reasonably be considered two independent samples. It would no doubt have been preferable theoretically to have data on more than 1 year, and even on the entire period from adolescence to youth. However, from our point of view, Dunford and Elliott's study (1984) on a national sample of American youths shows that data stretching over more than 2 years' time are of little use because they use that criterion as a cutting point to construct their variable. The facts reported by these

TABLE 6.1. Degree of criminal activity (%*) at time 1 (first interview) and time 2 (second interview after 2-year interval) for adolescent sample.

Time 1:	Time 2: Cutoff points				
Cutoff points†	0	1, 2	3–9	10–24	Total
0	14 (3.1)	17 (3.7)	8 (1.8)	1 (0.2)	40 (8.8)
1, 2, 3	22 (4.8)	54 (11.8)	50 (11)	9 (2)	135 (29.6)
4–10	11 (2.4)	64 (14)	128 (28.1)	26 (5.7)	229 (50.2)
11–21	1 (0.2)	10 (2.2)	17 (3.7)	24 (5.3)	52 (11.4)
Total	48 (10.5)	145 (31.8)	203 (44.5)	60 (13.2)	456 (100)

*All percentages calculated on the total sample.
† Number of crimes.

authors establish that a very small number of subjects are active for more than 2 years. Dunford and Elliott constructed their typology of delinquent careers from the illicit activities reported over only 2 years, even if they had five data collections concerning the same subjects. It must be pointed out, however, that with our sample of wards of the court it is possible to consider all the self-reported delinquency as occurring on a continuous basis, because the base rate is sufficiently high for the illicit activity as a whole, annually and by types of infraction.

To construct a typology that described offending patterns, we again made use of the procedure employed in a first attempt (Fréchette & Le Blanc, 1980, 1987), but used a refined and corrected version based on the results reported in the preceding chapters. The variable that described persistence was constructed with the aid of what Davis (1963) called a turnover table, the cross-tabulation of the results at $time_1$ by the results at $time_2$. The basic variables were the degree of criminal activity at the time of each data collection, assessed with the aid of answers to 28 questions on reported delinquency. The delinquency score is calculated in the following way: Since the categories of response were ordinal (never, once or twice, several times, often), and considering that the base rates are very low for each infraction among the general population, we dichotomized each type of behavior according to presence-absence and then summed up the results. The score of variety stretches from 0 to 28. This type of measurement is strongly correlated with frequency and other components of self-reported delinquency. Hindelang et al. (1981) showed that this is the most valid and most efficient variable among the many they have tried.

Table 6.1 was constructed by cross-tabulating the results obtained with this variable during $time_1$ with those obtained during $time_2$. As just mentioned, we counted on the presence of large differences in frequencies to determine the cutoff points. Because of this careful examination of the distribution of frequencies it appeared preferable not to use the same cutoff points at $time_1$ and $time_2$. In the first case the assembled values are 0 and then 1, 2, or 3; next 4 to 10; and 11 to 21; in the second case they are 0, 1, or 2; then 3 to 9; and from 10 to 24. For all practical purposes, the four categories in the table represent respectively the absence of criminal activity and a level that is a low, average, or high rate of activity. This difference in the cutoff points is due to the fact that the degree of delinquency is higher at $time_1$ than at $time_2$, the medians being respectively 4.55 and 3.25, and also to the fact that the greatest differences in frequencies appear at different places. It is interesting to note that the cutoff points used find their equivalents in other studies, such as the typology of Dunford and Elliott (1984) where, in a first category, the absence of illicit activity and little activity are combined. As for the other categories that resemble ours, the first is placed at 3 and the second goes from 4 to 11.

A comparison between the illicit activity before and after a 2-year interval gives us two symmetrical distributions with a gamma of .51. Analysis of Table 6.1 shows that there are 14 subjects (3.1%) without any offense at time 1 or time 2. Table 6.1 also shows that there are seven different ways of becoming involved in crime:

1. Some activities only at time 1 (6%)
2. Some offenses only at time 2 (6%)
3. A small amount of crimes at time 1 and time 2 (11.8%)
4. A medium amount of offenses at both times (28%)
5. A regression of illicit activity toward a medium or low level (20%)
6. A progression in crime toward a medium or high level (19%)
7. Activity becoming stabilized at a high level of frequency (5.3%)

These seven patterns of offending are reduced to six in Table 6.2 by adding together categories (1) and (2).

Taking these six patterns of criminal activity into account, two basic components come into play, persistence and intensity. To include another major component, escalation, we cross-tabulated these six types with gravity, graded according to the absence or presence only once at $time_1$ or $time_2$ or presence at $time_1$ and $time_2$ of four of the most serious crimes included in our questionnaire: burglary, motor vehicle theft, fighting using a weapon, and theft of more than $50.00 (1974 value). Gamma is .45 between intensity and gravity of the acts. Examination of Table 6.2 shows a typology comprising six categories, the first category being characterized by absence of illicit activity and containing 3% of the subjects and the five remaining categories representing the different offending patterns.

First there is *occasional* illicit activity, a matter of several crimes (one, two, or three), rarely serious, committed once; 13% of the subjects fall into this category. Then there is *intermittent* offending for 32% of the sample, few crimes occurring at different times, generally during both the first and second half of adolescence; also included in this offending pattern is little criminal activity at $time_1$ and $time_2$

TABLE 6.2. Continuous degree of criminal activity by presence of serious offenses: Adolescent sample (%).

Degree of criminal activity	Number of subjects committing serious offenses: 0	Time 1 or 2	Time 1 & 2	Total
0	14[a] 3.1			14 3.1
1	54[b] 11.8	6 1.3		60 13
2	52[c] 11.4	2 0.4		54 11.8
3	69 15.1	22 4.8		91 20
4	107[d] 23.5	16[f] 3.5	5[f] 1.1	128 28.1
5	64[e] 14	19 4.2	2 0.4	85 18.6
6	4 0.9	9 2	11 2.4	24 5.3
Total	364 79.8	74 16.2	18 3.9	456 100

[a] No offending.
[b] Occasional offending.
[c] Intermittent offending.
[d] Minor continuous offending.
[e] Major continuous offending.
[f] Serious persistent offending.

as well as regressive activity from one period to the other. It should be noted that out of the 145 subjects whose delinquency is serious and occasional only 16% (24 subjects) are in this category.

The last three offending patterns show criminal activity that is persistent in quantity and duration but that includes serious crimes only in the last case. Thus, 24% of the subjects show a stable and medium activity or *minor continuous*, which means that they produced between 3 and 10 illicit acts during the year preceding the data collection. There are 15% of adolescents who show a stable and abundant, or *major continuous* criminal activity, with more than 10 offenses at $time_1$ and $time_2$. Finally, 14% of the adolescents in our sample manifest stable illicit activity, sometimes of medium but more often of high intensity, which occurs regularly with serious crimes committed intermittently or continuously; this is *serious persistent* activity.

Before establishing the internal consistency and validity of this typology, it is interesting to compare the distribution obtained for the Montreal adolescents with that of Dunford and Elliott (1984) for a national sample of American adolescents. Their typology of career offenders was constructed with the frequency of the crimes grouped according to three categories (0 to 3, 4 to 11, and 12 and over), taking the gravity into account, the crimes of Uniform Crime Report

Part 1, and working with five waves of data. By combining these two variables, they defined five types: nonoffender, noncareer, nonserious career, serious career, and patterned serious career. The nonoffenders, who represented 49% of their sample, are our abstainers, our occasional delinquents, and our intermittent delinquents, representing 48% of our sample. It seems unfortunate that Dunford and Elliott put the abstainers and occasional delinquents together, particularly since they did not indicate the proportion each group represented. Their group of persistents represented 51% of their sample, whereas ours accounts for 52%; their noncareer group corresponds to our delinquents who show medium or very stable activity, 38% in our sample against 41% in theirs.

Certain differences between the two typologies merit some comments. The first, just mentioned, is due to the fact that Dunford and Elliott, being interested only in serious criminal careers, considered it unnecessary to distinguish between nonoffenders and the others. Furthermore, their criteria for persistence was more severe than ours, both in gravity (UCR Part 1) and in duration (5 years), which explains the slight overrepresentation we get of subjects whose illicit activity is abundant, stable, and serious, with 14% to their 10%. By being still more exacting and using the criterion of the serious career they found 2.5% of their subjects involved; our comparable proportion is 2.4%, according to Table 6.2. As for the respective merits of the two typologies, it must be remembered that Dunford and Elliott's typology is more exacting than ours in its definition of serious delinquency, whereas ours focuses more on all models of criminal conduct. As to the difference in degree, this is due to the higher level of crime in the United States, as we have had occasion to establish earlier on.

In short, taking stock of the data given above, some derived from a previous study (Fréchette & Le Blanc, 1980), and some from Dunford and Elliott (1984), we can say that about 5% of adolescents abstain from all illicit activity, that 45% engage in occasional or intermittent criminal activity, and that the remaining 50% are involved in persistent activity, not serious for about 40%. Of the other 10%, 2% to 3% can be considered the perpetrators of a particularly abundant, constant, and serious criminal activity. There are thus five basic offending patterns: occasional, intermittent, minor continuous, major continuous, and serious persistent.

Having constructed this typology of offending patterns, the question arises as to its internal consistency and its validity. Table 6.3 affords some data that provide an answer. If we rely on the diverse types of reported delinquency (which are indirectly included in the construction of the typology, such as petty theft, major theft, aggression, vandalism, and a variety of these), we can conclude that the consistency of the variable constructed is satisfactory. On the one hand, the proportion participation progresses evenly with the escalation of the offending patterns and the chi squares are statistically significant to $p \leq .0001$. On the other hand, the medians increase as well and the analyses of variance are similarly statistically significant to $p \leq .0001$. Elliott et al. (1987), incidentally, reported similar results.

As to validity, the typology can be evaluated in three ways: with the aid of different measures of delinquency and self-reported deviance; by using official delinquency as a criterion; or by making use of social, psychosocial, or psychological variables. Since we are limited in this book to the study of criminal activity, we shall focus on the first two ways of establishing validity. However, we might mention that each offending pattern corresponds to a specific social, psychosocial, and psychological profile (see Dunford & Elliott, 1984; Elliott et al., 1987; Fréchette & Le Blanc, 1980, 1987).

According to Table 6.3, other measures, such as degree of illicit drug consumption, rebellion at school or against the family, and general delinquency (which includes not only criminal acts but other infractions as well, of the Traffic Code, for example) distinguish clearly between the offending patterns, as much with the chi squares as with the analyses of variance. With regard to official delinquency, the results are not as convincing, however. In fact, the frequency of the convictions and their variety agree with the offending patterns, but the differences are not statistically significant with the other indices of official delinquency. We find that Elliott et al. (1987) obtained results that agree with the frequency of arrest.

The last way of verifying the validity of this typology based on reported delinquency consists of constructing an equivalent typology with the convictions and in verifying the agreement between the two. Using the frequency of convictions (grouped as follow: 0, 1, and 2 to represent occasional and intermittent activity; 3 and more to characterize persistent activity) and the gravity of the crimes (no crimes with violence, one or several crimes with violence), it was possible to reconstitute the same sequence of patterns. However, considering that only 9% of the sample of adolescents had been convicted between the ages of 7 and the mid-20s, it seemed more appropriate to consider only the three principal choices: abstinence, occasional activity, and continuous activity, which gave us more substantial frequencies. Table 6.4 presents the cross-tabulation of typologies of the reported illicit activity and official delinquency. The gamma is .48 between the two and the chi square is statistically significant to $p \leq .01$. Persistent delinquent activity such as reported by the subject himself is confirmed by numerous convictions; medium activity is followed by a limited number of convictions. Elliott et al. (1987) reported similar associations between their typologies of official and reported criminal careers.

This agreement between the offending patterns, evaluated on the basis of reported and official delinquency, is highly significant, particularly in view of the differences previously noted and which have criminologists constantly debating these two ways of studying criminal activity. The agreement should be interpreted as solid proof of the existence of specific ways of acting out. There are two basic methods of expressing delinquency, the first by occasional offending and the second by persistent illicit activity, with possibly other secondary methods. Occasional activity takes two forms, one restricted to a single delinquent act, in general of little gravity, occurring during adolescence or possibly at the beginning of adulthood, the other involving intermittent activity, that is several crimes of

TABLE 6.3. Internal consistency and validation of offending patterns: Adolescent sample.

	None	Occasional	Intermittent	Minor continuous	Major continuous	Serious persistent	$p \leq$
Self-reported							
Minor theft							
Presence	36.7	31.8	64.8	84.1	73.5	93.5	.0001
Number*	1.87	1.14	1.68	2.55	2.44	4	.001
Major theft							
Presence	0	11.4	5.5	0	0	58.1	.0001
Number	0	1	1	0	0	1.32	.05
Vandalism							
Presence	10	6.8	24.1	46.7	38.2	66.1	.0001
Number	2	0	1.2	1.36	1.37	2.46	.001
Aggression							
Presence	26.7	31.8	64.8	73.8	76.5	91.9	.0001
Number	1.17	1.14	1.54	1.84	1.87	3.56	.001
Variety of crimes							
Presence	46.7	59.1	82.8	99.1	97.1	100	.0001
Number	1.28	1.22	1.85	2.08	1.91	3.17	.001
Use of drugs							
Presence	23.3	18.2	33.8	57	38.2	59.7	.0001
Number	2.25	1.3	2	1.58	187	2.81	.05

Rebellion							
Presence	83.3	93.2	97.9	100	100	100	.0001
Number	2.42	2.85	5.1	6.25	5.77	7.3	.001
General delinquency							
Number	5.07	179	6.58	11.22	7.39	10.07	.001
Official							
Frequency							
Presence	3.3	2.3	6.2	7.5	8.8	25.8	.0001
Number	7	27	2	2	2.17	2.16	.001
Precocity							
Number	21	17	18.25	17	15.5	20.16	
Variety							
Number	4.5	0	1.25	1.4	1.33	1.23	.05
Gravity							
Number	75.8	9.6	10.27	6.4	10.14	13.21	
Violence							
Presence	0	0	1.4	1.9	0	3.2	
Number	0	2	5	1	0	1	
Duration							
Number	2	8	1.87	2	1.83	2.05	.01

*Median number of crimes.

TABLE 6.4. Self-reported and official offending patterns (%) for adolescent sample.

Self-reported	Official: None	Occasional	Continuous	Total
None	14	0	0	14
H	(100)			(3.1)
V	(7)			
Occasional	194	6	5	205
H	(94.6)	(3.2)	(2.4)	(44.9)
V	(50.1)	(23.1)	(33.4)	
Continuous	161	9	5	175
H	(92)	(5.1)	(2.9)	(38.4)
V	(38.8)	(34.6)	(33.3)	
Serious	46	11	5	62
H	(74.2)	(17.7)	(8.1)	(13.6)
V	(11.1)	(42.3)	(33.3)	
Total	415	26	15	456
	(91)	(5.7)	(3.3)	(100)

Gamma = .48; chi square: 27.21, df = 6, $p \leq .001$.
H: percentages are calculated on the row total.
V: percentages are calculated on the column total.

little gravity over a relatively short period or a period of several years. In the case of persistent criminal activity, it, too, can take several forms in terms of extent and gravity. Minor continuous activity refers to the commission of a medium number of crimes (between 3 and 10) over a period of several years but without the use of violence against anyone. Major continuous activity refers to an appreciably greater number of crimes (10 and more) over a period of several years, again without the use of violence. Finally, serious persistent activity goes beyond other offending patterns in quantity, duration, and gravity.

Our study has led to two conclusions. First, it is possible to construct a general typology of offending patterns that is consistent and valid, while limiting consideration to criminal activity alone. Second, this general typology has proven to be broadly applicable, since the same categories emerge in two cultural contexts, in Quebec and the United States.

Offending Patterns in a Delinquent Sample

A typology of persistent activity can be approached in two ways. The first is to use the measures of continuity, frequency, and violence to create more numerous and better differentiated patterns of offending. The second is to call upon our knowledge of the mechanisms underlying the development of the illicit activity, particularly activation and escalation. In the following pages we shall turn these two options to good account by constructing a typology with each of them, first using the indices of development and then those of intensity. Finally, we propose a classification that integrates both of these aspects.

Developmental Offending Patterns

To round out the developmental perspective, we make use of two key elements in the process of activation and escalation, the degree of precocity and the evolution by stages.

Precocity is included because it is a variable that precedes frequency, duration, and variety and because it has emerged very clearly as a sign of future acceleration, diversification, and above all, stabilization. An analysis of the distribution of cases on precocity, as well as their correlation with frequency, duration, and variety, shows that three periods can be distinguished: childhood, before the age of 11; the beginning of adolescence, between childhood and the middle of adolescence (age 15½); and the period between mid-adolescence and adulthood. It has become clear that it is in the first of these periods that the effect of activation (the frequency of the illicit activity being the most important) is felt the most, with the second period not far behind. For these reasons precocity was chosen as the first dimension of our typological analysis of the criminal activity of delinquents.

The development by stages is the second focal point of this typology. Choice of this aspect is due to the major observation made during our analyses, that the dynamics of criminal activity conforms to a hierarchic model of evolution. Delinquents, however, do not all start at the same stage and do not necessarily go through all the stages. We noted four types of evolution. First we have subjects whose crimes are limited to what is typical of one stage; most often it is the stage of explosion and then the stage of conflagration, in proportions of about three fifths and one third of these subjects, respectively. The crimes here are relatively serious, perhaps burglary for the first stage and automobile theft for the second, but they are not abundant and do not include a great variety. Second we have subjects who go through two stages; the central point is most often the stage of explosion, with burglary the main crime; most commonly subjects go through the stage of exploration (shoplifting and vandalism) to the stage of explosion or from that stage on to conflagration. Third are those who go through three stages; usually exploration, explosion, and conflagration. Finally, some subjects go through four stages or more (more than four is exceptional).

These two elements, precocity and evolution by stages, can obviously be applied only to recurring delinquency (in recent works, generally more than three infractions), which can therefore be qualified as persistent. It must be remembered that the sample of delinquents shows a platikurtic distribution of reported crimes, different from the asymmetrical distribution in the case of adolescents. Consequently, the subjects with occasional (one crime) or intermittent (several crimes) criminal activity are few, only 6% of the sample. They can be compared with the group of most serious offenders in the adolescent sample, those we refer to as having a continuous type of offending pattern.

TABLE 6.5. Typology of persistent delinquency: Precocity by stages (%), delinquent sample (N = 190)

Precocity	Number of stages 1	2	3	4 or 5	Total
Before age 11	1[a] 0.5	14 7.4	41[b] 21.6	25 13.1	81 42.6
11–14	8[c] 4.2	33[d] 17.4	28[e] 14.7	11 5.8	80 42.1
15 up	9 4.7	13 6.8	4 2.1	3 1.6	29 15.3
Total	18 9.5	60 31.6	73 38.4	39 20.6	190 100

Chi square = 44.71, df = 6, p = .0001; gamma = −.57.
[a] Early mildly aggravated offending.
[b] Early aggravated offending.
[c] Late nonaggravated offending.
[d] Late mildly aggravated offending.
[e] Late aggravated offending.

Table 6.5 cross-tabulates precocity in relation to the various stages. We must point out that we used the 196 delinquent subjects who were re-interviewed in their mid-20s and who reported all the criminal acts they committed up to that point; furthermore, the results proved the same when we used subjects who were interrogated twice during their adolescence (396 subjects) or all subjects interrogated once (470 subjects). Here we are not presenting the last two. There is lack of information concerning them, since all were not reinterviewed on reaching adulthood. We consider however the group of 196 to constitute a representative sample of all delinquents (see chap. 1).

First, Table 6.5 shows that the two periods when criminal activity begins—childhood and the first half of adolescence—applies to about 42% each of the subjects, while the group that emerges during the second half of adolescence or at adulthood includes only 15% of subjects. Moreover, it can be seen that 38% of the subjects go through three stages, 32% go through two, and 21% go through four or five, whereas only 10% are active during one. The correlation between the two variables is very strong, the gamma being −.57 and the chi square (= 44.71, df = 6) is statistically significant (p = .0001). Thus, the more precocious the criminal activity, the more stages of criminalization the offender will go through.

Looking further on, we find five persistent offending patterns classified in order of their intensity. The *late nonaggravated* pattern accounts for 9% of delinquents; criminal activity begins during the first half of adolescence or after midadolescence and consists of crimes typical of only one stage, generally explosion or conflagration, with burglary or motor vehicle theft. The *early mildly aggravated* pattern takes on 8% of delinquents; they begin their activities before the age of 11 and commit crimes typical of two stages, exploration (shoplifting, vandalism) or conflagration (motor vehicle theft, armed robbery, etc.). The *late mildly aggravated* pattern involves 24% of delinquents; two thirds begin their activities between ages 11 and 14 and others after the age of 15; their crimes cover two stages in much the same order as the preceding type.

These first three offending patterns are minor expressions of recurrent illicit activity. The following two are major expressions of this type of activity. About two thirds of delinquents go through three stages and the remaining third go through four stages or more. The most frequent stages are exploration, explosion, and conflagration, or two of these plus outburst. What differentiates the two, then, is the age at which criminal activity starts: 24% of delinquents fall into the *late aggravated* offending pattern and 35% are in the *early aggravated* offending pattern.

This complementary typology of offending patterns provides important configurations that mark the development of criminal activity, as described in the previous chapter. Its internal consistency and validity can be verified by referring to other parameters of illicit activity. As shown in Table 6.6, in terms of internal consistency the results are clear when we refer to the six measures of self-reported delinquency—frequency, precocity, gravity, violence, variety, and duration. The medians increase with the rise in intensity of the persistent criminal activity, and the analyses of variance are statistically significant to at least $p = 0.05$ and generally to $p < .001$ for the sample of 196 subjects as well as the entire sample. The quality of the classification is thus confirmed.

In exactly the same way, with the same data on self-reported and official delinquency, it is possible to come to an identical conclusion regarding validity. In both cases it is clear that with frequency, variety, gravity, and duration the medians vary from one pattern to another, very much as might be expected, but in terms of precocity and violence the results seem to be less convincing (which might be explained by certain factors mentioned previously, in particular the wide use of diversion in our justice system).

Intensity of Offending Patterns

Another way of constructing a typology of recurrent or persistent delinquency is by referring to the characteristics of the illicit activity. The patterns would be drawn according to the frequency of the infractions and the frequency of violent crimes, as was done with the typology built for the general population or the one of Dunford and Elliott (1984). Analysis of the distributions of frequency for these two variables makes it possible to grade them as follows: for frequency, the levels 0 to 20, 21 to 85, 86 to 999, and 1,000 and over; and for crimes of violence levels of 0, 1, 2 and 3, and 4 and over. Table 6.7 presents cross-tabulations of these two variables. Six types of persistent criminal activity emerge, three of them with no crimes of violence. First is the pattern with low frequency (13% of the subjects), next with medium frequency (11% of the subjects), and last with high frequency (14% of the delinquents). Another two include crimes of violence, either occasional or intermittent, the first showing low or medium frequency (17% of the subjects) and the second high frequency (17% of the delinquents). Finally, a

TABLE 6.6. Internal consistency and validation of the developmental persistent offending patterns: Delinquent sample (medians, analysis of variance).

	Pattern						
	Late nonaggravated	Late mild aggravation	Early mild aggravation	Late with aggravation	Early with aggravation	$p \leq (n = 190)$	$p \leq (n = 470)$
Self-reported							
Frequency	6	48.5	20.25	80	86.5	.001	.001
Precocity	14.63	7.75	13.19	12.61	8.13	.001	.001
Gravity	30.09	90.22	67.41	612.06	590.24	.01	.001
Violence	1.5	5	2.75	7	9	.05	
Variety	1.35	3.29	3.32	6.5	6.75	.001	.001
Duration	5	8.12	3.44	7.37	11.2	.001	.001
Official							
Frequency	2.83	3.5	8	14.5	50.5	.05	.001
Precocity	14.5	14.87	14.86	14.85	14.05		.05
Variety	1.9	3	3.83	5.3	5.25	.01	.001
Gravity	16.54	25.61	69.48	101.02	100.4	.05	.001
Violence	1	1.5	3.12	3.25	3.25		.01
Duration	1.5	3.17	5.5	5.72	6.64	.01	.001

TABLE 6.7. Typology of persistent delinquency: Frequency of criminal activities and degree of violence (%).

Frequency*	Violence* 0	1	2–3	4+	Total
0–20	25[a] (13.1)	12[b] (6.3)	8 (4.2)	0	45 (23.6)
21–85	20[c] (10.5)	4 (2.1)	8 (4.2)	16[d] (8.4)	48 (25.1)
86–999	13[e] (6.8)	6[f] (3.1)	13 (6.8)	18 (9.4)	50 (26.2)
1,000 +	13 (6.8)	6 (3.1)	8 (4.2)	21 (11)	48 (25.1)
Total	71 (37.2)	28 (14.7)	37 (19.4)	55 (28.9)	191 (100)

Chi square = 32.96, df = 9, p = .001; gamma = .36.
*See text for description of grading.
[a] Low frequency of offending.
[b] Occasional with low or medium frequency.
[c] Medium frequency of offending.
[d] Serious with medium or high frequency.
[e] High frequency of offending.
[f] Occasional with high frequency.

pattern emerges in which the activities are marked by violence and are of medium or high frequency (29% of the subjects).

As shown in Table 6.8, this typology has internal consistency and validity as impressive as, if not more so, those of the developmental typology. This conclusion must be counterbalanced, however, by the fact that some of the measures serving to assess the internal consistency were used to construct the typology. The validity of this typology can be guaranteed in two ways. First, we can compare the patterns described above with those of Dunford and Elliott (1984). We find that our pattern combining a high level of frequency and high incidence of crimes of violence is exactly comparable to the serious career offenders category of these authors. Similarly, our patterns with low or high frequency and occasional violence are totally compatible with their nonserious career offenders category. Finally, our patterns of activity without violence but with a low, medium, or high degree of frequency are equivalent to that of what these authors called noncareer offenders. Our typology of intensity is more detailed than that of Dunford and Elliott but the generic types are equivalent.

Second, we can compare our classification with the one obtained by using the method of judges. Fréchette and Le Blanc (1980, 1987), for their sample of delinquents, used two judges (and an arbiter when it was necessary), who were to evaluate all data obtained from two interviews on self-reported delinquency during adolescence. The judges had to classify all subjects into one of six types, according to a number of criteria pertaining to continuity, quantity, gravity, and the nature of the crimes committed. These categories formed a graduated continuum of the intensity of the delinquency. Cross-tabulation of this judgmental classification and the statistical typology shows they are strongly associated, the

TABLE 6.8. Internal consistency and validation of the intensity of persistent offending patterns: Delinquent sample (medians, analysis of variance).

	Frequency			Low, medium frequency occasional violence	High frequency occasional violence	High frequency and violence	$p \leq$ (n = 190)	$p \leq$ (n = 470)
	Low	Medium	High					
Self-reported								
Frequency	6	38.5	122.5	13.83	172	86	.001	.001
Gravity	29.96	155.84	719.36	90.25	875.15	856.45	.001	.001
Precocity	13.5	10.5	11	13.07	9.8	10.19	.001	.001
Violence	0	0	0	1.75	2.77	37	.001	.001
Variety	2.06	3.63	3.83	4.17	6.33	7.66	.001	.001
Duration	4	6	9	4.25	9	10.37	.001	.001
Official								
Frequency	2.14	32	7	8	13.33	29.75	.001	.001
Precocity	13.87	14.25	15.22	14.75	14.56	14.22	.05	
Variety	1.9	2.87	3.12	4.08	5.22	7.22	.001	.001
Gravity	11.54	40.05	69.41	60.58	87.77	205.05	.001	.001
Violence	1	1.2	5	2.4	7.67	7.67	.001	.001
Duration	1.83	3.4	3.75	5	6.25	7.38	.001	.001

TABLE 6.9. Developmental and intensity typologies combined (%).

Developmental typology	Frequency: Low	Frequency: Medium	Frequency: High	Intensity typology: Low-medium frequency occasional violence	Intensity typology: High frequency occasional violence	Intensity typology: High frequency violence	Total
Late, non-aggravated	10[a] (5.3)	2 (1.1)	2 (1.1)	2[b] (1.1)	1 (0.5)	0	17 (8.9)
Late, mild aggravation	2 (1.1)	5 (2.6)	2 (1.1)	2 (1.1)	3 (1.6)	1 (0.5)	15 (7.9)
Early, mild aggravation	9 (4.7)	5 (2.6)	9 (4.7)	16 (8.4)	4 (2.1)	3 (1.6)	46 (24.2)
Late, with aggravation	1[c] (0.5)	3 (1.6)	3 (1.6)	8[d] (4.2)	14 (7.4)	17 (8.9)	46 (24.2)
Early, with aggravation	2 (1.1)	5 (2.6)	10 (5.3)	6[e] (3.2)	19 (10)	24 (12.6)	66 (34.7)
Total	24 (12.6)	20 (10.5)	26 13.7	34 (17.9)	41 (21.6)	45 (23.7)	190 (100)

Chi square = 89.9; df = 20, p = .0001; gamma = .49.
[a] Persistent minor.
[b] Persistent limited gravity.
[c] Persistent major.
[d] Late serious persistent.
[e] Early serious persistent.

chi square (= 111.34, df = 25) (p = .001) and the gamma .48. Furthermore, we note that the association with the first typology we constructed, the developmental typology, is slightly less strong (X^2 = 62.41, df = 20, p = .001; gamma = .32).

In view of these two conclusions, the validity of the typology of intensity can be considered satisfactorily established. Let us now see its exact association with the developmental typology and try to construct an offending pattern that combines both of these approaches.

Combined Offending Patterns

Comparison of the developmental and intensity typologies in Table 6.9 shows that they are associated. The chi square is statistically significant (X^2 = 89.9, df = 20, p = .0001) and the gamma is .49. Considering these results and those concerning the internal consistency and validity of each, the question is whether one is more pertinent than the other or whether it might not be better to choose a system that combines the two. The typology based on intensity, which includes three fundamental traits—continuity, frequency, and violence—has the advantage of being constructed in the same manner as the general typology in the preceding section. The developmental typology has the disadvantage of introducing a different perspective, but it has two important assets. It is built around aspects of criminal activity that are rarely considered in criminology, activation and escalation, which gives it a new perspective. Whereas the association gamma between the two variables used for the construction of the intensity typology is .36 that between the variables in the developmental typology is .57. These figures indicate a much more clearly marked independence of the components of the first than the second.

These two advantages led us to choose the developmental typology since, while it remains compatible with the general typology, it is actually complementary to it, because it introduces aspects that are both essential and new and that are missing in the typology of intensity. For those who prefer a combined typology, Table 6.9, by the grouping it proposes, illustrates the result of such a combination. The categories are as follows: nonaggravated or mildly aggravated activity without violence, which is generally late and whose frequency is usually low, which means that the subjects involved (24%) practice recurrent or *persistent minor* activity. Aggravated activity without violence, that starts early and whose frequency is generally high, means that 14% of delinquents are engaged in *persistent major* activity. Nonaggravated or mildly aggravated activity with occasional violence, which starts early and whose frequency is low or medium and which accounts for 18% of the sample, is activity of *persistent limited gravity.* Aggravated activity with occasional or repeated violence that starts late and occurs with high frequency means that 21% of delinquents pursue a *late serious persistent* activity. Finally, the serious persistent activity with aggravation and violent crimes, an early start, and high frequency, practiced by 26% of delinquents, can be called *early serious persistent* activity.

This typology, which combines intensity and method of development, has an internal consistency and validity that is entirely satisfactory according to Table 6.10. Furthermore, its consistency is very strong, since the gamma it presents with the two typologies is impressive, .84 with the typology of intensity and .74 with the developmental typology. Its association with the judgmental typology, developed by Fréchette and Le Blanc (1987), is considerable with a gamma of .39.

Its principal advantage lies in the fact that it covers the total reality of criminal activity in a very comprehensive way and under all the aspects we considered in previous chapters. This is an important asset, but its practical and technical disadvantages must not be forgotten. Practically speaking, its complexity makes it more difficult to use. Technically, the criticism of Brennan (1987) on the subject of the artificiality of categories is pertinent here; already a typology constructed with the aid of two variables has been affected by the relatively arbitrary limitations placed on each. Clearly a typology combining intensity and development and implying the addition of several variables (four in this case) would involve an accumulation of errors due to the limitations and grouping effects.

Until an appropriate technical solution to the problem of artificial categories is found, one criterion remains for assessing the value of a typology–replication. Regarding our general typology of illicit activity, we have been able to conclude that it is a valid replication of that of Dunford and Elliott (1984) and we get an interesting corroboration from each of them. The same can be considered true

Table 6.10. Internal consistency and validation of the combined persistent offending patterns: delinquent sample (medians, analysis of variance).

	No aggravation & violence	Aggravation without violence	No aggravation with violence	Late with aggravation & violence	Early with aggravation & violence	$p \leq (n = 190)$	$p \leq (n = 470)$
Self-reported							
Frequency	18.5	42.5	14.17	105	93.5	.01	.001
Precocity	12.93	8.5	13.33	12.56	8.44	.001	.001
Gravity	51.11	244.46	103.94	856.45	640.29	.01	.001
Violence	0	0	2.5	7	9		
Variety	2.5	4.75	3.83	6.78	7.65	.001	.001
Duration	5.25	8	4.5	7.63	11.25	.001	.001
Official							
Frequency	3.42	5.5	8.15	17.25	16.75	.05	.001
Precocity	14.6	14.8	15.06	14.81	14.94		.05
Variety	2.56	2.1	5	6	6	.001	.001
Gravity	25.58	48.5	72.31	104.81	106.2	.05	.001
Violence	1.17	1.67	3.1	3.33	3.37		.01
Duration	2.75	3.1	5.62	5.94	7	.01	.001

with the typology of the intensity of criminal activity. This hypothesis, however, is yet to be verified along with the developmental and combined typologies.

Summary

In this chapter, we were able to construct a typology of offending patterns comprising five types of involvement in criminal activity: abstinence, occasional activity, intermittent activity, persistent minor activity, and persistent major activity. In addition, a complementary typology with the components of intensity and development was constructed to refine the basic typology, this time taking only persistent delinquency into account—persistent minor activities, persistent major activities, persistent limited gravity, early serious activities, and late serious activities. These typologies in sequence offer a number of advantages technically, practically, and theoretically.

At the technical level, we have followed as closely as possible the recommendations of Brennan (1987) concerning construction of these monothetic typologies. The content is very specific and limited by descriptive and evolutive parameters as well as by the mechanisms of development of this type of activity; furthermore, it is limited to a single interpretation of the criminal phenomenon. The operational measures are of good quality because the variables were chosen with careful attention to pertinence, given the conceptual framework and our assurance that in selecting only the most reliable, they would not be redundant.

A major criticism of the construction of these typologies could be the artificiality of the categories. Even though we applied strict criteria in selectivity of cutoff points for the different variables, and all variables are of a continuous nature, the fact remains that our typologies have this weakness. We believe, however, that our cutoff points are not arbitrary, since they are independently similar to those of Dunford and Elliott (1984); it also turns out that, thanks to present and past analyses (Fréchette & Le Blanc, 1980) of our frequency distributions, the limits that we have chosen for our categories differ from those of Dunford and Elliott only about one infraction. Finally, the homogeneity of the variables at the base of each typology, the homogeneity of the classifications that compose them, the internal consistency shown on the basis of other measures of self-reported delinquency, and the external validity evaluated by means of the official delinquency, are technical guarantees that ensure the value of the principal typology and the complementary one. Obviously, there is still progress to be made on two procedures, the selection of cutoff points and the homogeneity of the classification, but only new technical solutions will make such progress possible.

From the practical point of view, the advantages of these typologies are evident because they combine two characteristics often seen as contradictory, scope and descriptive accuracy (as Brennan, 1987, called them). Scope refers to the range of phenomena to which it applies, while descriptive accuracy refers to the relevance to particular aspects of the phenomena. The general typology of offending patterns makes possible a description of all types of activities on a continuum from abstinence to the most serious activity. The typology of persistent activities, on the other hand, gives precision, describing specific forms too rare among the general population to warrant categories, but well founded with delinquent subjects.

Considering the scope and precision of our typologies, it is possible to foresee their practical use in the following way (we will come back to this in the next chapter). The general typology of criminal activity could serve two functions: It could guide the design of social policy vis-à-vis delinquency and it could be used for screening delinquents. In the first case, the following orientations would be given: Occasional and intermittent criminal activities could be dealt with by primary preventive measures, whereas persistent activities could be the object of secondary or tertiary prevention. In the second case, the use of the general typology could enable agents of the justice system to distinguish between persons who would require no intervention, the occasional offenders, and those who should receive some kind of help, the situational delinquents. The complementary typology, which concerns persistent criminal activities because it makes a clear distinction between specific forms of serious criminal activities, could serve to determine clinical action, the selection and application of various types of intervention, whether punishment, neutralization, or treatment.

The theoretical significance of our typologies of offending patterns, or of any other system constructed by a scientific method, is still difficult to evaluate, even if the internal consistency and validity attain the best technical standards available in the social sciences. The typologies we propose compare advantageously with the principles advanced by Brennan (1987). Their theoretical quality is confirmed in a number of ways, among others by convergence with the results obtained by other authors, by clarity of the definitions of the various categories, by the absence of reductionism, by recourse to a known nomenclature, and by their comprehensiveness and specificity.

The clarity of the categories seems to us particularly apparent, given the fact that they are constructed on the basis of a finite number of variables and that for each one the boundaries are limited with precision, whether it be the categories of intensity based on the frequency of the infractions and the frequency of crimes of violence in the case of the general typology, or the precocity and evolution by stages in the typology of persistent activities. Also, since we propose a general typology comprising six categories and a complementary one with five, our approach cannot be accused of reductionism.

Finally, the convergence of the results, so necessary for backing up the theoretical significance of the constructs, is not limited to the fact that our categories replicate those of Dunford and Elliott (1984) or of Elliott et al. (1987). The categories are also akin to the categories of occasional and persistent minor and major activity in studies done by teams in Philadelphia (Wolfgang et al., 1972, 1987) and London (Barnett, Blumstein & Farrington, 1987; Blumstein et al., 1985b; Farrington, 1983; D.J. West, 1982). The terms differ widely, for example, one time offenders, recidivists, chronics, serious career offenders, nonserious career offenders, persisters. It would be a good thing if criminologists could make an effort to use the same terms. We suggest the following continuum: *occasional activity* (one offense), *intermittent activity* (several crimes with some time in between), *persistent minor activity* (a limited number of crimes but no violent crimes against individuals) and *persistent major activity* (numerous crimes accompanied by repeated crimes with violence). The persistent activities could be divided into five patterns: *minor, major, limited gravity, early serious*, and *late serious*. The lines of demarcation between these degrees of intensity would vary according to whether we were dealing with self-reported delinquency, arrest, or conviction.

7
A Criminological Agenda: Research, Theory, Policy, Decision Making, and Intervention

From the very beginning we decided to study only one of the three levels of interpretation of the criminal phenomenon. In the criminological literature, a distinction is made between three specific levels, referred to as the criminality level, the criminal level, and the crime level. The empirical part of our examination of this last level is now finished. We have used three areas for the analysis of criminal activity—the offense, the offending, and the patterns of offending—each calling for particular constructs and specific procedures for combining the basic variables. Let us look briefly at these constructs and procedures.

At the first level of analysis, the offense was described in terms of the methods of execution and the conditions that support it. To do this we used 14 categories of crime; for each of them we analyzed the choice of victim, the psychological and material preparation, the execution itself (in particular the use of instruments and of physical and/or psychological violence), the kind of accomplices (whether present, their number, and age), and the accompanying conditions (such as tension during and after, and the nature of the motivation). On the basis of this analysis it was possible to describe the types of acting out and to characterize their evolution throughout the three periods of life that we had placed under observation, the first and second half of adolescence and youth to the mid-20s. The major fact that emerged here was the aggravation of the criminal activity, which becomes more and more serious and sophisticated with time, and more and more like an occupation.

At the second level of analysis, the offending was examined with the aid of several parameters. By combining these we were able to discover the dynamics of the development of illicit activity. Descriptive parameters such as participation, frequency, variety, gravity, use of violence, and types of crime, or evolutive parameters such as age of onset, duration, age of offset, and transfer, were combined to show the process of activation (which depends on the mechanisms of acceleration, diversification, and stabilization), of escalation (which is shown by the gradation of the crimes and depends on a recurrent pattern of progression through the stages of exploration, explosion, conflagration, and outburst), and of desistance (which we deduced from the mechanism of deceleration, specialization, and culmination). The main conclusion here is that the development of criminal activity is not a matter of chance, that progress through stages of illicit activity occurs with a strong degree of predictability and according to a hierarchic model.

At the third level of analysis, that of patterns, we synthesized the results of the two previous levels. To do this we constructed typologies describing the methods used in perpetrating the crimes as well as the principal manifestations of criminal activity. In the first case the analysis revealed three forms of acting out, namely hedonistic, impulsive, and utilitarian. In the second it revealed two complementary typologies. The first, which applies to the entire gamut of illicit activities, is based on continuity, frequency, and gravity of the crimes and makes it possible to distinguish between occasional and persistent offending, with or without precocity and/or gravity. The second typology makes an even finer distinction between the manifestations of persistent offending by combining two components, intensity and evolution. Given the precise criteria of internal consistency and validity, these typologies are reliable instruments for describing manifestations of criminal activity.

Equipped with these instruments and having the empirical results described in the five preceding chapters, we consider it important now to conclude this study by reexamining several of the basic questions to which criminology, from the start, has tried to provide answers. In this regard we take the position adopted by pioneers in the field (Szabo, Le Blanc, Deslauriers, & Gagné, 1968; Wolfgang & Ferracuti, 1967), who see criminology as an applied science, hence both a science and a profession. That is why at this stage we propose an agenda covering each of these perspectives. To satisfy the requirements of the discipline as a science, and taking into account the mandate to develop our knowledge and verify it empirically, we will discuss the theoretical implications of our results and the direction that future research should take. To meet the needs of the professional component, particularly action at the policy and clinical levels as well as intervention at the individual level, we will examine the implications of our results on practice.

Consequently, this chapter will have two main sections. In the first we propose guidelines for future empirical research by discussing the consequences of our results in terms of criminological theories; in the second we indicate the direction of crime policies that stem from our observations.

Scientific Implications

Discussion of the scientific significance of our observations comes back quite naturally to questions of method and theory. It is necessary, then, to describe the scope and limitations of our data if we want to get an idea of the most promising areas for future research. Moreover, we would not be able to shy away from theoretical extrapolations concerning the two levels of analysis, the offense and the offending, or explanatory factors, or avoid taking a position concerning the nature of the theories that should be favored. Each of these issues will be dealt with in such a way as to evaluate the scope of our theoretical models and of our results, given the level of knowledge in the current criminological literature.

Research

Under this heading we intend to discuss the methodological and technical characteristics that seem to us the most effective to guarantee the development of research. From this point of view we will discuss the longitudinal approach, the outline of a research plan, procedures for the collection and analysis of the data, the conceptualization and assessment of offending, as well as the matter of replication.

Design

We have first to admit to an important limitation concerning the nature and the scope of our data which stems from the fact that we tried to cover every criminal activity committed by our subjects from childhood to adulthood with only three interviews, using the method of self-reported crime, which, in addition, was strictly retrospective. This methodological weakness is compensated, it seems to us, by the use of two samples, one representing members of the general population, the other comprising delinquents convicted by the court.

Second, since we have specified the characteristics of our research plan and see how it corresponds to current or recommended practices. We have chosen to adopt a developmental rather than a cross-sectional approach; it goes without saying that such a choice involves the study of changes over time within the individual rather than study of differences between individuals. This approach depends on a basic prerequisite: the capacity to place events in sequence. The main features of the design would then be to repeat measurements at different intervals, for instance, every 6 months or every year, and this for an extended period with a large representative sample of the population. Or, if we were to follow the design proposed by Farrington et al. (1986c), multiple cohorts of at least 1,000 subjects would be followed for 6 years, from birth to the age of 6, from age 6 to 12, from 12 to 18, and from 18 to 24. Such a design would require a representative cohort of the population and at least one cohort of delinquents.

It is true that in our research design, the emphasis is on the development of offending from a life-span perspective, so that a developmental theory of offending can be elaborated. To achieve this objective, however, we do not think it necessary to have all four periods of 6 years, although we agree fully with the idea of having two types of samples. Since our first concern is with the processes involved in offending (activation, escalation, and desistance) and not with descriptive or evolutive parameters as such, because this would limit us to synthetic descriptions, and since, as we have shown earlier, these processes do not stand out in a representative sample of the population because of the low base rate for most crimes, we have favored the use of cohorts of known delinquents, as recommended by Cernkovich et al. (1985).

The successive cohort design proposed by Farrington et al. (1986c) can, of course, adequately respond to epidemiological questions relating to the participation and frequency of offending. It can also enable identification of the factors responsible for the initiation of offending. Moreover, it can be very helpful in understanding the causes of occasional offending, which is the dominant type of offending in the case of a representative sample of the population or a specific age cohort. As these authors acknowledged, however, the number of repeaters would be very small in this type of sample; in our experience it would not permit the study of processes of offending or even of the factors underlying the continuation of offending. The complexity and diversity of the processes involved in the elaboration of a developmental theory of offending require the use of a large sample of repeaters.

It should also be noted that a design using four successive cohorts has some important defects. First, it does not take into account the transitory periods from the family to school, from elementary to secondary school, from school to work, and so on, mainly because the cutting points on the continuum are situated exactly in the middle of these periods. We think researchers should focus on these transitional periods because it is well known that they are sources of much turbulence (major textbooks put a great deal of stress on these transitions: Conger & Petersen, 1984; Kagan & Moss, 1962; Offer, 1969; and others). These periods are 4 to 8 years (entry in school), 10 to 14 years (puberty and transfer to secondary school), and 16 to 20 years (leaving school and entering the work place). A longitudinal design must make sure that the same individuals are followed through these periods in order to verify whether these transitions are as important for the development of offending as they are for physical and psychological development.

Second, a design of this type overlooks the present knowledge that cohort or generation effects are stronger than age effects (Nesselroade & Baltes, 1984) and even stronger than gender effects (Le Blanc et al., 1988) when personality is the dependent variable. This means that the results obtained with an older cohort cannot be put end to end with the results of a younger cohort to infer the entire development. An alternative strategy would be to have successive and overlapping cohorts that are studied for a longer period, for example, from ages 3 to 13, ages 10 to 20, and ages 16to 26. A duration of 10 years for such a study is not much longer than the 6 years proposed by Farrington et al. (1986c) and appears to be approximately the average length of the duration of offending. With such questions in the air, the fact remains that replications in different cultures and for different generations is the only appropriate scientific solution to the problem of cohort effects, all other strategies having major limitations.

It may appear that the ideal procedure would be to apply the self-reported delinquency method every year—some ongoing research is even using a time lapse of 6 months between data gatherings—from infancy to the middle of the 40s, if we are to have a life-span perspective. Gathering data on large samples at such intervals is very costly, even more so if long interviews are contemplated to gather comprehensive personal data. If we take into account how offending develops, however, we are not convinced that it is necessary.

Looking at our data on participation and frequency and on the developmental stages in offending, it is evident that yearly changes are neither very pronounced nor very regular between childhood and adulthood. From childhood to the end of adolescence, the changes taking place over a 2-year period or more are definitely more evident. After adolescence, the changes seem to occur at an even slower pace.

There are also no sound technical reasons for choosing such a short recall period to counterbalance memory lapse, according to Weis's (1986) findings based on empirical studies in cognitive psychology and in survey methodology. It has even been shown by Hindelang et al. (1981) that longer periods of recall are more efficient than shorter ones in terms of reliability and validity, and these measures present stronger associations with correlates.

One can conclude, then, that there are no real disadvantages in having longer intervals of time between data gathering on self-reported delinquency—even 3 or 4 years. The best rule, it seems, is always to make sure that the time lapse approximates the changes in the causal factors. Since we know very little about the sequence of the causal factors themselves, especially in relation to offending, it is best to be very cautious and to test various intervals. Looking at the results of the London longitudinal study, as reported in West and Farrington (1973, 1977) and in Farrington (1986b), the problem is even more complex, since the effect of certain factors (low social class or parent's criminality, for example) appears to survive through long intervals whereas the impact of other factors (labeling or leaving school, for instance) should be studied at shorter intervals.

In sum, our recommendation would be to gather data on a large sample of youngsters at risk for at least a 10-year period covering the important transitional stages of life. The spacing of data gathering could be 3 to 4 years, because for salient events the respondents do not always make a clear distinction between the past year and a longer period of time (see Weis, 1986). Finally, the data collections should be adapted to the nature of the causal factors, since some have an effect during very short periods while others require a much longer period of time.

Method of Data Gathering

Aside from the advantages and disadvantages of our research plan, our use of a semistructured interview is in line with current practice in studies on self-reported delinquency. If we had followed what is now advocated in the most recent methodological study (Hindelang et al., 1981) and in the latest review (Weis, 1986) of the question, as well as taking into account what has been proposed at the NATO Advanced Research Workshop on the measurement of self-reported delinquency (Klein, 1988), our self-reported delinquency instrument would have had the following characteristics: It would have been a nonanonymous self-administered questionnaire; the questions would have pertained to salient crimes; the questions would have been long enough to be very specific; the questions would have included a recall period of 1 year or less; the questions would have concerned frequency; the questions would have been open-ended; the criminal events would always have been the same for the duration of the research; and the questionnaire would have been devised in such a way that any trained interviewer could have administered it. We feel the method we used complies with most of these requirements.

Furthermore, though it was determined several years after the beginning of our study that there is no real difference between methods of administration, whether for the semistructured or structured interview or the self-administered questionnaire (Hindelang et al., 1981), we still support the semistructured interview for studying the development of criminal activity because of the need in criminology today to acquire a solid knowledge of the changes in offending within the individual. It is not our contention that a semistructured interview is superior to a questionnaire. This question has been discussed at length with regard to self-reported delinquency without any clear recommendations being arrived at (see Belson & Beeson, 1969; Gold, 1966; Hardt & Bodine, 1965; Hood & Sparks, 1970; Klein, 1988; Nettler, 1974). We believe, however, that at the present time it has a specific advantage for the development of knowledge on offending, since we need to know a lot more about the dynamics of criminal activity.

The authors just cited acknowledge interesting features of the semistructured interview approach. It provides direct personal contact with the subjects, which helps to reduce general or specific resistance against reporting crimes and to create conditions that encourage better communication; it provides a way of controlling cognitive errors and of mitigating the consequences of motivational delay; it prevents insufficient validity and reliability, since the interviewer is able to probe; and it allows immediate control of the veracity of the crimes reported, because questions can be asked about the modus operandi, the situation, and so on.

The two features of the semistructured interview that seem to us most important for the heuristic development of knowledge about offending are its greater precision in obtaining information and in sorting out the sequence of events. Not only is it possible to explore many aspects of crime perpetration in detail to arrive at a more precise evaluation of its seriousness, frequency, and so on, but it is also easy to construct a time chart of the criminal events in which someone has participated and to investigate the causal factors. These informations are of a great value when there is a lack of basic knowledge, which is presently the case with the development of offending.

Obviously, the use of the semistructured interview raises the question of the characteristics of the interviewer. Even though characteristics such as age, sex, and race do not seem to play an important role in surveys on crime (Hindelang et al., 1981), it is our experience that not only should these structural characteristics be considered, but also interpersonal skills. In our project, better skilled persons produced more detailed data.

In short, our argument is that in the state of present knowledge on the development of offending and the ordering of causal factors, there is a need for data-gathering techniques that produce more detailed information. The semistructured interview is not superior per se to the self-administered questionnaire or the structured interview, but it is more appropriate because of this need and because of its ability to place the data in sequence. If we were to start the same research again, we would still use a semistructured interview for these reasons.

Techniques of Data Analysis

Development in the study of offending became bogged down to a large extent because of the almost exclusive use of an essentially statistical approach, along with the use of transition matrices and simple Markov models. We do not intend to discuss again the limitations of the statistical approach; we have already done so and J. Cohen (1986) went into several of these limitations at length. We will simply point out three major weaknesses. First, the transition matrices and the Markov sequences take into account only one parameter of illicit activity, participation in such-and-such a type of crime, thus completely ignoring the frequency and evolutive parameters (precocity, duration, age at termination). Furthermore, as J. Cohen (1986) pointed out, the Markov technique is incapable of taking the subjects' previous criminal activities into account. Second, most of the studies using the statistical approach fail to furnish a picture of criminal activity as a whole, which should be the very purpose of the developmental approach; such studies are often satisfied presenting the sequence constituted by two criminal events and, even when they consider several successive pairs, they fail to present an overall view. Third, this approach, which was meant to establish a high level of quality and mathematical sophistication, proved to be premature because it had not sufficiently encouraged researchers to adopt a heuristic attitude; they got involved in verification and replication before they could rely on good conceptual development or before the most elementary aspects of reality had been adequately explored.

We tried to avoid these errors. By comparison, our data on the processes of activation, escalation, and desistance, while they had the advantages of coming from a good-sized sample and of revealing hidden delinquency, were processed by simple techniques rather than by complex mathematical methods, and above all, were analyzed in such a way that all criminal activity was seen in perspective rather than just being reduced to crime switching.

Conceptualization and Measuring of Offending

We would like to point out that certain contributions have been extremely important for our work, such as those of Wolfgang et al. (1972), who introduced, implicitly or explicitly, most of the concepts we are using, and of Blumstein et al. (1986) and Loeber (1982, 1987), who made a masterly effort to update all the concepts and various measures available. Even if our evaluation of the contributions of others may have appeared negative at times, it must be pointed out that the principal weakness is not so much in the definition of the parameters of criminal activity as in the method used to examine the mechanisms and processes of development of this activity.

That is why we have borrowed the descriptive parameters (participation, frequency, variety, gravity, direction) and the evolutive parameters (age of onset, duration, age at termination, crime switching, transfer) from various studies where they are clearly defined and differentiated from one another, while taking into account the fact that the processes, such as activation, escalation, and desistance, are often dealt with implicitly or without any clear formulations being given. This can produce confusion whether at the conceptual or the empirical levels that cannot be dissipated unless criminologists agree on meanings and on procedures for measuring processes.

To solve this problem, we have followed the recommendation of Duncan (1984), who suggested defining variables by using a combination of basic elements. For us, the basic elements were the descriptive and evolutive parameters, and the combination of one or several of them enabled us to put forward eight mechanisms belonging to three processes. These processes are activation, which includes the mechanisms of acceleration (connection between precocity and frequency), diversification (the impact of precocity on variety), and stabilization (the consequences of precocity on duration); escalation, which involves the gradation of the crimes (deduced from precocity, duration, gravity, the age of desistance, types of crime, and age) and progression through the stages of illicit activity (emergence, exploration, explosion, conflagration, and outburst); and desistance, which comes about in three ways: through deceleration (the relation between frequency and the age the crimes stop), specialization (the connection between variety and the age the crimes stop), and culmination (when a given level of gravity is reached).

This conceptual plan has supported a thorough description of activity and its development. We think it dissipates the confusion that we find today in the literature, both at the conceptual and operational levels. However, the value of this conceptual plan and the method of constructing the underlying variables cannot be confirmed without replication.

Replication

As definitive verification of his results, the good researcher includes a replication of his or her work (for a discussion of replication, see Selvin, 1965). An adequate methodological replication involves the use of the same methods and draws data from the same milieu. This means a comparable sample in every respect, the same procedures in collecting the data, and common instruments and methods for the construction of identical variables. It is extremely rare that a true replication is published in the criminological literature; what we find are different researchers who address the same question with an assortment of methods. Consequently, it is essential that criminologists seriously set about performing this scientifically fundamental task.

If we want to construct general theories, it is necessary also to replicate studies in different cultural contexts. Criminological theories are in large measure American, and may suffer from quite a large degree of ethnocentrism. Our work has shown major differences between the level of offending among Francophones of Quebec and that of Americans. It would be particularly interesting to replicate our study in the United States and elsewhere so as to guarantee the generalization of our conclusions on the development of criminal activity.

Not only do we need replications in diverse cultures but also over time. Our results are valid for the period from the mid-1970s to the mid-1980s, but are they valid for the time before or after that? There are two possible ways of answering this question: reanalyze the data of previous longitudinal studies or repeat the same study in the coming years.

Theorization

In the last few years criminology has taken a renewed interest in theorization [as shown by the study of Meier, 1985; by the Albany Conference, 1987; and by the recent issue of *Criminology* 25(4)]. We must not forget several attempts at integration at the substantive and empirical level in this regard. Since the classic works on integration of A.K. Cohen (1955a), and of Cloward and Ohlin (1960), the integrative movement has taken several forms, doing, unification, combination, incorporation, and elaboration. A few of the more recent examples can be mentioned. Pearson and Weiner (1985) proposed theoretical unification by elaborating a common conceptual framework for two levels of explanation, crime and criminality. Elliott, Huizinga, and Ageton (1985), to develop a theoretical synthesis, combined together strain, control, and cultural deviance theories, while Thornberry (1987) has opted for the last two theories and included a developmental perspective. Denno (1985), to arrive at a theoretical incorporation, mixed biological considerations and human development ideas in the study of social control and cultural variations in crime. Finally, Le Blanc (1986a) suggested a theoretical elaboration in which he developed the conceptual framework expounded by Hirshi (1969); starting with the concept of social bonds, he introduced the idea of social constraints, of psychological functioning and conformity to the adolescent role.

For the theorization we propose now, we have not followed these various paths. We are relying more on two orientations that do not appear in the literature. First, we will try to construct a theory on the mechanics of crime, and second, we will look for explanatory factors, whether antecedents, correlatives, or causes, applicable to the two levels of analysis of crime previously mentioned, the offense and the offending. Thus, we will put forward two types of theories, explanatory theories based on the causes of crime and mechanical theories, showing the internal dynamics of crime.

A Crime Theory

If we accept the three criteria of Blalock's (1969) definition of a theory, namely, that it should have a conceptual plan, a group of propositions that compare two or more variables at a time, and propositions that maintain the connections between them, we certainly have all the elements that make possible the elaboration of a multilayered and mechanical theory of crime.

The formulation of this theory is as follows: Crime is composed of two interlocking levels of analysis, the offense and the offending. These levels of analysis are interrelated in such a way that the offending becomes the sum of all the offenses [$O = o_1 + o_2 + o_3 + \ldots + o_n$ (O, offending; *o*, offense)]. Each of these levels of analysis should be described with the help of the parameters and the patterns we have presented. A pattern is the combination of specific characteristics belonging to different parameters [$P_1 = p_{1.1} + p_{2.3} + p_{3.1} + \ldots; P_2 = p_{1.3} + p_{2.1} + p_{2.1} + p_{3.3} + \ldots, P_n$, (*P*, pattern; *p*, parameter)]. Finally, each level of analysis of crime should be dealt with according to two complementary perspectives, static and dynamic, the first concerning the convergent relations between the parameters and the second their successive relations [($D = s_1 < s_2 < s_3 < \ldots, s_n$) (*D*, dynamics; *s*, a specific state)].

The conceptual plan here comprises three levels of analysis, offending, offense, and patterns: a set of parameters and two perspectives, static and dynamic. Five propositions help specify the relationships between these elements; these propositions are formalized moreover with mathematical equations. Finally, this theory is multilayered, according to Lenski's (1988) meaning of the term, since it is a broadly inclusive general theory establishing a set of covering principles from which a series of more limited theories can be derived. We shall now present specific theories concerning each level of analysis.

The Offense

For this first level of analysis, 13 parameters were used, separated into the following categories: knowledge of the victim, preparation (psychological, material), use of instruments, complicity (presence, age, number of accomplices), use of violence (physical, verbal), tension (during, after), and motivation (hedonistic, utilitarian). Let us see first how these parameters combine from the statistical and dynamic point of view, then how they can be used to construct the patterns.

Analysis of the connection between these parameters shows that perpetration of the crime varies with the nature of the crime and age of the offender. It takes different forms in the case of three major categories of crimes—theft, personal attack, and drug trafficking. Moreover, the form becomes more aggressive and the execution more sophisticated as the age of the offender increases, a clear distinction taking place between the first and second half of adolescence and between adolescence and youth. In the sequence of parameters that mark the execution of the crime, the motivation governs the modus operandi; it conditions the degree of preparation and the nature of the complicity, which in turn depend on the type of victim, while the situation determines the degree of violence used.

With the help of these 13 parameters, it was possible to construct a general pattern and three specific configurations of illicit activity. Generally, crime is an attack on an anonymous victim, committed with accomplices, prepared and motivated by a mixture of utilitarianism and hedonism, and producing little tension during or after the act. Specifically, we detected three types of crime—utilitarian, impulsive, and hedonistic. The first is planned and prepared in advance, is carried out with a small number of accomplices, and is primarily for material gain. The second is characterized by the use of violence, is associated with a state of intoxication, and the victim, whether person or place, is usually known to the offender. The third is the search for excitement in a group. Burglary is most often associated with the utilitarian type of crime, motor vehicle theft and misdemeanors are the most frequent hedonistic crimes; impulsive crimes usually take the form of attacks against people and thefts with violence.

These are elements that must be ordered to analyze the perpetration of crime adequately and also to determine the mechanics that govern the acting out. In criminology, this theory of the perpetration of common crimes can be added to the two major theories formulated to describe criminal behavior. The theory of de Greef (1947, 1955) on crimes of passion and on crimes associated with mental illness essentially concerns acts against individuals. It is based on a complex process of psychological and material preparation comprising three phases: reserved approval, formulated consent, and crisis. The other theory is the theory of professional crime which emphasizes technical skills, a high level of planning and preparation, and the accessibility of mechanisms for the disposal of stolen goods; it is mainly derived from the biographies of criminals and it is summarized by Hagan (1987). This type of perpetration is especially marked in cases of fraud, pickpocketing, burglary, receiving stolen goods, armed robbery, motor vehicle theft, and first degree murder.

These two theories discuss only the internal dynamics of crime and are thus incomplete, since they neglect important explanatory factors, whether those operating at the time the crime is committed or those less immediate, awaiting favorable conditions. All these questions are part of what Sutherland (Sutherland & Cressey, 1960) already in 1960 called situational or dynamic explanations of crime and that we now call routine activity theories (Cohen & Felson, 1979, Felson & Cohen, 1980) or rational choice theories (Clarke & Cornish, 1985; Cornish & Clarke, 1986). We shall come back to these in the next section.

The Offending

This second level of analysis of crime is conceptually as complex as the one on the offense. It comprises two classes of elements, descriptive parameters (participation, frequency, variety, gravity, direction, and crime mix) and evolutive parameters (precocity, duration, age at desistance, transfer). We can even say that the proposal based on these parameters constitutes a much more elaborate

TABLE 7.1. Formalization of propositions relating to the theory of the development of criminal activity.

$$d_{tl} = S(p)$$
$$f_{tl} = A[S(p)] = A(d)$$
$$v_{tl} = D[S(p)] = D(d)$$
$$f_{tl}, v_{tl} = \mathrm{Ac}\{A_{tl}\ [S(p)], D_{tl}[S(p)]\} = \mathrm{Ac}(A_{tl}, D_{tl})$$
$$\mathrm{td}, p, g, d, t = G(a)$$
$$\mathrm{St} = s_1 < s_2 < s_3 < s_4 < s_5$$
$$P = s_1 + s_2 + s_3 + s_4 + s_5$$
$$t_{tn} = \mathrm{De}\ (f_{tn-1})$$
$$t_{tn} = \mathrm{Sp}\ (v_{tn-1})$$
$$C = s_{max} = t_{tn}$$

Key to abbreviations

Mechanisms and and processes			Parameters
S:	Stabilization	p:	Precocity
A:	Acceleration	f:	Frequency
D:	Diversification	d:	Duration
Ac:	Activation	v:	Variety
G:	Gradation	td:	Types of crime
St:	Stage	s:	Each stage
De:	Deceleration	t:	Age at cessation
Sp:	Specialization	s_{max}:	Stage of maximum gravity
C:	Ceiling	$t_{1...n}$	*time 1 . . . n*
P:	Progression		

conceptual whole. It involves three processes (activation, escalation, and desistance), and eight mechanisms (acceleration, stabilization, diversification, gradation, progression through stages, deceleration, specialization, and saturation). Moreover, the method of combining these parameters is precise and systematic and controls interactions between two or more parameters. Let us now enumerate the essentials that constitute this theory of the development of criminal activity; they are presented in the form of equations in Table 7.1 and were previously illustrated as models in Figures 5.1 through 5.9.

The development of illicit activity includes three phases – emergence or activation, consolidation or escalation, and desistance or saturation. Activation refers to the autostimulation of criminal activity, directly accomplished by stabilization and indirectly by diversification and acceleration. Stabilization is due to the multiplying effect of precocity on duration – the earlier the illicit activity begins, the longer it persists [$d_{tl} = S(p)$]. Acceleration is affected by the impact of precocity on the frequency throughout the duration; in other words, the sooner the illicit activity begins, the longer it lasts and the higher frequency it attains

$$f_{tl} = A\ [S(p)] = A(d)$$

Diversification is the mechanism by which precocity influences variety indirectly by the expedient of duration, and here the earlier the illicit activity begins, again, the longer it lasts and the more it involves different types of crimes

$$V_{t1} = D\,[\mathrm{S}(p)] = D(d)$$

Activation, then, is a result of the combination of stabilization, acceleration, and diversification; hence the earlier the onset of illicit activity, the longer it lasts and the more frequent and varied it becomes

$$f_{t1},\ V_{t1} = \mathrm{Ac}[A_{t1}(S(p)],\ D_{t1}[\mathrm{S}(p)] = \mathrm{Ac}(A_{t1},\ D_{t1})$$

The consolidation of criminal activity takes place through the process of escalation: Offenders progress from minor crimes to major crimes according to a hierarchic model. They do not all start at the same stage, nor do they go through all the stages. The gradation of the crimes can be deduced from the interaction between the following parameters: the types of crime, starting age, duration, age when stopped, gravity, and age

$$\mathrm{td,\ p,\ g,\ d,\ t)} = G\,(a)$$

On the basis of gradation of the crimes, five stages were identified: emergence, exploration, explosion, conflagration, and outburst

$$\mathrm{St} = s_1 < s_2 < s_3 < s_4 < s_5$$

Consolidation of the illicit activity, then, takes place by progression through these stages, generally several adjacent ones; when it covers all stages, it can be expressed in the form:

$$P = S_1 + S_2 + S_3 + S_4 + S_5$$

We come now to desistance, which is linked with saturation. After a certain time the activity culminates, whether in terms of frequency or variety, and so on. Desistance begins with deceleration and specialization; then a ceiling is reached with culmination. Deceleration refers to the diminution of frequency that precedes the end of the illicit activity, according to the principle that the higher the frequency the sooner the end

$$t_{\mathrm{tn}} = \mathrm{De}\,(f_{\mathrm{tn}-1})$$

Specialization is the reduction in variety before the illicit activity stops, according to the rule, the greater the specialization, the more quickly the criminal activity will end

$$t_{\mathrm{tn}} = \mathrm{Sp}\,(v_{\mathrm{tn}-1})$$

The ceiling is the maximum level of gravity that has been reached and been maintained over a given period prior to the decline of the criminal activity

$$C = S_{\mathrm{max}} = t_{\mathrm{tn}}$$

From a developmental perspective, criminal activity should be seen as an activity that has a beginning, runs its course, and has an end. As justly noted by Blumstein et al. (1986) and Farrington et al. (1986c), of particular importance to give it a correct interpretation, is taking into account the different factors underlying its emergence and development.

It must be remembered also that we used a statistical analysis centered on the converging relation between the parameters of criminal activity. Two major observations have to be emphasized. First, these parameters present different levels depending on the categories of crime. It is a mistake to think of criminal activity as constant and uniform: Participation, frequency, duration, and so on vary in intensity with different categories of crime. Each category has to be studied separately.

Second, many parameters of criminal activity seem redundant at first, because there is evidence of strong correlations between them (frequency, variety, gravity, and duration, for example). We have shown, however, that this deduction is fallacious: The parameters maintain an acceptable level of influence when they are controlled each in turn or when previous or consequential variables are taken into account, such as precocity and the age at which the crimes stop. Hence the models in Figures 5.8 and 5.9 show both activation and saturation; they show that precocity, as an independent variable, acts on the intermediary variables duration, frequency, and variety. These, in turn, cause the variable desistance (or the age at which the criminal activity stops) to fluctuate.

Besides this integrated pattern for determining the way criminal activity is structured, it proved worthwhile to construct two typologies of offending patterns, each marked by a specific combination of parameters as well as by an unequivocal consistency and validity. We thus constructed a general typology of offending that covers all criminal activity and a complementary typology that concerns only persistent activity. The former suggests five fundamental patterns—occasional, intermittent, minor continuous, major continuous, and persistent grave criminal activity. The latter suggests five categories of persistent activities—those of a minor level, of a major level, of limited gravity, late serious activities, and early serious activities.

Thus we elaborated, verified, and formalized a theory of offending, and more particularly a theory of the development of criminal activity. Although its replication and further study remain to be done, this theory already makes it possible to better conceptualize offending—the key dependent variable in criminology—and to more easily detect the causes of offending.

Explanatory Theories

Since we were dealing with two overlapping levels of crime analysis, the offense and the offending, we at first favored two types of explanation, one for each level of analysis. Subsequently, however, we decided to take an integrative and unified theoretical approach. This is in line with the classic conception of crime in criminology (see Szabo et al., 1968; Wolfgang & Ferracuti, 1967), that is to say, the conception that puts the accent on the interaction of personal and social factors, not the current perspective, which is strictly sociological (see Elliott et al., 1985, or the Albany Conference, 1987). It is integrative also in the sense that $B = f(P,E)$ to cite Lewin's (1933) celebrated formula, where behavior (*B*) is a function of the interaction between the person (*P*) and the environment(*E*). If we adapt this formula to our levels of analysis, it becomes: for the perpetration of the crime, $o = P\ (S)$ (o, offense; P, person; S, situation) and for criminal activity, $O = P\ (E)$ (O, offending; P, person; E, environment).

This integrative conception, in which social and psychological factors, while interacting, each play their own role, has a unifying effect on our two levels of analysis. As we have shown, personal as well as environmental factors serve to support the explanation both of the perpetration of the crime and of the criminal activity. The relationship between the two levels is maximized by the fact that we are faced with a single plan of interpretation, that of the crime, but it is examined from two angles, as an isolated act and as an activity (we avoid dealing with the other two levels, the criminal and criminality). This relationship could also be promoted by the choice of a single theoretical orientation, control theory, which Empey (1978) stated is the only perspective in explaining behavior. In this orientation, theoretical formulations in both psychology and sociology adopt the same assumptions, a common underlying logic, and similar content.

Before tracing the theoretical orientations we believe are pertinent for each level of analysis, it is important that we distinguish the categories of factors to which we refer. Let us remember that Hirschi and Selvin (1967) proposed three criteria of causality: A and B should be statistically associated, A should be prior to B, and the association between A and B should not disappear when the effects of other variables are removed. For the purpose of our discussion, let us define correlates as variables statistically associated with the offense or the offending, and causes as variables that match this criterion and for which causal order can be established. Since our comments concern causes, let us also define three categories of variables: antecedent conditions, structural variables, and personal variables.

Antecedent variables can be age, sex, race, temperament, prior experience of crime, and so on. These are variables that have to be controlled, as Hirschi and Selvin (1967) strongly argued. They cannot be thought of as causal variables because they are connected with the length, the starting age, or the prior experience of crime as such. Structural variables, or risk factors, refer to specific events or situations: unguarded premises, studying or working, one-parent or two-parent family, having delinquent friends, criminality of parents, and so on. Personal variables concern such factors as attachment, commitment, personality, motivation, and so on and refer to the attitudinal dimension. These last two groups of variables remain independent from crime. By keeping these distinctions in mind, we can discuss various explanations for the perpetration of crime and for criminal activity, our intention being not to propose a completely worked out theory, but to open up some valid avenues for exploration.

Explanations of the Offense

Criminologists have always concentrated on the immediate situation to explain the perpetration of a crime (see Pinatel, 1963; Sutherland & Cressey, 1960). Only recently have more integrative formulations been proposed concerning the nature and the role of the immediate factors. Felson and Cohen (1980) spoke of life situations that cause the convergence of the subject's delinquent capacity, interest in a target, and vulnerability of that target. Hough et al. (1980) introduced two types of variables, conditions favorable to the infraction and absence of risk. Cusson (1986) spoke of the potential delinquent and the accessibility and vulnerability of the target. West (1982) described three categories of variables: the crime-prone person, precipitating events, and opportunities. Cornish and Clarke (1986) suggested four models: initial involvement, event, continuing involvement, and desistence from a particular type of crime; and for the first offense they proposed eight groups of variables: background factors, previous experience, general needs, solutions perceived, solutions evaluated, reaction to chance event, readiness, and decision.

All these theories have two characteristics in common: (a) They make a distinction, more or less explicitly, between personal factors and situational factors—a distinction necessary for an integrative approach, and (b) they make a distinction between preceding factors, precipitating ones, and active causes, thus affording a useful classification of the causes. For some authors, the antecedents signify the condition of a potential delinquent, whereas for others it is the background factors and previous experience. Thus, for Cornish and Clarke (1986), the crime-prone person is one whose needs are general (money, excitement, etc.), who has had previous experience (with crime, the law, etc.), and who has certain personal characteristics (psychological: temperament, intelligence, etc.; social and demographic: upbringing, type of family, discipline, sex, class, and so on). As to the immediate causes or structural factors, they are the routine activities (drinking, proximity, hanging around, etc.) and the opportunities for crime (unguarded property, poorly lit streets, easy victims, reward, etc.).

It is possible, then, to envisage an integrative theory of the perpetration of crime in the case of the first level of analysis, following the example of a number of criminologists who have already established the outlines. Our more specific contribution is in compiling an inventory of pertinent factors; in separating the categories of factors, the predisposing (antecedents) and precipitating (structural and personal factors); and in determining, by means of precise propositions, the connection between the various factors.

Explanation of Offending

It is possible to think of a unified theory for the two levels of analysis, on condition that the following principle is brought into play: the behind-the-scene factors, called the antecedents, that are used to explain the perpetration of crime, must stay instrumental when explaining criminal activity. But, given the definition of offending, which stipulates that it is the sum of all the individual crimes, it is clear that the immediate causes of each act cannot appear as such in the explanation of offending. For this reason, in any global consideration of delinquent activity, the role and the impact of the antecedents must be reevaluated. Some remain the same (sex, temperament, etc.), whereas others become structural causes (type of family, school attendance, delinquent peers, etc.) and still others are personal factors (attachment, social control, upbringing, and so on).

Another principle that should guide any theorizing about offending is the need to distinguish between the factors of emergence and those of development. With the same concern for preciseness a number of researchers have recently proposed important distinctions. Blumstein et al. (1986) and Farrington et al. (1986a) suggested distinguishing between explanations bearing on participation and those concerning frequency. Ferdinand (1987) recommended recognition of the fact that explanations of conformity as well as nonconformity exist and he classified existing sociological theories accordingly. Finally, Thornberry (1987) stated that theories should contain concepts that differ according to the stage of life, adolescence or youth, the stages we are generally concerned with in criminology.

Always maintaining the basic distinction between occasional offending and persistent offending, as we have done throughout this book, we found promising ground for the elaboration of integrative theories on one or the other of these two phenomena. The first, the emergence of general illicit activity during adolescence, as reflected by participation, comes under the heading of theories of conformity. Similarly, the development of this activity, as shown by activation and escalation, calls on complementary theories or theories that emphasize certain amplifying factors.

The volatile nature of occasional offending makes it immediately clear that explanations cannot be sought in factors, conditions, and causes connected with past experience. We know, moreover, that macrosociological factors, such as the impact of the mass media, the economic situation, social class, and so on, cannot account for such offending satisfactorily. Offending of this type occurs quite the same way in every era, in every Western society, and in all classes of society. The explanation must be sought in the drift, to cite Matza (1964), that occurs during adolescence. In this context, particular mechanisms operate that are responsible for the emergence of illicit activity; we have clarified these mechanisms by means of an integrative theory of behavior control (Le Blanc, 1986a, 1988), which was based on Hirschi's (1969) theory.

Speaking very generally, this theory can be formulated as follows: Delinquent activity appears in proportional relation to the weakness of the control mechanism of people's behavior. This weakness is due to tenuous links with society (little attachment to anyone and uncertain commitment to social institutions), to retarded psychological development (an enduring primitiveness and an unyielding antagonism), and to a lack of social control (weakened external social controls and unachieved internalization of norms). The momentary weakness of one or the other of these factors leads directly to activity of varied intensity or leads to it indirectly through a process of marginalization at school, reinforced by the choice of deviant peers, which can seriously complicate the assumption of a social role.

These influential factors, however, are not linked haphazardly. In fact, two elements interact constantly, the social ties and the personal attitudes. We are unable to say which has priority as far as influence is concerned. These elements make the difference, since they determine the receptivity of the adolescent toward social control and the demands of social life. Moreover, it is actually these sources of control that act as a sort of barrier against the pressure toward illicit activity. In the absence of dynamic behavior control, a lack of conformity to the adolescent role develops, which is concretized in conflicts at school and attachment to delinquent or deviant peers and is supported by insufficiently close ties and retarded psychosocial development.

It is this nonconformity that has proved the strongest indication if imminent delinquent behavior. We were able to show that such offending is not due to a loosening or break with social ties or to wrong psychological development, but rather to insufficient social control that occurs with a lack of parental supervision, momentary problems in adapting to school, and association with deviant peers who encourage the emergence of this illicit activity. This underlying dynamic can be referred to as an ambiguous attitude toward society.

Turning now to persistent offending, particular factors again emerge in explanation. By comparative analysis (Fréchette & Le Blanc, 1987), we established social criminogenic factors that influence adolescents – antecedents that have the weight of veritable antisocial determinants. The main ones are the indirect consequences of a negative early environment, since these youngsters often come from socioeconomically disadvantaged milieus; they have acquired major social handicaps, such as maladjustment or failure at school, a reputation of being a mischief maker, behavior problems, and so on. They have been the object of successive and ineffective interventions by the social services and justice system; their marginal behavior has become more accentuated in their immediate community and at school, and they have established an attachment to delinquent peers. In such a context, it is not surprising that they have never developed an adequate attachment to their parents or persons in authority or made a commitment to social institutions and values (social success, for example). It is perfectly understandable, then, that a person who is not more attached to society cannot be subject to social control.

In short, these delinquents are "unsocialized," to use the concept of Mucchielli (1965). However, the strong determinants that we have just mentioned have not proved to be the basic reason for persistent offending. Rather, it is among the criminological factors of a psychological nature, especially in an ever-present egocentricity, that we have found the basis of this undersocialization. In this regard, our analyses (Fréchette & Le Blanc, 1987) show that the psychological aspects have a greater influence than the social conditions, which confirms Mannhein's (1965) "principle of the transformer." The assertion that the personality characteristics constitute the foundation of persistent offending is confirmed by the following facts: Juvenile delinquents evince subnormal psychological functioning; the gravity of their offending covaries very well with the intensity of their psychological deficiencies; the variables that best distinguish conventional adolescents one from the other are social, whereas those that best discriminate between types of juvenile delinquents are psychological; the specific psychological component capable of clearly distinguishing the occasional delinquent from the persistent delinquent comes to the fore sharply at mid-adolescence and is present from then on. It was possible to show that if delinquents become deeply involved in criminal activity, it is because of the persistence of a dominant egocentric orientation in their personality. Instead of progressing toward allocentricity, toward reciprocity, even altruism, they become firmly established in this egocentricity. According to our assessments, it is the psychosocial areas, with hyposociality, involving impoverished relations with others and supported by psychoaffective elements, insecurity for one, that contribute to delinquent behavior. Moreover, this persistent offending based on an egocentricity that is consolidated little by little to become closely linked with undersocialization is expressed at mid-adolescence in the form of four delinquent syndromes (see Fréchette & Le Blanc, 1987).

Practical Implications

This book, in trying to develop a precise knowledge of offending, answers one of the most important objectives of criminology as a science. Our discipline is also an applied science, and that is why this last section is devoted to the practical implications of our findings. The problem of delinquency, while urgent, is a difficult one. In a way, the urgency lies in the fact that the delinquents of today are the parents of the future. As it is becoming ever more clear that antisocial behavior is persistent among the population and stable from one generation to the next, it becomes a matter of urgency to develop effective procedures for detection and diagnosis as well as appropriate policies and methods of intervention. At the same time, the prevalence and incidence of delinquency have taken on disquieting proportions, a fact that has been noted for a long time in our industrialized societies. There are now so many individuals who deviate so largely and with such persistence from socially prescribed or tolerated patterns of behavior that dealing with all of them with any success has become impossible.

Apart from grand principles and grandiose declarations of intention, the crucial question remains; Who will we choose as a subject for intervention? Are there any valid criteria by which one can judge which individuals are more in need of protection or special treatment? It is to clarify these questions that we submit the following ideas on policies, decision making, and intervention vis-à-vis delinquents.

Policies

The facts we have examined in this book convince us that crime presents a multitude of guises. Readers who have followed us this far will surely be convinced that criminal activity is not a simple or homogeneous phenomenon. That is why we believe we should not speak of delinquency but of delinquenc*ies* (Fréchette & Le Blanc, 1987).

Two Styles of Offending

Offending has serious social repercussions because of its high frequency, objective gravity, and precocity. Offending is predominantly a problem of youth. It is a conduct that intensifies rapidly and declines suddenly. But the most important characteristic is the fact that there are two clearly divergent types of offending, situational and chronic.

Let us briefly go over the differences between these two types of criminal activity. Situational offending consists of infrequent offenses that tend to be so harmless, or even insignificant, that they well might constitute some of the ordinary hazards of life, the price that has to be paid to adapt to our complex social life and to learn the social norms and the limits of what is permitted in society. Chronic offending, on the other hand, is a conduct that is part of the lifestyle of the subject; it is integrated into his activity given the fact that it is precocious, voluminous, heterogeneous, serious, persistent, and of such scope that it denotes an antisocial way of life and indicates a probable adult criminal career. It is evident that the diverse authorities – parents, educators, police, judges, social workers assigned to youth – cannot deal in the same way with these two types of offending. The procedures of prevention, control, and treatment cannot be based on the same principles or be applied in the same way in both cases. These two forms of offending clearly call for different strategies.

Let us recall the most outstanding divergences that emerged between the two, as shown in our comparative study in chapters 3 to 5 of a representative sample of adolescents as opposed to juvenile delinquents, and the distinction between occasional activity and persistent activity that showed clearly in the typological analysis in chapter 6. Whether in terms of participation, frequency, nature, diversity, duration, or precocity, the dimensions of the offending of the wards of the court, self-reported of official, differ spectacularly from those of the offending of the adolescents. The criminal activity of the former is massive and its gravity and persistence leave no doubt, whereas that of the latter is incidental, less serious delinquency that could be what we have called an epiphenomenon of the maturing process (Fréchette & Le Blanc, 1987). Our typological analysis supports this difference, for in the sample of adolescents the illicit activities are occasional and intermittent, whereas in the second sample of delinquents they are persistent.

The difference is also evident in the dominant social and psychological characteristics of each group (see the analyses of Fréchette & Le Blanc, 1987). The adolescents get average scores according to the norm in psychological tests and show no major family, school, or social handicaps. The wards of the court, on the other hand, seem to be grappling with a sort of breakdown in communication that makes it very difficult for them to integrate into social structures. There is a consistent twisting of reality that makes them insecure and weakens the links with their family circle; it brings considerable difficulty in submitting to control, which makes them vulnerable vis-à-vis the most elementary requirements of social life; and finally, it culminates in a rejection of the conventional ways of functioning, which leads them to seek refuge in marginal groups and even look for excitement in defying authority.

Action on Two Fronts

Generally speaking, our data point to the need to dedramatize most of the criminal acts committed by adolescents, and, since there is a great deal of tolerance already, mainly due to the mechanisms of diversion, it is necessary to maintain this tolerance and even increase it. In the case of situational offending, a policy of tolerance is essential.

In the case of chronic offending, however, different rules are necessary. Here criminal activity tends to be concentrated at the beginning of adolescence, and by age 15 it has become a problem of considerable magnitude. In responding to the problem, it is essential to remember that it is due to difficulties inherent in this phase of development and that the probability is strong that these difficulties will last for a long time. Nonetheless, powerful forces can still act favorably in such a way that delinquency, even though serious, will lessen considerably under the joint effect of various factors, such as police and judicial control, intervention of the social services, expectations of family and friends (especially the "girlfriend"), integration into the labor market, psychological maturation, future requirements, and so forth. Neutralization or even psychological and social rehabilitation can be undertaken to straighten out these youngsters.

The differences in the methods of intervention required are obvious. Where situational offending is concerned, there must be social tolerance, and more particularly diversion, protection, conciliation, support, and a return to freedom and to the subject's natural milieu. For chronic offending, judicial control must take precedence, as well as neutralization of the behavior, guidance, social reeducation, and intensive supervision. The important thing in every approach to the problem of offending is to modulate the intervention, especially in the case of differences as crucial as these.

In short, in the light of this first distinction, intervention in the matter of delinquency could and should be done in accordance with two requirements that, while strict, are radically different. The first is to let spontaneous social and psychological reconstruction play their roles as far as possible. This means that it might be wiser to not intervene or at least to wait as long as nonintervention has no ill effect. The second, on the contrary, recommends early intervention, forcefully and for a long time, in order to prevent youngsters from becoming antisocial and to avoid their ability to function as adults being compromised. Considering this twofold reality, the most important element is differential prediction: Some delinquents require nonintervention or minor intervention, others require massive intervention. This is the challenge of applied criminology.

An Appropriate Legislative Framework

If scientists, politicians, practitioners in the criminal justice system, and caregivers in institutions were to agree to establish this principle of differential action regarding policy in matters of delinquency, an appropriate legislative framework would be the necessary instrument for such an approach. For example, in Quebec, recent federal (Young Offenders Act, 1982) and provincial (The Youth Protection Act, 1984) legislation furnishes a legislative framework entirely appropriate for the application of a differential strategy of intervention (we feel that this is far from being the case for adult crime because of the limited room for diversion).

In the first place, these Acts specify the meaning of offending and limit it to infractions of the Criminal Code. In itself, such a restrictive position facilitates the work of differentiation that decision makers constantly have to do and obliges them to effect selective screening of juvenile delinquents. Because of this, in turn, in the current administration of justice and in the social service system, the persons involved are forced to refine their instruments and show discernment, since the legal definitions limit the diversity of the problems they have to face.

Second, in the judicial and administrative framework that has been established, a vast list of measures has been provided, from alternatives to imprisonment, which include strategies such as reconciliation with the victim, restitution, or community work, to a choice of diverse possibilities, such as supervision in the community, supervision following detention, probation, and so on. The presence of such varied measures has obliged those in charge to take into account the pertinence of each of them to the needs of each delinquent. This variety is exactly what our study of delinquency indicates is needed; the tolerance we prescribe for the occasional delinquent finds an answer in diversion and closing of the file or in alternative measures that can be applied according to the gravity of the act. At the other extreme, chronic offending requires other types of measures, supervision at liberty or treatment in institution, depending on the degree of involvement in criminal activities.

Third, not only does the variety of measures encourage a differential approach, but the judicial process itself encourages such an approach by mechanisms such as legal representation and appeal, which afford the choice of a satisfactory measure for each particular case. Then there is the increasingly important role of specialists in the social sciences who participate in the selection of delinquents who have to answer for their acts before the courts: They advise judges by means of the presentence report; they carry out the measures ordered; and they determine the end of the measures, subject to the approval of the judicial authority. These specialists strengthen the application of the differential principle, because to carry out their jobs they must distinguish as effectively as possible between the juvenile delinquents and the others.

If there is any question, however, that the legislation is not entirely suitable, it is because of the age of responsibility, set by law at 12 years. This regulation is not important where situational offending is concerned, since such offending rarely occurs at this age. With regard to chronic offending, however, this limit can be an obstacle to the need for early intervention. Here, in fact, the study of self-reported delinquency shows a starting age of about 10; the study of official delinquency shows that it, too, begins before age 12. It is possible that the delay in taking action with the power and guarantees of the judicial apparatus means that at the very moment the criminal conduct emerges and before it is consolidated, a promising occasion for intervention is missed. Without reference to the generational transmission of delinquency (see D.J. West, 1982, for example) or to indirect influences stemming from a poor environment during childhood (poverty, broken home, antisocial father, etc.; see Rutter & Madge, 1976), it is interesting to note, in an early perspective, that the appearance of the delinquent conduct is preceded by or is concomitant with serious problems of integration and functioning at school. This is particularly the case for chronic delinquents (see West & Farrington, 1973, 1977; Farrington, 1985). There could be detection even before the appearance of official delinquency; it would no doubt be useful to be able to use all our expertise, all our professional resources, and all our ability to act in such a case, since intervention could occur at a particularly crucial moment.

Decision Making

The construction of offending patterns has made it possible to better characterize both qualitatively and quantitatively the various forms of criminal activity for situational as well as chronic delinquency. It is important to note, too, that it is by determining the basic mechanisms governing the development of illicit activity, particularly its stabilization and progression through stages, that one is able to identify the significant criteria for the prognosis of chronic adult crime. According to these two series of results, it is possible to facilitate the difficult and complex process of decision making even with a diverse delinquent population.

Let us look first at the characteristics that differentiate situational offending from chronic offending. Whether hidden or official, it emerges later, at mid-adolescence, with fewer and less serious crimes. Although we exceed the strict level of interpretation of crime here, it can also be established that the behavior is partly due to a lack of sufficient parental supervision, to maladjustment at school, and to belonging to a marginal group of youths (Fréchette & Le Blanc, 1987). Limiting ourselves to the most significant behavioral characteristics of this form of offending, we must now decide which of them can best indicate the diagnosis and the types of social measures available.

At the present time, the official reaction has three aspects: (a) The police officer observes the infraction and formulates a request to start proceeding, (b) the crown prosecutor studies whether court action is appropriate for a specific infraction, and (c) the director of youth protection, in the case of a minor, considers the use of alternative measures. At each of the three levels, personnel have the discretionary power to separate situational offending from chronic offending. They use this power all the time, based on the behavioral data (nature and gravity of the crime, recidivism) and objective data on the adolescents (age, for example) (for Quebec, see Le Blanc, 1971; Trepanier & Marceau, 1985).

Although practices at the first two levels are based on a long tradition and are supported by legislative statutes and strict regulations, they tend to neglect the criterion of precocity. An infraction committed at a tender age is met with non-intervention and tolerance by the Quebec police and judges, just as it is in the United States (Gottfredson & Gottfredson, 1980). (Incidentally, our results operate in another direction. It would no doubt benefit the police and judicial courts if they were to ask more often for the opinion of specialists in the social sciences when an adolescent commits a crime before the age of 14, and especially before the age of 12, since it could be a sign of a serious delinquent orientation. Our data clearly show that precocity is an important support of the stabilization of criminal conduct and is a prerequisite of potential escalation.)

It is just as important that the social agencies also look for signs of situational offending, the supervision of the parents, the functioning at school, and association with peers. This verification can be done very quickly by an experienced practitioner, by a brief interview with the adolescent and his parents, a telephone call to the school, and a study of the grounds for the request to institute proceedings. It could also be done by using a standardized short questionnaire that would investigate the above themes. Such a questionnaire would make it possible to calculate whether the offense belongs to one or the other of the two major forms of offending. This last method would probably be as effective as the first, considering that we already get 80% correct predictions with the analysis of the discriminant function that we did (Fréchette & Le Blanc, 1987).

The basic elements leading to making a decision are actually available, the criteria are known, and our variables can serve as parameters. Why, then, is today's practice not more strict, more precise, and at the same time more efficient, saving time and energy? Why are we so afraid to classify? Why do we put off intervention so much (certain youngsters require it early if we want to maximize our chance of success)? It must be remembered that official delinquency is a pale reflection of hidden delinquency, a fact well established in our analyses in chapters 3, 4, and 5. It is necessary, therefore, that the decision in each case be based on the latter as much as possible, in order to be more reliable and have greater validity.

Chronic offending, for its part, seems to be a complex problem that depends on a number of supporting factors, so that to ascertain the young delinquent's real condition requires a three-dimensional model, comprising not only behavioral aspects but also social and psychological aspects, as our analyses show (Fréchette & Le Blanc, 1987). The data describing each of these basic aspects should lead to the criminological diagnosis. Concerning the first, which has been studied at length in this book, what is needed is to update the dynamics of official crime, and especially hidden crime. It is for this reason that a thorough knowledge of the way the criminal activity is expressed is the first prerequisite for a pertinent diagnosis. For the second, the key elements are the extent of undersocialization, serious social handicaps, and insufficient or poor social ties. This information is particularly useful in choosing an appropriate measure. Finally, for the third, the personality structure is the target, and all measures that give access to it become pertinent.

To create this three-way model, in which the diverse interacting elements are defined, it is not so much the nature of the instrumentation that counts but the pertinence of the information. What the instruments must look for are specific symptoms. For example, it is of the utmost importance to be able to assess the extent of the escalation patterns, the quality of personal ties, the influence of deviant peers, and so on. A diagnosis of this kind cannot be made by means of a mechanized and cumulative collection of information, but should be the result of interpretation. Once gathered, the data should be analyzed and interpreted in the light of criminological knowledge and clinical experience. The specific effect of such a diagnosis on the handling of cases and on the strategy of intervention will not only better answer the specific needs of the various categories of delinquents but will also permit what we call *guided intervention*, that is, intervention in which the agencies and persons in charge put their efforts where the need is greatest.

In comparing adolescents who were involved in offending with those who were not, we were unable to come up with an answer to the crucial question of how to detect nascent delinquency. To discover what is not yet evident brings up considerable methodological and ethical problems (see Farrington & Tarling, 1985). However, our data are very explicit and show that grave persistent criminal activity is a phenomenon connected with a particular phase in a person's development, that of preadolescence, and that other forms of serious illicit activity also appear before mid-adolescence. These observations demonstrate the importance of detection, because criminal orientation seems to set in at a relatively tender age and quickly stabilizes. These facts indicate that, if we are seeking to increase the effectiveness of our intervention, we must take action before behavior patterns become set and before they are recognized officially by the agencies of social control and justice.

A number of recent works show that criminologists can be more effective than they think with regard to identifying children, from the age of 6, 7, or 8, who are at risk of adolescent offending and those at risk of chronic adult crime or violent crime (see Loeber & Dishion, 1983, for a review of the literature; Farrington, 1985, did a comparative analysis of methods; Blumstein et al., 1985a; Farrington & Tarling 1985b; and Husmann, Eron, Lefkovitz, & Walder, 1984, reported some very interesting data on this question). What is more, a sequential procedure for the detection of children at risk of offending is known; it suggests the gradual elimination from a base population of youngsters who are not at risk, progressively using more and more precise and complex sources of information and instruments. This procedure has been used in some studies in criminology (Briggs, Wirt, & Johnson, 1961; Loeber, Dishion, & Patterson, 1984; Marineau, Fréchette, Limoges, & Le Blanc, 1971).

Intervention

As we have based our approach to social policies and the mechanisms of decision making on the distinction between situational offending and chronic offending, we shall end with some proposals regarding intervention strategies that should be implemented for each of these types of illicit activity.

For Situational Offending

A large majority of youngsters from age 12 to 18, regardless of their social status, become involved in offending toward mid-adolescence. This offending takes the form of a few infractions of little gravity, notably vandalism and petty theft. These acts seem to be an expression of the vicissitudes of the process by which youngsters learn to adhere to the social norms of conduct and to integrate them. The phenomenon, being temporary and situational, naturally calls for the tolerance we spoke of or even for what Schur (1973) called radical nonintervention.

This form of illicit activity, by its very nature, does not lend itself to detection. It is almost impossible to predict who will find themselves in circumstances conducive to involvement in offending. Prevention focused on the offender is impracticable here. The only step that is appropriate is what Gibbens (1969) called first level prevention – it consists of action within the community. This can only be very nonspecific, but it can improve the quality of life of the adolescent and the general population.

In this kind of prevention, society seeks the revitalization of its institutions: school, family, working structures, and community organizations. A social development model of this kind requires two strategies: first, to improve the upbringing skills of parents, of educator in the school, and of religious leaders; second, to establish a true youth policy favoring the integration of young people at work and in community life. The most recent formulations of these comprehensive models of primary prevention are those of Hawkins, Oastaie, Bele, and Morrison, (1980) and of Johnson, Cohen, and Bird (1981) in the United States; of Rutter and Giller (1983) in England; and of Waller and Weiler (1984) in Canada, all of whom rely on the theory of social control.

Since in this context potential delinquents are the entire population of adolescents, and since the offending consists in suddenly succumbing to temptation, a particularly pertinent defensive strategy is to center on the potential victim and his or her milieu. Opportunity theories prescribe all sorts of means to reduce opportunities for acting out depending on the type of crime, in particular, by controlling the material and physical accessibility of targets and by increasing the offender's risk of apprehension and identification (see Hough et al., 1980, and Newman, 1972). The object of the first type of action is to increase the defense of the target (the use of unbreakable materials, padlocks, grills, etc.), to eliminate certain targets (cash, storage, and so on), to lessen the means of committing crimes (control of firearms, plastic objects in bars), and to reduce the profits from stolen objects (markings, elimination of receiving). At the same time, in a second type of action, the risk of identification and arrest must be increased by police patrols and community efforts (neighborhood watch) and by technical equipment (public lighting, development of the area).

If these strategies of primary prevention are sufficient in the case of situational offending, it is hardly likely that they would be able to reduce chronic offending. To grapple with this type of crime, marked by the processes of activation and escalation, there must be recourse to more direct and stronger means.

For Chronic offending

Chronic offending is expressed in diverse forms. It is thus important to have a varied list of means of control from early detection techniques and differential diagnoses to very strong methods of intervention. The need is urgent in view of the fact that a large number of delinquents of this type end up in adult crime, with all the serious consequences it entails (prolonged incarcerations, negative social status, the disgrace of a criminal record, the break with social life, and so on). At adolescence, however, their activity can be regarded as a call for help, a way of telling us they have major problems of adjustment. This is a challenge that must be met efficiently and quickly.

In the face of persistent criminal activities, prevention is applied in two ways, either through what Gibbens (1969) classified as secondary prevention, including all action taken to prevent the development of the criminal activity among persons at risk, or as tertiary prevention, intervention aimed at preventing recidivism among persons who have already committed crimes. The tactics currently used in our societies today are deterrence, neutralization, and treatment. They can be applied in the natural milieu or in a training center, and there are numerous and varied means for sustaining each tactic, according to the survey of Hawkins et al. (1980) and of Finckenauer (1984).

We must mention, however, that this whole array of intervention methods has been judged ineffective by representatives of a certain school of thought in criminology. According to them, these methods, program, and measures produce no general elimination or even substantial reduction of recidivism. A great many reviews of studies have been done in this regard, among them those of Lipton, Martinson, and Wilks, (1975), Lundman and Scarpitti (1978), Romig (1978), Wright and Dixon (1977), and Cusson (1983). On the other hand, more recent works (Feldman, Caplinger, & Wodarshy, 1983; Kobrin & Klein, 1983; Le Blanc 1983a; Murray & Cox, 1980; Palmer, 1978; Ross & Gendreau, 1980) show that the effect of measures or treatment is one of reducing the individual level of offending, but that this effect is subject to the influence of individual characteristics. Given these variable results according to types of individuals, it is evident that the differential diagnosis constitutes the key mechanism of articulation between the diverse forms of expression of illicit activity and the entire range of means available. No measure, no method of intervention, can claim to have the maximum effect on all delinquents. To match each case with the appropriate measure seems to be the best way of substantially increasing the effectiveness of our practices.

With regard to the three major tactics used to combat chronic offending, namely, deterrence, neutralization, and treatment, the criteria for choosing the type of intervention are clear. Deterrence can be attained in two ways, the strengthening of moral control or the fear of punishment. With this category of delinquent, considering their psychological deficiencies, their late development, and the degree of their undersocialization, it appears—and here we agree with Cusson's (1983) analysis of moral control—that the positive form of deterrence would be most unlikely to influence such subjects. As for the fear of punishment, criminological studies indicate that general deterrence, with its certainty and/or severity of punishment, or specific deterrence, the impact of the punishment on the probability of recidivism, have only a momentary and general effect on true delinquents, that is, on those who have adopted offending as a way of life (see the works of Cusson, 1983, and of Finckenauer, 1984, in this regard).

In the case of neutralization, which Western societies have been using for ages, incarceration and probation are called for. The rates of recidivism, shown by many studies, speak for themselves. For the juvenile delinquents we have studied, they are 85% for incarcerated subjects and 60% for those placed on probation (Le Blanc, 1985b). Neutralization is effective while the subject is under restraint, but has little impact over the long term (see Blumstein et al., 1986, and Gottfredson & Hirschi, 1986). Research results indicate that the more structured the offending, the less the effect of neutralization.

Since the effectiveness of treatment is also uncertain, as mentioned above, the only potentially more appropriate measure for chronic offending is early detection together with specific or guided prevention (see the arguments of Farrington et al., 1986c). Its object is to anticipate and eliminate incipient maladjustments, preferably when the subject is very young, for example by focusing on aggressive children during childhood (see Patterson, 1982; Patterson, Reed, Jones, & Conger, 1972); or when they start school (see Tremblay & Charlebois, 1988). This approach really seems the most promising, since it is essential to prevent an antisocial orientation from developing. In other words, maladjustment paving the way to delinquency and possibly criminality must be nipped in the bud. It is important for the subjects themselves, so that they can escape what is often a terrible fate, possibly ending in self-destruction or death; also for the community, since the potential for destruction increases considerably when subjects cross this threshold (and once they have reached it, they can even pass it on to the next generation; Favard, 1983). However, until the appropriate early prevention mechanisms have been both implemented and evaluated, it is imperative that we ask ourselves what curative intervention would be the most effective.

With persistent delinquents, the strategy of intervention should not focus only on the criminal activity. Social and psychological factors must be taken into account. Therefore, going more deeply into our analysis, we arrived at a typology of delinquents who have been through the courts, and, on the basis of their offending patterns, we have been able to identify explicit configurations with social and psychological characteristics. These are to a great extent mutually exclusive (see Fréchette & Le Blanc, 1987). For each of them, we found the essential orientations of the intervention, the measures being chosen according to their pertinence and differential effectiveness.

In short, a true clinical approach is possible. Our knowledge now enables us to better differentiate between offending patterns and thus to better conciliate the social objectives – the protection of society, aid to the youth, and an answer to the personal needs of the maladjusted – through policies and better modulated strategies of intervention. To develop a similar model of clinical action, the first thing to be done is to reduce the competition between organizations and professions. At the same time we must set up structures capable of taking action, structures that should be based on scientific knowledge and practice, and set in operation a true model of differential intervention. This school of thought and this differentialist discourse are still too little regarded in criminology.

Postscript

From the very beginning of this work, we set out to demonstrate the need to conceptualize and operationalize the phenomenon of crime with more precision. To do this, we chose to limit ourselves to one level of interpretation, the one concerned with criminal activity. We then proposed two levels of analysis, the offense and the offending, and for each a list of parameters. We analyzed our data in two different ways: a synthetic description by means of diverse parameters and a developmental analysis.

The synthetic description contributed in three ways to criminological knowledge, through the presentation of original data, through a comparison of self-reported and official delinquency, and through a comparison of our data with those of other researchers. The developmental analysis represents, in our opinion, our most interesting contribution to knowledge on criminal activity. It offers a perspective that shows how criminal activity starts, is consolidated, and is finally dropped. The start is a process of activation submitted to a dynamic of stimulation that depends on stabilization, acceleration, and diversification. The consolidation comes from a process of escalation by which the offender progresses from minor infractions to more serious crimes. We could describe this process because we were able to show a gradation of the offenses. Finally, abatement of illicit activity appears after a saturation point is reached; this desistance depends on deceleration, specialization, and culmination reaching a ceiling. Not only have we identified these mechanisms, but we have also proposed a formalized theory of the development of illicit activity. Finally, we have found avenues that can lead to an explanation of criminal activity and to policies, decision making, and intervention, connected as solidly as possible with our knowledge about crime.

We cannot end this work without mentioning two problems that face researchers in their task of developing scientific knowledge—the difficulties of reconciling first creativity and replication and second, generalization and elaboration. The improvement of theories requires creativity, the ability to leave the beaten track and suggest new solutions. On the other hand, empirical research requires replication. Generally speaking, the value of creativity is put ahead of replication in criminology. A theory is verified once, then immediately modified by another researcher, and then tested. The fact is there is little replication in our discipline. There is no doubt that these two requirements should be put on the same footing; the policy of publishing scientific reviews could be a strong lever in this regard if it explicitly encouraged precise replications.

As to the second problem, researchers have a natural tendency to try to formulate generalizations, laws of general application, rather than developing their conceptualization. To favor the first over the second has the disadvantage of maintaining criminological theories at a level of generality that in the end can paralyze the field. The only way to give these two opposite perspectives equal value is to constantly reaffirm the need for both of them.

Appendix A
The Self-reported Questionnaire

1. During the past 12 months, did you purposely damage or destroy musical instruments, sport supplies, or other school equipment?
2. During the past 12 months, did you purposely damage or destroy public or private property that did not belong to you?
3. During the past 12 months, did you take some school property worth $5.00 or more?
4. During the past 12 months, did you purposely damage school building (windows, walls, . . .)?
5. During the past 12 months, did you take a motorcycle and go for a ride without the owner's permission?
6. During the past 12 months, did you take a car and go for a drive without the owner's permission?
7. During the past 12 months, did you purposely destroy a radio antenna, tires, or other parts of a car?
8. During the past 12 months, did you "beat up" someone who hadn't done anything to you?
9. During the past 12 months, did you take something from a store without paying?
10. During the past 12 months, did you threaten to beat up someone to make him do something he didn't want to do?
11. During the past 12 months, did you get into a place (a movie, a game, or a performance) without paying the admission price?
12. During the past 12 months, did you use a weapon (stick, knife, gun, rock, . . .) while fighting with another person?
13. During the past 12 months, did you use stimulants (speed, pep pills, etc. . . .) or hallucinogens (LSD, STP, THC, etc. . . .)?
14. During the past 12 months, did you have a fist fight with another person?
15. During the past 12 months, did you take something of large value (worth $50.00 or more) that did not belong to you?
16. During the past 12 months, did you gamble for money with persons other than your family members?
17. During the past 12 months, did you sell any kind of drugs?

18. During the past 12 months, did you break into and enter somewhere to take something?
19. During the past 12 months, did you carry a weapon (chain, knife, gun, etc. . . .)?
20. During the past 12 months, did you take something of some value (between $2.00 and $50.00) that did not belong to you?
21. During the past 12 months, did you purposely set a fire in a building or in any other place?
22. During the past 12 months, did you take and keep a bicycle that did not belong to you?
23. During the past 12 months, did you take something of little value (worth less than $2.00) that did not belong to you?
24. During the past 12 months, did you trespass anywhere you were not supposed to go (e.g., vacant house, railroad tracks, lumber yard, etc. . . .)?
25. During the past 12 months, did you use marijuana or hashish?
26. During the past 12 months, did you make anonymous phone calls (not say who you were)?
27. During the past 12 months, did you use opiates (heroin, morphine, opium)?
28. During the past 12 months, did you send in a false alarm?
29. During the past 12 months, did you buy, use, or sell something that you knew had been stolen?
30. During the past 12 months, did you drive a car without a driver's license?
31. During the past 12 months, did you have sexual relations (other than kissing) with a person of the same sex?
32. During the past 12 months, did you skip school without a legitimate excuse?
33. During the past 12 months, did you have sexual relations (other than kissing) with a person of the opposite sex?
34. During the past 12 months, did you take part in a gang fight between adolescents?
35. During the past 12 months, did you run away from home for more than 24 hours?
36. During the past 12 months, did you tell your parents (or those who replace them) that you would not do what they ordered you to do?
37. During the past 12 months, did you take money from home without permission and with no intention of returning it?
38. During the past 12 months, did you get drunk on beer, wine, or other alcoholic beverages?
39. During the past 12 months, did you "fool around" at night when you were supposed to be home?

Appendix B
The Semistructured Interview

1. Questions:
   1. Have you ever comitted any crimes?
      (If yes)
   2. What crimes? (from the most recent to the earliest)
   3. How old were you? (for each)
   4. What was your very first crime?
   5. How old were you?
   6. How were your latest crimes carried out?
   7. Did you plan your offenses? (premeditation)
   8. Did you have any accomplices?
      (If yes)
   9. Who were they?
   10. Were they older or younger than you?
   11. What was your role?
       (If not, or if subject no longer has any)
       12. Why do you operate alone?
   13. Did you use any tools?
       (If yes)
   14. Why?
   15. Was there any violence during your crimes?
       (If yes)
   16. What sort of violence?
   17. Why was there violence?
   18. Did you drink or take drugs when you committed your crimes?
       (If yes)
   19. Which did you take?
   20. Who was the victim or victims in each of your crimes?
   21. Why did you choose this victim?
   22. Why did you commit your crimes (What promped you?)
   23. How did you feel while committing each of your crimes?
   24. After each crime where you afraid of being arrested?

25. How many times have you been arrested?
    (If arrested)
26. At what age the first time?
27. For what crime or crimes were you arrested?
28. How many times have you appeared before a judge?
29. What were you convicted for (what was the judge's sentence?)
30. At what age were you convicted for the first time?
    (If the subject had been placed in an institution)
31. To what institution were you (will you be) sent?
32. What was the reaction of your family and your school to these arrests and convictions?

2. Codification

Codification of the variables relating to each type of crime:

Frequency: approximate number

Age: -At the start
-At the end

Instrument

Recourse to the use of an instrument of some sort, making the delinquent activity more effective, easier, etc.

1. No instrument used
2. Used seldom (less than half the crimes committed)
3. Used frequently (half or more occasions)
4. No information

Preparation

Crime planned (ahead of time), organization of the activity, and/or systematic repetition (using the same method as usual)

1. No preparation
2. Preparation seldom
3. Preparation frequent
4. No information

Accomplices

1. None
2. A small number
3. A significant number
4. No information

If accomplices present:

Number of accomplices

Fill in the number if one crime, or if several crimes, fill in the usual number of accomplices (or the closest approximation to this number) for each occasion

9. Nine accomplices or more

Age of accomplices

1. Same age level (within a span of 2 years) or more than half the occasions with accomplices

2. Various ages on more than half the occasions
3. Half and half (the occasions)
4. No information

Specific age of accomplices
1. Older than the subject by at least 1 year or more (for all or the majority of accomplices)
2. The same age as the subject (for all or the majority of accomplices)
3. Younger than the subject
4. No information

Participation of the subject in group crimes

Role played in the preparation and/or execution of the crime
1. Active role (in decisions, carrying out crime) on half the occasions or more with accomplices
2. Passive role (onlooker, present by chance or involuntarily, a "follower," etc.) on more than half the occasions
4. No information

Physical violence

Use of force involving physical consequences for the victim (any physical contact)
1. None
2. Rare physical violence
3. Frequent physical violence
4. No information

If there is physical violence:

Nature of the violence
1. No weapons (bare hand only)
2. Occasional use of weapons (on less than half the occasions of violence) (guns, knives, dangerous objects, etc.)
3. Frequent use of weapons (half the occasions or more)
4. No information

Psychological violence

Use of any kind of pressure other than physical, such as intimidation, alone or with a group, brandishing a weapon, threatening reprisals, etc., to compel the victim
1. Never
2. Sometimes
3. Often
4. No information

Intoxication

Consumption of alcohol, drugs, or any other product before and/or during the perpetration of the crime and relative to the crime
1. No
2. Sometimes
3. Often
4. No information

Knowing the victim

Victim known, i.e., person and/or place that is known by the subject, that is familiar to him

1. Not known
2. Sometimes
3. Often
4. No information

Motivation – hedonistic, gratifying

Any act committed for fun, kicks, the need to show off (including peer pressure) to get attention, and of a markedly impulsive nature

1. No hedonistic motivation
2. Some hedonistic motivation
3. Significant hedonistic motivation
4. No information

Utilitarian aspect

Any act committed because of material need, for the lure of gain, for certain advantages, or in a spirit of vengeance

1. No utilitarian motivation
2. Some utilitarianism
3. Significant
4. No information

Reaction

During the act

1. No nervous reactions (cool, as usual)
2. Some nervous reaction
3. Significant nervous reaction (fear, tension)
4. No information

After the act

1. No nervous reaction (content, cool, indifferent)
2. Significant reaction (anxious, fearful, guilty)
3. No information

Arrest

Fill in the number mentioned

References

Akman, D., & Normandeau, A. (1968). The measurement of crime and delinquency in Canada: A replication study. *Acta Criminologica* 1:135–173.

Albany Conference (1987). *Theoretical Integration in the Study of Deviance and Crime: Problems and Prospects.* Department of Sociology, University of Albany, Albany, NY.

Alexander, F., & Staub, H. (1934). *Le criminel it sis juges.* Paris: Gallimard.

American Psychiatric Association (1980, 1987 rev.). *Diagnostic and Statistical Manual of Mental Disorders.* Washington, D.C.: American Psychiatric Association.

Amir, M. (1971). *Patterns of Forcible Rape.* Chicago: University of Chicago Press.

Andersen, C. (1963). Le comportement criminel des anormaux mentaux. *Colloque sur les délinquants anormaux mentaux.* Paris: Cujas.

Aries, P. (1962). *Des siècles d'infance.* Berlin: Knopf.

Arnold, W.R., & Brungardt, T. (1983). *Juvenile Misconduct and Delinquency.* Boston: Houghton Mifflin.

Bachman, J.G., O'Malley, P.M., & Johnston, J. (1978). *Youth in Transition: Adolescence to Adulthood. Change and Stability in the Lives of Young Men.* Ann Arbor, MI: Institute for Social Research.

Barnett, A., Blumstein, A., & Farrington, D.P. (1987). Probabilistic models of youthful criminal careers. *Criminology* 25(1):83–107.

Barnett, A., & Lofaso, A.J. (1985). Selective incapacitation in the Philadelphia cohort data. *Journal of Quantitative Criminology* 1:3–36.

Becker, H.S. (1963). *Outsiders, Studies in the Sociology of Deviance.* New York: The Free Press.

Becker, H.S. (1970). *Sociological Work: Method and Substance.* Chicago: Aldine.

Belson, W., & Beeson, M. (1969). Identifying difficulties and facilitating factors in getting information from boys about their stealing and about associated matters: An exploratory study. The Survey Research Center, London School of Economics.

Bennett, T., & Wright, R. (1984). *Burglars on Burglary.* Aldershot, Hants, England: Gower.

Biron, L., Caplan, A., & Le Blanc, M. (1975). La construction de l'échantillon, la cueillette des données et leur préparation. Montréal, Research Group on Juvenile Maladaptation, University of Montréal.

Biron, L., Caplan, A., & Le Blanc, M. (1977). La relance: Échantillonnage, cueillett et préparation des donées. Research Group on juvenile maladaptation, University of Montréal.

Blalock, H.M. (1969). *Theory Construction: From Verbal to Mathematical Formulations.* Englewood Cliffs, NJ: Prentice Hall.

Blalock, H.M. (1970). *Introduction to Social Research.* Englewood Cliffs, NJ: Prentice Hall.

Blumstein, A., & Moitra, S.D. (1980). The identification of "career criminals" from "chronic offenders" in a cohort. *Law Policy Quarterly* 2(3):321–334.

Blumstein, A., & Cohen, J., with Hshieh, P. (1982b). The duration of adult criminal careers. Final report submitted to National Institute of Justice, August 1982. School of Urban and Public Affairs, Carnegie-Mellon University, Pittsburgh, PA.

Blumstein, A., Cohen, J., & Das, S. (1985a). Crime-type switching in criminal careers. Unpublished paper. Urban Systems Institute, School of Urban and Public Affairs, Carnegie-Mellon University, Pittsburgh, PA.

Blumstein, A., Farrington, D.P., & Moitra, S. (1985b). Delinquency careers: Innocents, desisters and persisters. In Tonry, M., & Morris, N. (Eds.): *Crime and Justice: An Annual Review of Research (Vol. 6).* Chicago: University of Chicago Press.

Blumstein, A., Cohen, J., & Farrington, D.P. (1988a). Criminal career research: Its value for criminology. *Criminology* 26(1):1–35.

Blumstein, A., Cohen, J., & Farrington, D.P. (1988b). Longitudinal and criminal career research: Further clarifications. *Criminology* 26(1):57–74.

Blumstein, A., Cohen, J., Roth, J.A., & Visher, C.A. (1986). *Criminal Careers and "Career Criminals"* (Vols. 1 and 2). Washington, DC: National Academy Press.

Brennan, T. (1987). Classification: An overview of selected methodological issues. In Gottfredson, D.M., & Tonry, M. (Eds.): *Prediction and Classification, Criminal Justice Decision Making: Crime and Justice, A Review of Research (Vol. 9).* Chicago: University of Chicago Press, pp. 201–248.

Briggs, P.F., Wirt, R.D., & Johnson, R. (1961). An application of prediction tables to the study of delinquency. *Journal of Consulting Psychology* 25:46–50.

Brown, W.K., & Gable, R.J. (1980). Socialization of delinquents. *International Journal of Offender Therapy and Comparative Criminology* 24(1):58–66.

Bursik, R.J. (1980). The dynamics of specialization in juvenile offences. *Social Forces* 58:851–864.

Cameron, M.Q. (1964). *The Booster and the Snitch.* New York: The Free Press.

Caplan, A., & Le Blanc, M. (1976). Measuring delinquency: The homogeneous-heterogeneous issue. Paper presented at the 71st Annual Meeting of the American Sociological Association, New York.

Carroll, J., & Weaver, F. (1986). Shoplifters perceptions of crime opportunities: A process-tracing study. In Cornish, D.B., & Clarke, R.V.G. (Eds.): *The Reasoning Criminal: Rational Choice Perspectives on Offending.* New York: Springer-Verlag, pp. 19–38.

Cavan, R.S. (1962). *Juvenile Delinquency.* Philadelphia: J.B. Lippincott.

Cavan, R.S. (1969). *Juvenile Delinquency: Development, Treatment, Control.* 2nd ed. Philadelphia: J.B. Lippincott.

Cernkovich, S.A., Giordano, P.C., & Pugh, M.D. (1985). Chronic offenders: The missing cases in self-reported delinquency research. *The Journal of Criminal Law and Criminology* 76:705–732.

Chaiken, J.M., & Chaiken, M.R. (1982). *Varieties of Criminal Behavior.* Santa Monica, CA: Rand Corporation.

Chaiken, J.M., & Chaiken, M.R. (1984). Offender types and public policy. *Crime and Delinquency* 30:195–226.

Chaiken, J., & Rolph, J.E. (1985). *Identifying High-Rate Serious Criminal Offenders.* Santa Monica, CA: Rand Corporation.

Charbonneau, J.P. (1982). *Rapport de la commission parlementaire spéciale sur la protection de la jeunesse. Québec.* National Assembly of Québec.
Clarke, R.V.G. (1983). Situational crime prevention: Its theoretical basis and practical scope. In Tonry M., Morris, N. (Eds.): *Crime and Justice: An Annual Review of Research (Vol. 4).* Chicago: University of Chicago Press, pp. 225–256.
Clarke, R.V.G., & Cornish, D.B. (1985). Modeling offenders' decisions: A framework for research and policy. In Tonry M. & Morris, N. (Eds.): *Crime and Justice: An Annual Review of Research (Vol. 6).* Chicago: University of Chicago Press, pp. 147–185.
Clerckley, H. (1964). *The Mask of Sanity.* 4th ed. St Louis, MO: C.V. Mosby.
Clinard, M., & Quinney, R. (1967). *Criminal Behavior Systems: A Typology.* New York: Holt, Rinehart and Winston.
Cloward, R.A., & Ohlin, L.E. (1960). *Delinquency and Opportunity: A Theory of Delinquent Gangs.* New York: The Free Press.
Cocklin, J. (1972). *Robbery and the Criminal Justice System.* Philadelphia: J.B. Lippincott.
Cohen, A.K. (1955). *Delinquent Boys: The Subculture of the Gang.* Glencoe, IL: The Free Press.
Cohen, A.K. (1966). *Deviance and Control.* Englewood Cliffs, NJ: Prentice Hall.
Cohen, A.K. (1969). The study of social disorganization and deviant behavior. In Merton, R.K., Broom, L., Cottrell, L.S. (Eds.): *Sociology Today: Problems and Prospects.* New York: Basic Books.
Cohen, J. (1986). Research on criminal career: Individual frequency rates and offense seriousness. In Blumstein, A., Cohen, J., Roth, J.A., & Visher, C.A. (Eds.): *Criminal Careers and "Career Criminals"* (Vol. 1). Washington, DC: National Academy Press, pp. 292–418.
Cohen, L.E., & Felson, M. (1979). Property crime rates in the United States: A macrodynamic analysis 1947–1977, with ex ante forecasts for the mid-1980s. *American Journal of Sociology* 86:90–118.
Cohen, L.E., & Felson, M. (1980). Social change and crime rate trends: A routine activity approach. *American Sociological Review* 44:588-608.
Collins, J.J. (1981). Alcohol careers and criminal careers. In Collins, J.J. (Ed.): *Drinking and Crime.* New York: Guilford Press.
Conger, J.J., & Petersen, A.C. (1984). *Adolescence and Youth: Psychological Development in a Changing World.* New York: Harper & Row.
Cormier, B.M., Kennedy, J., Sangoviz, J., & Trottier, M. (1959). The natural history of criminality and some tentative hypotheses on its abatement. *Canadian Journal of Correction* 1(4):35–49.
Cornish, D.B., & Clarke, R.V. (1986). *The Reasoning Criminal: Rational Choice Perspectives on Offending.* New York: Springer-Verlag.
Corrado, R.R., Trépanier, J., & Le Blanc, M. (1983). *Current Issues in Juvenile Justice.* Toronto: Butterworths.
Cullen, F.T. (1985). *Rethinking Crime and Deviance Theory: The Emergence of a Structuring Tradition.* Totowa: Rowman & Allanheld.
Cusson, M. (1981). *Délinquant pourquoi?* Montreal: Hurtubise.
Cusson, M. (1983). *Le contrôle social du crime.* Paris: Presses Universitaires de France.
Cusson, M. (1986). L'analyse stratégique et quelques développements récents en criminologie. *Criminologie* 19(1):53–72.
Cusson, M., & Pinsonneault, P. (1986). The decision to give up crime. In Cornish, D.B., & Clarke, R.V. (Eds.): *The Reasoning Criminal: Rational Choice Perspectives of Offending.* New York: Springer-Verlag, pp. 72–82.

Datesman, S.K., & Aikin, M. (1984). Offense specialization and escalation among status offenders. *Journal of Criminal Law and Criminology* 75(4):1246–1275.

Davis, J.A. (1963). *Panel Analysis: Techniques and Concepts in the Interpretation of Repeated Measurements.* National Opinion Research Center, University of Chicago.

Debuyst, C. (1960). *Criminels et valeurs vécues: étude clinique d'un groupe de jeunes criminels.* Louvain: Publications Universitaires Béatrice.

De Greef, E. (1947). *Les instincts de défense et de sympathie.* Paris: Presses Univeristaires de France.

De Greef, E. (1955). Criminologie. In *Actes du 11e Congrès international de criminologie (Vol. VI).* Paris: Presses Universitaires de France.

De Greef, E. (1956). Le devenir, élément du processus criminogène: La durée condition de son étude. *Autour de l'oeuvre du Dr. E. de Greff.* Louvain: Editions Nauvelaerts.

Denno, D.H. (1985). Sociological and human development explanations of crime: Conflict or consensus? *Criminology* 23:711–741.

Duncan, O.D. (1984). *Notes on Social Measurement: Historical and Critical.* New York: Russell Sage Foundation.

Dunford, F.W., & Elliott, D.S. (1984). Identifying career offenders using self-reported data. *Journal of Research in Crime and Delinquency* 21(1):57–86.

Dunford, F.W., Elliott, D.S., & Huizinga, D. (1983). *Characteristics of Career Offending: Testing Four Hypotheses.* Project report no. 2 submitted to the National Institute of Justice. Behavior Research Institute, Boulder, CO.

Durkheim, E. (1956). *Les règles de la méthode sociologique.* Paris: Presses Universitaires de France.

Elliott, D.S., & Ageton, S.A. (1980). Recording race and class differences in self-reported and official estimates of delinquency. *American Sociological Review* 45:95–100.

Elliott, D.S., Dunford, F.W., & Huizinga, D. (1987). The identification and prediction of career offenders utilizing self-reported delinquency and official data. In Burchard, J.D., & Burchard, S.N. (Eds.): *Prevention of delinquent behavior: Primary prevention and psychopathology (Vol. 10).* Beverly Hills, CA: Sage, pp. 90–121.

Elliott, D.S., & Huizinga, D. (1980). Social class and delinquent behavior in a national youth panel. *Criminology* 21(2):149–178.

Elliott, D.S., Huizinga, D., & Ageton, S.S. (1985). *Explaining Delinquency and Drug Use.* Beverly Hills: Sage Publications.

Elmhorn, D. (1965). Study in self-reported delinquency among schoolchildren in Stockholm. In Christiansen, K.O. (Ed.): *Scandinavian Studies in Criminology* (Vol. 1). London: Tavistock.

Empey, L.T. (1978). *American Delinquency: Its Meaning and Construction.* Homewood, IL: Dorsey Press.

Erez, E. (1980). Planning of crime and the criminal career: Official and hidden offenses. *The Journal of Criminal Law and Criminology* 71(1):73–76.

Erez, E. (1987). Situational or planned crime and the criminal career. In Wolfgang, M.E., Thornberry, T.P., & Figlio, R.M. (Eds.): *From Boy to Man, From Delinquency to Crime.* Chicago: University of Chicago Press, pp. 122–133.

Erickson, M.L., & Empey, L.T. (1963). Court records, undetected delinquency and decision making. *Journal of Criminal Law, Criminology and Police Science* 54:456–469.

Farrington, D.P. (1973). Self-reports of deviant behavior: Predictive and stable. *Journal of Criminal Law and Criminology* 64:99–110.

Farrington, D.P. (1977). The effect of public labelling. *British Journal of Criminology* 17(2):112–125.

Farrington, D.P. (1979). *Juvenile Justice in England and Canada.* Ottawa, Solicitor General of Canada.

Farrington, D.P. (1981). The prevalence of convictions. *British Journal of Criminology* 2(2):173–175.

Farrington, D.P. (1982). Delinquency from 10 to 25. In Mednick, S.A. (Ed.): *Antecedents of Aggression and Antisocial Behavior.* Boston: Hingman, Kluwer.

Farrington, D.P. (1983). Offending from 10 to 25 years of age. In Teilmann-Van Deusen, K., & Mednick, S.A. (Eds.): *Prospective Studies of Crime and Delinquency.* Boston: Klumer Nyholf. pp. 17–38.

Farrington, D.P. (1984). Measuring the natural history of delinquency and crime. In Glow, R.A. (Ed.): *Advances in the Behavioral Measurement of Children (Vol. 1).* Greenwich, England: JAI Press.

Farrington, D.P. (1986a). Age and crime. In Tonry, M., & Morris, N. (Eds.): *Crime and Delinquency: An Annual Review of Research* (Vol. 7), pp. 189–250. Chicago, IL: The University of Chicago Press.

Farrington, D.P. (1986b). Stepping stones to adult criminal careers. In Olweus, D., Block, J., & Radke-Yarrow, M. (Eds.): *Development of Antisocial and Prosocial Behavior.* New York: Academic, pp. 359–384.

Farrington, D.P., Gallager, B., Morley, L., Ledger, R.J., & West, D.J. (1985a). Cambridge study in delinquent development: Long term follow-up. First annual report to the Home Office, Institute of Criminology, University of Cambridge, England.

Farrington, D.P., & Tarling, R. (1985b). *Prediction in Criminology.* Albany, NY: State University of New York Press.

Farrington, D.P., Gallager, B., Morley, L., Ledger, R.J., & West, D.J. (1986a). Cambridge study in delinquent development: Long term follow-up. Second annual report to the Home Office, Institute of Criminology, University of Cambridge, England.

Farrington, D.P., Gallager, B., Morley, L., Ledger, R.J., & West, D.J. (1987). Cambridge study in delinquent development: Long term follow-up. Third annual report to the Home Office, Institute of Criminology, University of Cambridge, England.

Farrington, D.P., Ohlin, L.E., & Wilson, J.Q. (1986c). *Understanding and Controlling Crime: Toward a New Research Strategy.* New York: Springer-Verlag.

Farrington, D.P., Snyder, H.S., & Finegan, T.A. (1988). Specialization in juvenile court careers. *Criminology* 26:461–487.

Farrington, D.P. (1985). Predicting self-reported or official delinquency. In Farrington, D.P., & Tarling, R. (Eds.): *Prediction in Criminology.* Albany, NY: State University of New York Press.

Favard, A.M. (1980). *Étude du devenir criminologique de quatre cohortes de naissance de la région bayonnaise.* Bayonne, France: Sauvegarde de l'enfance du Pays Basque.

Favard, A.M. (1983). La reproduction de l'inadaptation. *Les Cahiers du C.T.N.E.R.I.* 22:19–49.

Feeney, F. (1986). Robbers as decision-makers. In Cornish, D.K., & Clarke, R.V. (Eds.): *The Reasoning Criminal: Rational Choice Perspectives on Offending.* New York: Springer-Verlag, pp. 53–71.

Feldman, M.P. (1978). *Criminal Behavior: A Psychological Analysis.* New York: John Wiley.

Feldman, R.A., Caplinger, T.E., Wodarshy, J.J. (1983). *The Saint Louis Conundrum: The Effective Treatment of Antisocial Youths.* Englewood Cliffs, NJ: Prentice Hall.

Felson, M. (1987). Routine activities and crime prevention in the developing metropolis. *Criminology* 25(4):911–932.

Felson, M., & Cohen, L.E. (1980). Human ecology and crime: A routine activity approach. *Human Ecology* 8:384–406.

Ferdinand, T.N. (1987). The methods of delinquency theory. *Criminology* 25(4):841–863.

Ferri, E. (1905). *La sociologie criminelle (Vols. 1 and 2).* Paris: Alcan.

Finckenauer, J.O. (1984). *Juvenile Delinquency and Correction: The Gap Between Theory and Research.* New York: Academic Press.

Follman, J. (1972). Reported delinquency of college students and delinquents. *Psychological Report* 31(3):998.

Fréchette, M. (1970). Le criminel et l'autre: analyse des relations interpersonnelles de l'homme criminel. *Acta Criminologica* 3:11–102.

Fréchette, M. (1980). Portrait de la délinquance: Rapport final de la recherche sur le diagnostic et le prognostic de la délinquance grave. University of Montreal, Research Group on Juvenile Maladaptation.

Fréchette, M., & Le Blanc, M. (1978). *La délinquance cachée des adolescents montréalais,* Vol. 1 of final report, University of Montreal, Research Group on Juvenile Maladapation.

Fréchette, M., & Le Blanc, M. (1979). *La délinquance cachée à l'adolescence.* University of Montreal, Research Group on Juvenile Maladaptation.

Fréchette, M., & Le Blanc, M. (1980). *Pour une pratique de la criminologie: Configurations de conduites délinquantes et portraits de délinquants,* Vol. 5. University of Montreal, Research Group on Juvenile Maladaptation.

Fréchette, M., & Le Blanc, M. (1987). *Délinquances et délinquants.* Québec, Canada: Gaétan Morin.

Frum, H.S. (1958). Adult criminal offense trends following juvenile delinquency. *Journal of Criminal Law, Criminology and Police Science* 49:29–49.

Gabor, T., Baril, M., Cusson, M., Élie, D., Le Blanc, M., & Normandeau, A. (1987). *Armed Robbery: Cops, Robbers and Victims.* Springfield, IL: Charles C Thomas.

Gagnon, D. (1978). Histoire de la loi sur les jeunes délinquants. Unpublished master's thesis. University of Montreal, School of Criminology.

Gagnon, R., & Le Blanc, M. (1984). Le vol à main armée dans les systèmes de justice. International Center of Comparative Criminology, University of Montreal.

Garfinkel, H. (1967). *Studies in Ethnomethodology.* Englewood Cliffs, NJ: Prentice-Hall.

Gath, D., Tennent, G., & Pidduck, R. (1971). Criminological characteristics of bright delinquents. *British Journal of Criminology* 11:275–279.

Gibbens, T.C.N. (1969). *The Identification of Key Problems in Criminological Research.* Strasbourg, France: Council of Europe.

Gibbons, D.C. (1965). *Changing the Lawbreakers.* Englewood Cliffs, NJ: Prentice-Hall.

Gibbons, D.C. (1968). *Society, Crime and Criminal Career.* Englewood Cliffs, NJ: Prentice-Hall.

Gibbons, D.C. (1975). Offender typologies—two decades later. *British Journal of Criminology* 15:140–156.

Glover, E. (1960). *The Roots of Crime.* London: Imago Publishing.

Glueck, E.T. (1968). *Delinquents and Non-Delinquents in Perspective.* Cambridge, MA: Harvard University Press.

Glueck, S., & Glueck, E. (1970). *Toward a Typology of Juvenile Offenders.* New York: Grune & Stratton.

Glueck, S., & Glueck, E. (1974). *Of Delinquency and Crime.* Springfield, IL: Charles C Thomas.

Glueck, S., & Glueck, E. (1930). *Five Hundred Criminal Careers.* New York: Knopf.

Glueck, S., & Glueck, E. (1937). *Later Criminal Careers.* New York: The Commonwealth Fund.

Glueck, S., & Glueck, E. (1940). *Juvenile Delinquents Grown Up.* New York: The Commonwealth Fund.

Glueck, S., & Glueck, E. (1943). *Criminal Careers in Retrospect.* New York: The Commonwealth Fund.

Gold, M. (1966). Undetected delinquent behavior. *Journal of Research in Crime and Delinquency* 3:27–46.

Gold, M. (1970). *Delinquent Behavior in an American City.* Belmont, CA: Brooks/Cole.

Goodenough, W.H. (1944). A technique for scale analysis. *Educational and Psychological Measurement* 4:179–190.

Göppinger, H. (1987). *Life Style and Criminality.* New York: Springer-Verlag.

Gordon, R.A. (1976). Prevalence: The rate datum in delinquency measurement and its implication of the theory of delinquency. In Klein, M.W. (Ed.): *The Juvenile Justice System.* Beverly Hills, CA: Sage.

Gottfredson, M.R., & Gottfredson, D.M. (198). *Decisionmaking in Criminal Justice: Toward the Rational Exercise of Discretion.* Cambridge, MA: Ballinger.

Gottfredson, M.R., & Hirschi, T. (1986). The true value of lambda would appear to be zero: An essay on career criminals, criminal careers, selective incapacitation, cohort studies and related topics. *Criminology* 24(2):213–234.

Gottfredson, M.R., & Hirschi, T. (1987a). The methodological adequacy of longitudinal research on crime. *Criminology* 25(3):581–614.

Gottfredson, M.R., & Hirschi, T. (1987b). A propensity-event theory of crime. *Advances in Criminological Theory* 1:181–218. New Brunswick, NJ: Transaction Publishers.

Gottfredson, M.R., & Hirschi, T. (1988). Science, public policy and the career paradigm. *Criminology* 26(1):37–55.

Green, M.A. (1977). *The Incapacitative Effect of Imprisonment Policies on Crime.* Ph.D. Thesis, School of Urban and Public Affairs, Carnegie-Mellon University, Pittsburgh, PA (University Microfilms, Ann Arbor, MI).

Greenberg, D.F. (1975). The incapacitative effect of imprisonment: Some estimates. *Law and Society Review,* pp. 11:541–580.

Guttridge, P., Mednick, S.A., & Van Deusen, K. (1982). Violence in a Danish birth cohort. In Mednick, S.A. (Ed.): *Antecedents of Aggression and Antisocial Behavior.* Boston: Hingman, Kluwer.

Hagan, F.E. (1987). *Introduction to Criminology: Theories, Methods and Criminal Behavior.* Chicago, Nelson-Hall.

Hamparian, D., Schuster, R., Dinitz, S., & Conrad, J. (1978). *The Violent Few: A Study of Dangerous Juvenile Offenders.* Lexington, MA: Lexington Books.

Hardt, R.N., & Bodine, G.E. (1965). *Development of Self-report Instruments in Delinquency Research: A Conference Report. Syracuse,* NY: Youth Development Center.

Hare, R.D. (1970). Psychopathy and response to electrical stimulation. *Journal of Abnormal Psychology* 76:3–70.

Hausman, P., Beaufils, M., Boniver, M., & Kerger, A. (1982). *Le poids de l'inadaptation en milieu scolaire dans le processus delinquantiel.* Luxemburg University Foundation, Luxemburg Center for Social and Pedagogic Research.

Hawkins, J.D., Oastaic, M., Bele, M., & Morrison, S. (1980). *A Typology of Causes: Focused Strategies of Delinquency Prevention.* Washington, DC: Office of Juvenile Justice and Delinquency Prevention.

Healy, W., & Bronner, A.F. (1936). *Delinquency and Its Treatment.* New Haven, CN: Yale University Press.

Hempel, C.G. (1952). Typological methods in the natural and social sciences. *Proceedings, American Philosophical Association.* Philadelphia: University of Philadelphia Press, p. 84.

Hesnard, A. (1963). *Psychologie du crime.* Paris: Payot.

Hewitt, L.E., & Jenkins, R.L. (1946). *Fundamental Patterns of Maladjustment: The Dynamics of Their Origin.* Springfield, IL: State University of Illinois.

Hindelang, M.J. (1972). *Situational Influences on the Delinquent Act.* Rockville, MD: National Institute of Mental Health.

Hindelang, M.J., Hirschi, T., & Weis, J.G. (1981). *Measuring Delinquency.* Beverly Hills, CA: Sage.

Hirschi, T. (1969). *Causes of Delinquency.* Berkeley, CA: University of California Press.

Hirschi, T. (1979). Separate and unequal is better. *Journal of Research in Crime and Delinquency* 16(1):34–38.

Hirschi, T. (1987). *Exploring Alternatives to Integrated Theory.* The Albany Conference, May 1987. Department of Sociology, University of Albany, NY.

Hirschi, T., & Gottfredson, M.R. (1983). Age and the explanation of crime. *American Journal of Sociology* 89:552–584.

Hirschi, T., & Gottfredson, M.R. (1986). The distinction between crime and criminality. In Hartnagel, T. & Silverman, R. (Eds.): *Critique and Explanation: Essays in Honor of Gwyne Nettler.* New Brunswick, NJ: Transaction Books.

Hirschi, T., & Selvin, H.C. (1967). *Delinquency Research: An Appraisal of Analytic Methods.* New York: The Free Press.

Hood, R., & Sparks, R.R. (1970). *Key Issues in Criminology.* London: Weidenfeld and Nicholson.

Hough, J.M., Clarke, R.V.G., & Mayhew, P. (1980). Introduction. In Clarke, R.V.G., & Mayhew, P. (Eds.): *Designing Out Crime.* London: Her Majesty's Stationary Office.

Huseman, L.R., Eron, L.D., Lefkovitz, M.M., & Walder, L.D. (1984). The stability of aggression over time and generations. *Developmental Psychology* 20:1120–1134.

Jason, C-G. (1982). *Delinquency Among Metropolitan Boys.* Project Metropolitan, a longitudinal study of Stockholm cohort (17). Department of sociology. University of Stockholm, Sweden.

Jeffery, C.R. (1959). An integrated theory of crime and criminal behavior. *Journal of Criminal Law, Criminology and Police Science* 49(6):533–552.

Jesness, C.F., & Haapanen, R.A. (1982). *Early Identification of the Chronic Offender.* Sacramento, CA: Department of the Youth Authority.

Jessor, R., & Jessor, S.L. (1977). *Problem Behavior and Psychological Development: A Longitudinal Study of Youth.* New York: Academic Press.

Johnson, G., Cohen, G., & Bird, T. (1981). *A Guide to Delinquency Prevention Programs Based in School Activities: A Working Paper.* Washington, DC: Office of Juvenile Justice and Delinquency Prevention.

Jolin, A., & Gibbons, D.C. (1988). Age patterns of criminal involvement. *International of offender therapy and comparative criminology* 30:237–260.

Kagan, J., & Moss, H.A. (1962). *Birth to Marturity: A Study in Psychological Development.* New York: John Wiley.

Karpman, B. (1959). *Child and Juvenile Delinquency.* Washington, DC: Psychodynamics Monograph Series.

Kempf, K.L. (1987). Specialization and the criminal career. *Criminology* 25(2):399–420.

Klein, M. (1955). On Identification. In Klein, M., Heimann, P., & Money-Kyple, R.E. (Eds.): *New Directions in Psychoanalysis.* London: Tavistock.

Klein, M.M. (1984). Offense specialization and versatility among juveniles. *British Journal of Criminology* 24(2):185–194.

Klein, M.M. (1988). Measurement of self-reported delinquency. NATO Advanced Research Workshop, The Hague, Holland.

Kobrin, S., & Klein, M.W. (1983). *Community Treatment of Juvenile Offenders: The DSO Experiments.* Beverly Hills, CA: Sage.

Lab, S.P. (1984). Patterns of juvenile misbehavior. *Crime and Delinquency* 30(2):293–308.

Lagache, D. (1965). *Le modèle psychoanalytique de la personnalite: les modèles de la personnalité en psychologie.* Paris: Presses Universitaires de France.

Lagier, P.M. (1983). Programme de recherche Myosotis IV: Diagnostic et prognostic de la criminalité vraie chez les jeunes adultes; rapport d'étape 1981–1982. University of Montreal, Research Group on Juvenile Maladaptation.

Lagier, P.M. (1988). La vie quotidienne des jeunes adultes anciens pupilles de la Cour du Bien Être Social de Montréal. Programme de recherche Myosotis IV: Diagnostic et prognostic de la criminalité vraie chez les jeunes adultes. University of Montreal, International Center of Comparative Criminology.

Langan, P.A., & Farrington, D.P. (1983). Two-track or one-track justice? Some evidence from an English longitudinal survey. *The Journal of Criminal Law and Criminology* 74(2):501–527.

Le Blanc, M. (1969). *Délinquance juvénile: perspective épidémiologique et sigmatique.* Doctoral Thesis, University of Montreal, Départment of Criminology.

Le Blanc, M. (1971). La réaction sociale à la délinquance juvénile: une analyse stigmatique. *Acta Criminologica* 4:112–191.

Le Blanc, M. (1977a). La délinquance à l'adolescence: de la délinquance cachée et de la délinquance apparente. *Annales de Vaucresson* 14:15–50.

Le Blanc, M. (1977b). *La délinquance juvénile au Québec.* Québec, Quebec Official Publisher.

Le Blanc, M. (1983a). La délinquance cachée, une alternative aux statistiques criminelles. In *Connaître la criminalité: le dernier état de la question.* Actes de 31st Cours international de criminologie, Aix, France. Aix: Presses de l'Université Aix-Marseille.

Le Blanc, M. (1983b). *Boscoville, la rééducation évaluée.* Montréal: Harribise, HMH.

Le Blanc, M. (1985a). La loi sur les jeunes contrevenants et les intervenants du système de justice pour mineurs au Québec. *Annales de Vaucresson* 21:67–92.

Le Blanc, M. (1985b). De l'efficacité de l'internat québéçois. *Revue canadienne de psycho-éducation* 14(2):113–120.

Le Blanc, M. (1986a). Pour une approche intégrative de la conduite délinquante des adolescents. *Criminologie* 19(1):73–96.

Le Blanc, M. (1986b). La prédiction de la carrière criminelle. *Criminologie* 19(2):79–100.

Le Blanc, M. (1988). Designing a self-reported instrument for the study of the development of offending from childhood to adulthood: Issues and problems. NATO Advanced Research Workshop on the Measurement of Self-reported Delinquency. The Hague, Holland, June 26–30.

Le Blanc, M., & Beaumont, H. (1985). Description du fonctionnement d'un tribunal de la jeunesse en milieu urbain. Montréal, Consultation, Évaluation et Recherche sur l'Inadaptation Juvénile.

Le Blanc, M., & Beaumont, H. (1986). De la délinquance à la criminalité. Montréal, International Center of Comparative Criminology, University of Montreal.

Le Blanc, M., Biron, L., & Caplan, A. (1973). La délinquance juvenile comise, observée et subie. Montreal: Departement de criminologie, Universite de Montreal.

Le Blanc, M., & Brousseau, G. (1974). La prise de décision et la recommandation de l'agent de probation pour mineurs. *Revue canadienne de criminologie* 16(4):373–392.

Le Blanc, M., & Côté, G. (1986). Comparaison des adolescents en 1974 et 1985. In Tremblay, R.E., Le Blanc, M., & Schwartzman, A. (Eds.): *La conduite délinquante des adolescents de Montréal (1974–1985): étude descriptive et prédictive.* Montréal: School of Psycho-Education, University of Montreal.

Le Blanc, M., Loeber, R., & Côté, G. (1988). Temporal paths in delinquency: Stability, regression and progression analyzed with panel data from an adolescent and a delinquent male sample. *Journal of Quantitative Criminology.*

Le Blanc, M., & Pronovost, L. (1979). Le passage de l'école au travail et la délinquance. *Apprentissage et Socialisation* 2(2):69–73.

Le Blanc, M., & Pronovost, L. (1980). Transition statuaire et délinquance. *Revue canadienne de criminologie* 22:288–297.

Le Blanc, M., & Tremblay, R.E. (1987). Drogues illicites et activités délictueuses chez les adolescents de Montréal: épidémiologie et esquisse d'une politique sociale. *Psychotropes* 3(3):57–72.

Lemay, M. (1973). *Psychopathologie juvénile: les désordres de la conduite chez l'enfant et l'adolescent.* Paris: Fleurus (2 vol.).

Lemert, E.M. (1972). *Human deviance, social problems and social control.* Englewood Cliffs, NJ: Prentice-Hall.

Lenski, G. (1987). Rethinking macrosociological theory. *American Sociological Review* 53:163–171.

Lerner, R.M. (1986). *Concepts and Theories of Human Development.* New York: Random House.

Lewin, K. (1933). *Principles of Topological Psychology.* New York: McGraw-Hill.

Lipton, D., Martinson, R., & Wilks, J. (1975). *The Effectiveness of Correctional Treatment: A Survey of Treatment Evaluation Studies.* New York: Praeger.

Loeber, R. (1982). The stability of antisocial and delinquent child behavior. A review. *Child Development* 53:1431–1446.

Loeber, R. (1985a). Patterns and development of antisocial child behavior. In Whitehurst G.J. (Ed.): *Annals of Child Development* (Vol. 2). Greenwich, England: Jay Press.

Loeber, R. (1985b). Les débuts précoces et la progression de la carrière des jeunes délinquants. In Le Blanc, M. (Ed.): *Conduites délinquantes et personnalités criminelles.* Les cahiers de l'École de Criminologie (no. 20). Montreal: University of Montreal.

Loeber, R. (1986). Precursors to delinquency. Paper presented at the Conference on Explaining Crime, University of Leiden, Leiden, Holland.

Loeber, R. (1987). Natural histories of conduct problems, delinquency and associates substance use: Evidence for developmental progressions. In Lahey, B.B., & Kazdin, E. (Eds.): *Advances in Clinical Child Psychology* (Vol. 10). New York: Plenum.

Loeber, R., & Dishion, T.J. (1983). Early predictors of male delinquency: A review. *Psychological Bulletin* 94(1):68–99.

Loeber, R., Dishion, T.J., & Patterson, G.R. (1984). Multiple gating: A multistate assessment procedure for identifying youths at risk for delinquency. *Journal of Research on Crime and Delinquency* 21(1):7–32.

Loeber, R., & Le Blanc, M. (1988). Toward a developmental criminology. In Tonry, M., & Morris, N. (Eds.): Crime and Justice, an Annual Review (Vol. 11). Chicago, IL: The University of Chicago Press.

Loeber, R., & Waller, N. (1988). Artefacts in delinquency specialization and generalization studies. *British Journal of Criminology* (in press).

Loevinger, J. (1966). The meaning and measurement of ego development. *American Psychologist* 21:195–206.

Lombroso, C. (1899). *Le crime, causes et remèdes.* Paris: Alcan.

Luckenbill, D.F. (1977). Criminal homicide as a situated interaction. *Social Problems* 25:176–186.

Lundman, R.J., & Scarpitti, F.R. (1978). Delinquency prevention, recommendations for future projects. *Crime and Delinquency* 24(2):207–220.

Maguire, M. (1982). *Burglary in a Dwelling.* London: Heinemann.

Mailloux, N. (1971). *Jeunes sans dialogue.* Paris: Fleurus.

Mannheim, H., & Wilkins, L.T. (1955). *Prediction Methods in Relation to Borstal Training.* London: Her Majesty's Stationary Office.

Mannheim, H. (1965). *Comparative Criminology (Vol. 2).* London: Routledge and Kegan Paul.

Marceau, B. (1985). Le délinquant violent devant la science et devant la loi. Doctoral Thesis, School of Criminology, University of Montreal.

Marineau, D., Fréchette, M., Limoges, T., & Le Blanc, M. (1971). Projet de prévention spécifique et criminologie. *Revue canadienne de criminologie* 13(3):233–250.

Mathias, R.A., DeMuro, P., & Allinson, R.S. (1984). *Violent Juvenile Offenders: An Anthology.* San Francisco: National Council on Crime and Delinquency.

Matza, D. (1964). *Delinquency and Drift.* New York: John Wiley.

Mayr, G., von (1917). Statistics and Gesellschaftslehe. *Kriminelstatistik* 3:45 et seq.

McCord, J. (1979). Some child-rearing antecedents of criminal behavior in adult men. *Journal of Personality and Social Psychology* 37(9):1477–1486.

McCord, J. (1981). Consideration of some effects of a counseling program. In Martin, S., Sechrest, L., & Redner, R. (Eds.): *New Directions in the Rehabilitation of Criminal Offenders.* Washington, DC: National Academy Press, pp. 394–405.

McCord, J. (1982). A longitudinal view of the relationship between paternal absence and crimes. In Gunn, J., & Farrington, D. (Eds.): *Abnormal Offenders, Delinquency, and the Criminal Justice System.* Chichester, England: John Wiley, pp. 113–128.

McCord, W., & McCord, J. (1956). *Origins of Crime.* New York: Columbia University Press.

McCord, W., & McCord, J. (1959). *The Psychopath: An Essay on the Criminal Mind.* New York: D. Van Nostrand.

Mednick, S.A., & Baert, A.E. (1981). *Prospective Longitudinal Research. An Empirical Basis for the Primary Prevention of Psychological Disorders.* Oxford, England: Oxford University Press.

Meier, R.F. (1985). *Theoretical Methods in Criminology.* Beverly Hills, CA: Sage.

Meisenhelder, T. (1977). An exploratory study of exiting from criminal careers. *Criminology* 15(3):319–334.

Mergargee, E.E., & Bohn, M.J. (1979). *Classifying Criminal Offenders.* Beverly Hills, CA: Sage.

Moitra, S.D. (1981). *Analysis of Sentencing Policies Considering Crime Switching Patterns and Imprisonment Constraints.* Ph.D. Dissertation, School of Urban and Public Affairs, Carnegie-Mellon University, Pittsburgh, PA.

Moore, M., Estrich, S.R., McGillis, D., & Spelman, W. (1984). *Dangerous Offender: The Elusive Target of Justice.* Cambridge, MA: Harvard University Press.

Morange, E.R. (1979). *La criminalité réelle à Aix-en-Provenence.* Doctoral Thesis, University of Law, Economy and Sciences of Aix-Marseille, France.

Morris, A., & Giller, H. (1987). *Understanding Juvenile Justice.* London: Croom Helm.

Moyer, S. (1975). *La déjudiciarisation dans le système judiciaire pour les jeunes et ses répercussions sur les enfants: recension de la documentation.* Ottawa, Research Division, Solicitor General of Canada.

Mucchielli, R. (1965). *Comment ils deviennent délinquants: genèse et développement de la socialisation et de la dissocialité.* Paris: Éditions Sociales Françaises.

Mulvey, E., & LaRosa, J.F. (1986). Delinquency cessation and adolescent development: Preliminary data. *American Journal of Orthopsychiatry* 56(2):212–224.

Murphy, F.J. (1946). The incidence of hidden delinquency. *American Journal of Orthopsychiatry* 16:689–696.

Murray, C.A., & Cox, L.A. (1979). *Beyond Probation: Juvenile Correction and the Chronic Delinquent.* Beverly Hills, CA: Sage.

Nesselroade, J.R., & Baltes, P.B. (1984). Sequential strategies and the role of cohort effects in behavioral development: Adolescent personality (1970–72) as a sample case. In Mednick, S.A., Harway, M., & Finello, K.N. (Eds.): *Handbook of Longitudinal Research: Birth and childhood cohorts.* New York: Praeger.

Nettler, G. (1974). *Explaining crime.* Toronto: McGraw-Hill.

Newman, O. (1972). *Defensive Space: Crime Prevention Through Urban Design.* New York: Macmillan.

Nye, F.I., & Short, J.F. (1957). Scaling delinquent behavior. *American Sociological Review* 22:326–331.

Nye, F.I., Short, J.F., & Olson, V.J. (1958). Socio-economic status and delinquent behavior. *American Journal of Sociology* 63:381–389.

Offer, D.E. (1969). *The Psychological World of Teenager.* New York: Basic Books.

Ohlin, L.E. (1969). *A Situational Approach to Delinquency Prevention.* Washington, DC: Office for Juvenile Justice and Delinquency Prevention.

Ohlin, L.E. (1974). Organizational reform in correctional organism. *Handbook of Sociology* 63:381–389.

Palmer, T. (1979). *Correctional Intervention and Research.* Toronto: Lexington.

Patterson, G.R. (1982). *A Social Learning Approach. Vol. 1: Coercive Family Process.* Eugene, OR: Castalia.

Patterson, G.R., Reid, J.B., Jones, R.R., & Conger, R.E. (1972). *Families with Aggressive Children.* Eugene, OR: Castalia.

Pearson, F.S., Weiner, N.A. (1985). Toward an integration of criminological theories. *The Journal of Criminal Law and Criminology* 76:116–150.

Petersilia, J., Greenwood, P.W., & Lavin, M. (1978). *Criminal Careers of Habitual Felons.* Santa Monica, CA: Rand Corporation.

Peterson, M.A., & Braiker, H.B. (1980). *Doing Crime: A Survey of California Prison Inmates.* Report R-2200-DOJ. Santa Monica, CA: Rand Corporation.

Pinatel, J. (1963). *Traité de criminologie.* Paris: Dalloz.

Pinatel, J. (1970). *La Société criminogène.* Paris: Calman-Lévy.

Platt, A.M. (1969). *The Child Savers. The Invention of Delinquency.* Chicago: University of Chicago Press.

Podgorecki, A. (1976). *Problèmes de Psychologie Sociale.* (Panatwowe Wydawnictwo Naukowe). Varsovie, Vodopira.

Polk, K., Alder, C., Basemore, G., Blake, G., Cardray, S., & Coventry, G. (1981). *Becoming Adult: An Analysis of Maturational Development From Age 16 to 30.* Washington, DC: Center for Studies of Crime and Delinquency, National Institute of Mental Health.

Porterfield, A.L. (1946). *Youth in Trouble.* Fort Worth, TX: Leo Potishman Foundation.

Quay, H.C. (1965). Personality and delinquency. In Quay, H.C. (Ed.): *Juvenile Delinquency.* New York: Litton.

Quetelet, A. (1835). *Sur l'homme et le développement de ses facultés, ou essai de physique sociale.* Paris: Bachelier.

Rand, A. (1987). Transitional life events and desistance from delinquency and crime. In Wolfgang, M.E., Thornberry, T.P., & Figlio, R.M. (Eds.): *From Boy to Man, from Delinquency to Crime.* Chicago: University of Chicago Press, pp 134–162.

Rankin, J.H., & Wells, L.E. (1985). From status to delinquent offenses: Escalation. *Journal of Criminal Justice* 13:171–180.

Reed, J.P., & Baali, F. (1972). *Faces of Delinquency.* Englewood Cliffs, NJ: Prentice-Hall.

Reiss, A.K. (1988). Co-offending and criminal careers. In Tonry, M., & Morris, N. (Eds.): *Crime and Justice: A Review of Research (Vol. 10).* Chicago: University of Chicago Press.

Remschmidt, H. (1978). Recent results of juvenile delinquency research—West Germany. *Praxis der Kinerpsychologie und Kinderpsychiatrie* 27(2):29–40.

Reppetto, T. (1974). *Residential Crime.* Cambridge, England: Ballinger.

Robins, L.N. (1966). *Deviant Children Grown Up.* New York: Robert E. Krieger.

Robins, L.N. (1980). Epidemiology of adolescent drug use and abuse. In Furcel, E.F. (Ed.): *Psychopathology of Children. Medicine* 8:611–622.

Robins, L.N., & Ratcliff, K.A. (1979). Risk factors in the continuation of childhood antisocial behavior into adulthood. *International Journal of Mental Health* 7:96–116.

Robins, L.N., & Wish, E. (1977). Childhood deviance as a developmental process: A study of 223 urban black men from birth to 18. *Social Forces* 7:96–116.

Robinson, S.M. (1960). *Juvenile Delinquency.* New York: Holt, Rinehart & Winston.

Rocher, G. (1968). *Sociologie générale: regards sur la réalité sociale.* Montréal: Hurtubise.

Rojeck, D.G., & Erickson, M.O. (1981). "Delinquent careers: A test of the career escalation model. *Criminology* 12:5–28.

Romig, D.A. (1978). *Justice for Our Children: An Examination of Juvenile Delinquent Rehabilitation Programs.* Lexington, MA: Lexington.

Ross, R.R., & Gendreau, P. (1980). *Effective Correctional Treatment.* Toronto: Butterworths.

Rutter, M., & Giller, H. (1983). *Juvenile Delinquency: Trends and Perspectives.* London: Penguin Books.

Rutter, M., & Madge, N. (1976). *Cycles of Disadvantage.* London: Heinemann.

Rutter, M., Tizard, J., & Whitmore, K. (1970). *Education, Health and Behavior.* New York: John Wiley.

Sarnecki, J. (1985). *Delinquent Networks.* Stockholm: The National Council for Crime Prevention.

Sarrasin, M., Caplan, A., & Le Blanc, M. (1977). Construction des échelles de délinquance. Research Group on Juvenile Maladaptation, University of Montreal.

Schrag, C. (1971). *Crime and Justice: American Style.* Rockville, MD: Center for Studies of Crime and Delinquency, National Institute of mental Health.

Schur, E.M. (1973). *Radical Nonintervention: Rethinking the Delinquency Problem.* Englewood Cliffs, NJ: Prentice-Hall.

Seelig, E. (1956). *Traité de criminologie.* Paris: Presses Universitaire de France.

Sellin, T.E. (1958). Recidivism and maturation. *National Probation and Parole Association Journal* 4:241–250.

Sellin, T.E., & Wolfgang, M.E. (1964). *The Measurement of Delinquency.* New York: John Wiley.

Sélosse, J. (1983). Délinquance et délinquants: réflexions sur l'articulation entre psychologie criminelle et psychologie judiciaire. *Bulletin de psychologie* 36(5–10): 209–216.

Selvin, H.C. (1965). Durkheim's suicide: Further thoughts on a methodological classic. In Nisbet, R.A. (Ed.): *Émile Durkheim.* Englewood Cliffs, NJ: Prentice-Hall.

Shannon, L.W. (1978). A cohort study of the relationship of adult criminal careers to juvenile careers. Paper presented at the International Symposium on Selected Criminological Topics, Stockholm, 1978.

Shannon, L.W. (1982). *Assessing the Relationship of Adult Criminal Careers to Juvenile Careers.* Urban Community Research Center, University of Iowa, Iowa City.

Shaw, C.R. (1931). *The Natural History of a Delinquent Career.* Chicago: University of Chicago Press.

Shinnar, R., & Shinnar, S. (1975). The effect of the criminal justice system on the control of crime: A quantitative approach. *Law and Society Review* 9:581–612.

Shoemaker, D.J. (1984). *Theories of Delinquency: An Examination of Explanations of Delinquent Behavior.* New York: Oxford University Press.

Short, J.F. (1985). The level of explanation problem in criminology. In Meier, R.F. (Ed.): *Theoretical Methods in Criminology.* Beverly Hills, CA: Sage.

Short, J.F. (1987). Exploring integration of the theoretical levels of explanation: Notes on juvenile delinquency. In *The Albany Conference. Theoretical Integration in the Study of Deviance and Crime: Problems and Prospects.* Albany, Department of Sociology.

Shover, N. (1983). The later stages of ordinary property offender careers. *Social Problems* 31(2):208–218.

Shover, N. (1985). *Aging Criminals.* Beverly Hills, CA: Sage.

Siegel, S. (1956). *Nonparametric Statistics for the Behavioral Sciences.* New York: McGraw-Hill Book Company.

Smith, D.E., Smith, W.R., Noma, E. (1984). Delinquent career-lines: A conceptual link between theory and juvenile offenses. *The Sociological Quarterly* 25:155–172.

Soothil, K.L., & Gibbons, D.C. (1978). Recidivism of sexual offenders: A reappraisal. *British Journal of Criminology* 18:267–276.

Sparks, R.F., Greer, A., & Manning, S.A. (1982). Crime as Work: Theoretical Studies. Newark, NJ: Rutgers University.

Stinchcombe, A.L. (1987). *Constructing Social Theories.* Chicago: University of Chicago Press.

Sullivan, D.E., Grant, M.W., & Grant, J.D. (1957). The development of interpersonal maturity: Application of delinquency. *Psychiatry* 20:373–385.

Sutherland, E.H. (1937). *The Professional Thief.* Chicago: University of Chicago Press.

Sutherland, E.H., & Cressey, D.R. (1960). *Principles of Criminology,* 6th ed. Chicago: J.B. Lippincott.

Szabo, D., Le Blanc, M., Deslauriers, L., & Gagné, D. (1968). Interprétations psychoculturelles de l'inadapatation juvénile dans la société de masse contemporaine. *Acta Criminologica* 1:9–134.

Tappan, P.W. (1949). *Juvenile Delinquency.* New York: McGraw-Hill.

Teilman Van Deusen, K., Mednick, S.A. (1984). *Prospective Studies of Crime and Delinquency.* Boston, MA: Kluwer-Nijhoff Publishing.

Thomas, C.W. (1976). Are status offenders really so different? *Crime and delinquency* 22:438–455.

Thornberry, T.P. (1987). Toward an interactional theory of delinquency. *Criminology* 25(4):863–892.

Thrasher, F.M. (1927). *The gang: A study of 1313 gangs in Chicago.* Chicago: University of Chicago Press.

Tolan, P.H. (1987). Implications of age of onset for delinquency risk. *Journal of Abnormal Child Psychology* 15(1):47–65.

Tracy, P.E. (1987). Race and class differences in official and self-reported delinquency. In Wolfgang, M.E., Thornberry, T.P., & Figlio, R.M. (Eds.): *From Boy to Man, From Delinquency to Crime.* Chicago: University of Chicago Press.

Tremblay, R.E., & Charlebois, P. (1988). La prévention précoce des comportements antisociaux chez les enfants turbulents: l'étude longitudinale-expérimentale de Montréal. Research Group on Psychosocial Maladaptation, School of Psychoeducation, University of Montreal.

Trépanier, J., & Gagnon, R. (1984). La déjudiciarisation à la cour du Bien-Être social de Montréal. School of Criminology, University of Montreal.

Trépanier, J., & Marceau, B. (1985). La justice des mineurs. In Szabo, D., & Le Blanc, M. (Eds.): *Traité de criminologie empirique: le phénomène criminel et la justice pénale au Québec.* Montreal: Presses de l'Université de Montréal.

Visher, C.A., & Roth, J.A. (1986). Participation in criminal careers. In Blumstein, A., Cohen, J., Roth, J.A., & Visher, C.A. (Eds.): *Criminal Careers and "Career Criminals"* (Vol. 1). Washington, DC: National Academy Press.

Wadsworth, M. (1979). *Roots of Delinquency: Infancy, Adolescence and Crime.* Oxford, England: Martin Robertson.

Walker, N. (1977). *Behavior and Misbehavior: Explanations and Nonexplanations.* New York: Basic Books.

Waller, I., & Weiler, D. (1984). *Crime Prevention Through Social Development.* Ottawa: Canadian Council for Social Development.

Walsh, D. (1986). Victim selection procedures among economic criminals: The rational choice perspective. In Cornish, D.B., & Clarke, R.V. (Eds.): *The Reasoning Criminal: Rational Choice Perspectives on Offending.* New York: Springer-Verlag.

Weis, J.G. (1979). *Jurisdiction and The Elusive Status Offender: A Comparison of Involvement in Delinquent Behavior and Status Offenses.* Report of the Juvenile Justice Assessment Center. Washington, DC: U.S. Government Printing Office.

Weis, J.G. (1986). Issues in the measurement of criminal careers. In Blumstein, A., Cohen, J., Roth, J.A., & Visher, C.A. (Eds.): *Criminal Careers and "Career Criminals"* (Vol. 2). Washington, DC: National Academy Press.

Werner, H. (1957). The concept of development from a comparative and organismic point of view. In Harris, D.B. (Ed.): *The Concept of Development.* Minneapolis: University of Minnesota Press.

West, D.J. (1969). *Present Conduct and Future Delinquency.* New York: International Universities Press.

West, D.J. (1982). *Delinquency: Its Roots, Careers, and Prospects.* London: Heinemann.

West, D.J., & Farrington, D.P. (1973). *Who Becomes Delinquent?* London: Heinemann.

West, D.J., & Farrington, D.P. (1977). *The Delinquent Way of Life.* London: Heinemann.

West, G.W. (1984). *Young Offenders and the State: Canadian Perspective on Delinquency.* Toronto: Butterworth.

Wikström, P-O. (1987). *Patterns of Crime in a Birth Cohort: Age, Sex and Class Differences.* (Project metropolitan: a longitudinal study of a Stockholm cohort no. 24.) Department of Sociology, University of Stockholm.

Williams, J.R., & Gold, M. (1972). From delinquent behavior to official delinquency. *Social Problems* 20(2):209–229.

Wilson, J.Q., & Herrnstein, R.J. (1985). *Crime and Human Nature.* New York: Simon and Shuster.

Wolfgang, M.E. (1958). *Patterns of Criminal Homicide.* New York: John Wiley.

Wolfgang, M.E. (1967). The viable future in criminology. In Szabo, D. (Ed.): *Criminologie en action: bilan de la criminologie contemporaine dans ses grands domaines d'application.* Montréal: Presses de l'Université de Montréal.

Wolfgang, M.E., & Ferracuti, F. (1967). *The Subculture of Violence.* London: Tavistock Publications.

Wolfgang, M.E., Figlio, R.M., & Sellin, T. (1972). *Delinquency in a Birth Cohort.* Chicago: University of Chicago Press.

Wolfgang, M.E., Figlio, R.M., Tracy, P.E., & Singer, S.I. (1985). *The National Survey of Crime Severity.* Washington, DC: U.S. Department of Justice, Bureau of Statistics.

Wolfgang, M.E., Thornberry, T.P., & Figlio, R.M. (1987). *From Boy to Man, From Delinquency to Crime.* Chicago: University of Chicago Press.

Wright, W.E., & Dixon, M.C. (1977). Community prevention and the treatment of juvenile delinquency. *Journal of Research in Crime and Delinquency* 14(1):35–67.

Yockelson, S., & Samenow, S.E. (1976). *The Criminal Personality. Vol. 1. A Profile for Change.* New York: Jason Aronson.

Zimmerman, J., & Broder, P.K. (1980). A comparison of different delinquency measures derived from self-reported data. *Journal of Criminal Justice* 8:147–162.

Zimring, F.E. (1982). *The Changing Legal World of Adolescence.* New York: Free Press.

Author Index

Y

Z

Subject Index

G

H

I

J

L

M

O

MIX
Papier aus verantwortungsvollen Quellen
Paper from responsible sources
FSC® C105338

If you have any concerns about our products,
you can contact us on
ProductSafety@springernature.com

In case Publisher is established outside the EU,
the EU authorized representative is:
Springer Nature Customer Service Center GmbH
Europaplatz 3, 69115 Heidelberg, Germany

Printed by Libri Plureos GmbH
in Hamburg, Germany